TONIC WATER

Fluid, dynamic approaches towards Environmental Leadership

WANO URBONAS

CONTENTS

THE PURPOSE

Leaders are survivors with a story to tell—ours is about dismemberment, incapacitation and the gory details of a crew held captive. We have never been in greater need of full-strength, high octane environmental leadership. Gangrenous leadership continues to limit the ability of agencies, organizations and individuals to collaboratively and effectively tackle the causes of air, land, water and wildlife impairment—we are captivated by the cause, while imprisoned in our efforts.

I am confident that **Tonic Water** will <u>excavate and energize leadership capacity within our conservation communities</u>, transforming dull, light-green programs into fluid, dynamic bright green tomorrows. We shall overcome our chronic Environmental Leadership (EL) deficits by delivering a message in a bottle--one chock full of conservation conundrums, environmental prophecies, self-deprecating humor and swigs of blasphemy (aimed at pseudo- leaders, oblivious directors, underperformers and back-burner EL). Go ahead and grasp this bottle with both hands, pry it open and devour its contents of environmental ambition and conservation thirst—it is your EL truth serum. I dare you!

Our environmental community thinks not in terms of cluttered toolsheds, but of unique airsheds, watersheds and foodsheds, with someone at the helm providing direction and a semblance of a vision. Admittedly, environmental proponents are not the toast inside the toaster, tweaked to a predictable finish, then smothered with someone else's political conviction. We are more like, heaven forbid, beads of Styrofoam—fragile, dependent, pervasive lightweights that are taken for granted, disposed of, displaced, misplaced or replaced. We are in dire need of strong leadership, but before we flex our muscle, we need to purposefully build it! Environmental gods and goddesses the likes of John Muir, Aldo Leopold, Rachel Carson, Edward Abbey and others had an intense and endearing ecological message to share, and share they did—via cosmic green bodings of climatic turmoil. Likewise, **Tonic Water** is an essential and potent additive to every Environmental Leadership Survival Kit, conjuring up stellar songs to sing and vivid rants to rave.

This EL tonic book is about liberating one's conscious and unconscious abilities for the betterment of you, and yes, society as well. Never will a page in this book go by without a reference to (or reverence for) our environment, conservation or quality of life. **Tonic Water** speaks distinct EL lingo and spews out chunky insight about our impaired environmental communities until our readers are green in the face. We then briskly usher you outside to the fresh air and promote forms of environmental polygamy that require curiosity, flexibility and practice—toying with copious quantities of innovative, watershed-based leadership challenges and collaborative 'liquid linkages'.

This guide does not strive to be a green version of 'Chicken Soup for the Soul'—on the contrary, we intend to concoct an environmental gumbo of unsettling, gut-wrenching proportions, to the point where you can no longer stomach our current less-than- mediocre leadership efforts. We sincerely hope that you suffer an acute reaction, and consciously seek out a remedy to our rash of EL maladies, some self-inflicted.

Environmental leadership is extremely potent, but it is often concentrated in the wrong hands or in too few of them. We don't attempt to slay this almighty green dragon, but in its stead opt to deftly convert his / her respiratory actions from flame-broiled affliction and abuse, to positive energy, resource-sharing and communal affection. But this is not a warm & fuzzy 'you can do it' book—**Tonic Water** tells a relate-able story, unveils mysteries, advises EL discretion, nips at hind quarters, warns of severe natural / cultural ramifications and urges an enlightened rebirth of environmental leadership courage and conservation conviction.

Our environmental community is rarely communal. We often seek out carcinogens inside and outside our individual homes (and minds), creating 'Toxic Inventories' that we limit our exposure to. Yet we are inexplicably chastised for scrutinizing the internal machinations of our organizational culture—deemed as taboo, out of bounds, high security clearance required. Without being Hercule Poirot, the hazardous human waste that can be detected within our environmental arena include suppressants (rules), depressants (orders), relaxants (lack of motivation) and anti-oxidizers—they suck the life out of you!

Yet within these often-guarded chambers of boards and directors is an invisible vault of half-truths and deceptions—safe keeping for self-preservation. The kingdom truly believes that most errors are committed by staff servants and perhaps mid-level managers, not by the silky cream at the top. As an added slap, caustic board members can inflict sufficient animus to where a minority begins to feel compromised, paralyzed, and under the influence of an infective force. With closer examination, there will be a wide continuum as to where your Environmental Leadership ability currently sits (a bad sign) and where you want to go (cool)! We will attempt to perform a kinetic conveyance, transforming potential EL into a significant force to be reckoned with.

Our environmental flock has been cooped up too long—our green choices gnawed on by foxes guarding henhouses or by chickens pretending to be foxes. It's time to unlock our potential and take on a free range of environmental challenges by going on a jaw- dropping conservation leadership safari! I'll tell the story of this trek sort of Pee Wee Herman-style, seeking the brilliant green bicycle that eludes us somehow, someway.

By instilling environmental leadership principles, possibilities and potential into leadership equations, readers will progressively develop a thirst that provokes action and reaction, percussion and repercussions, with elements of EL regurgitation as a positive indicator. Collaboratively, we will expose the types of individuals and personality traits that result in Environmental Dysfunction (ED), will pester the status quo and their frigid environmental tendencies until the quo no longer has much status, and will sling mud (or worse) at environmental puritans that devote themselves to narrow niches at the ultimate expense of the broader community.

So, it's time to grab our green pitchforks and poke at environmental weaklings (and heavyweights alike) until their noxious dominion is punctured, exuding its infectious negativity until voided. We then promptly replenish it with truthful, organic thinking, verdant leadership potential and ecological oomph. That's the plan.

Tonic Water reveals to the reader that there is no single key to achieving EL success, but rather a combination of twists, turns, jabs and uppercuts that need personal attention and intense exercising. We acknowledge the significant, critical nature of our attempts to become more environmentally aware and active leaders, and we start by recognizing our weaknesses, our vulnerabilities, our addictions to standardized programming. We have to convene not only as a field of environmental leaders—we have to become leaders throughout our green fields! **Tonic Water** leads the way, unafraid to take a walk on the wild side.

INTRODUCTION

What on earth is that foul odor breaching the nucleus of our conservation communities? I hope that the stench dissipates quickly, while we can still breathe. What in the world is that lingering limburger emanating from the organizational board room, wafting through the administrative and managerial chambers, seeping into our trenches? I call it 'Brilliant Green Bile'.

As a lifelong conservationist and as a well-traveled environmental health professional, I've experienced poor, lackluster or non- existent environmental leadership at the Federal, State, county and community levels. I've gained considerable insight by engaging in environmental dialogue and performing environmental tasks (paid and volunteer) in both the public and private (non-profit) sectors. I know wastewater from holy water, and I'm fairly adept at discerning stagnant, decomposing programs from opportunistic, fluid approaches. Sharing many of my experiences with you would be my pleasure, if you can hold your nose.

We universally acknowledge that some gases are tasteless and odorless yet remain lethal to otherwise healthy environmental initiatives. The off gassing from rancid, righteous or downright timid organizations is enough to make one gag. Our apothecary guidance is meant to alert the environmental community and its leaders (or leaders-to-be) of the dangerous ramifications of piecemeal programming, bizarre decision-making, erroneous priority-setting and perhaps the biggest stink of all, underperformance. I can't stand the putrid smell! It leaves a nasty taste in my mouth. The search for un-bitter varieties of EL begins here and now!

Through this empirical, 'Tonical Transformation', I propose that we go forth and prosper, not in the staunch conservative or financial mindset, but in support of our roots, our nature and our culture. We will make

Bernie Sanders, Noam Chomsky, Yvon Chouinard, Alexandria Ocasio-Cortez and even Greta Thunberg proud of our environmental tendons and tendencies, by assisting from the inside-out. My ambition is to jettison the chronic environmental and conservation leadership encumbrances that have stymied organized efforts to advance our environmental initiatives—and I need your help!

But we can't go willy-nilly, as that is the current impression of enviro-fanatics, including myself. I will try to wreak the environmental havoc that is long, long overdue—pointing one finger at the root cause, and the other finger at our-selves (the rank within our ranks). And I will counterpunch my critical comments with some rosy optimism, hoping to share ways to alleviate ineffective environmental leadership.

Why environmental leadership, you might ask? To the best of my knowledge, there has never been a compelling Environmental Leadership guidebook, and there certainly has not been one like this. Prior to writing this Environmental Leadership guide, I took on the painstaking task of reading 19 leadership books. Several of them were actually pretty decent, yet dealt mostly with the business world or politics. Sure, we all have staff, mid & upper-level management and executive honchos, but we 'enviros' are a different sort of critter. We are diverse by nature (human and environmental), but are rarely stimulated by youth leadership, military leadership, business leadership or Christian leadership. Marketing scenarios, sales quotas, production capacity and paper- pushing cause us to doze off into Never, Never Land. We green leaders are not driven by money, force or God, but rather by precious people and precarious places.

We in the environmental arena can also be zealous bloodsuckers, fearful of revealing organizational secrets, panicky over competition, deceitful when it serves our purpose and forgetful when it comes to rewarding our guides. I've served under a few cutthroat leaders, but that's the extreme as opposed to the norm, where a simple chokehold stifles environmental dreams. I will spare you the agony of reading the multitude of leadership texts that do not aptly or artfully comprehend our ecological philosophies and complex communities / habitats. Generic self-help leadership books suggest basic 'ways to lead', while **Tonic Water** <u>delivers</u> <u>substantive green will and greener ways</u>.

When there's something ultra-special or unique that I picked up along my environmental jihad, I'll include it and attempt to add some high fiber earth muffin ingredients. We will dissect the abundant green manure that permeates our environmental entities and conservation culture. I'll also be using an ocean of watershed analogies and metaphors, in an honest attempt to saturate you with useful stuff. Swallow what you like, and then spit out the rest—it's your journey!

Let's say that you're concerned about certain ill feelings, some acute, some chronic, and try to self-diagnose. What does that obscure, fine print on your medication box state?

"*.. may cause dizziness, drowsiness, nausea, irritability, restlessness, dyspnea, apnea, diarrhea, anxiety, elevated blood pressure and other serious conditions… seek advice from your physician if such symptoms occur or re-occur…*"

Sorry to say, but that container is your cubicle at the workplace— your personal, volatile organic compound. Worse yet, you are both patient and physician. You get to write your own prescriptions!

I sincerely hope that you will consider this Environmental Leadership guide as anti-venom and not snake oil—but that will be your call, based on your clinical studies and professional inclinations. Let's not be the party of 'no', but the party of 'go'—

Go forward with environmental initiatives. Go get help from anywhere possible.

Go talk with strangers.

Go to meetings and events.

Go with a message, a vision and an objective or two (not three, two is plenty!).

Things could be dramatically worse, but this guidebook is not about reducing the threshold of pain and anguish—it's about introducing sustainable levels of environmental pleasure, or even ecstasy. Astute businesspeople are invited to read on and make the translation and transition to their leadership world. They are welcome to join our entourage, as most times we are worlds apart, yet sometimes strange bedfellows. Entrepreneurs can build upon these principles and ideas to create an even better outcome, shedding light on other non-sustainable leadership predicaments. But by and large, I'll be speaking and puking about our environmental communities and our ecological innards until I'm green in the face. With more time and experiences under your belt, you'll be raring to turn up the heat, provoking action and reaction that may be opposite, but are never truly equal.

With regards to environmental progressions and conservation initiatives, most U.S. counties are amply lame and somewhat extra- terrestrial. Meanwhile, our states are either drenched in bureaucratic gravy or so heavily processed to the point where we are in remote control of neighboring environmental community needs. This reality is tough to swallow and will require in-depth self and group analysis.

One should also note that 85% of Environmental Health resources at the county level are consumed by restaurant inspections and septic systems—not my idea of environmental priorities, unless they are researched, evaluated and deemed as priorities by the very public that they serve (are we asking the critical questions?). Yet these programs are in-fact sustainable, as they are linked to licenses and permit fees, while local issues such as watershed health, air pollution prevention and greenhouse gas emissions are always seeking funding sources—volunteers, contributions, grants and donors. I'll share many revealing anecdotes as we pedal uphill towards EL nirvana—are you ready, Pee Wee?

My wife just told me that environmental leadership is passé—she just heard on the radio how Norway is closing in on 100% renewable energy, so why am I wasting time writing ideas when there are scientists out there with the technical capacity to change our lives, literally overnight. She really got my goat, but talk about challenges—if I can't get my own wife to understand the basic premise of what I'm trying to do, then how do I convince you, my reader, my last vestige of hope, that I'm creating something better than Flubber or hula hoops?

Answer: I am providing you with an Environmental Leadership armory that may only sound intriguing if you are intrigued by Environmental Leadership as a potential solution to your current drudgery or drab programs.

If you're open-minded, adventurous and looking for possible learning tools (did I just call my wife closed-minded?), then I want your attention, so I can promote invention, not retention. This leadership guidebook is not for retentive persons, it is an innovative and progressive approach towards maintaining or enhancing the integrity of our air, land, water and wildlife. There's a reason why the owl turns her head in so many perplexing angles—let's follow her lead.

'Hey babe, take a walk on the wild side..'—
                    Lou Reed

CHAPTER I.
CONSERVATION RIPPLES AND WAVES OF CHANGE

Oh, the irony!

Bile, when put to its proper, balanced and best use (within an organism or organization) can aid in the digestion of fats and unwanted residue. Our livers need some bile to properly function. Yet due to man-made imbalances and system(ic) debilitation, most environmental organizations exude copious amounts of bile, oozing putrid practices right alongside the water cooler, en route to your swivel chair. The bitter pill of experiencing bile build-up can result in gallstone formation, Stonehenge mentality or the bitter truth— some might call it 'inconvenient'.

Few would argue with our need to aid digestion and improve absorption of nutrients within our team body. Raising reasonable doubt about program priorities and project implementation is usually sufficient to get those juices flowing. Yet while some of us salivate, others experience heartburn, and wish that we would just go away and leave well enough alone. That's not going to happen.

This guidebook aims to be perturbing, better yet, revolting! When we closely examine the repugnant acts of past and present environmental and conservation leaders, many of us will be one step closer to casting off allegiance to or subjugation by those in authority, and willing to engage in less vile, more alluring environmental leadership possibilities. At the very least, we will become less apt to perform perfunctory environmental tasks without questioning the rationale behind the approach. Due to our environmental propensity and conservation caring, we can no longer remain indifferent to the mundane, superficial or egregious acts that would ultimately erode our environmental leadership ambitions.

Are you feeling chopped, squeezed, backed into a corner? Plucked, grilled and placed in dicey situations? Or maybe simply ignored, isolated or under-appreciated? Who 'ya gonna call? How about 'nobody'? While these are commonly-occurring sensations within most types of organizations, we don't have to put up with it in the green world—in fact, we can't afford to put up with it, because it puts us down, down, down! We need to deal with these doldrums and deleterious issues within our daily earthly domain, emanating within our inner self. Like Santa Claus and the M&M guys, environmental chameleon-type leaders do exist, all too often.

Conventional leadership focuses on checking off boxes for each class taken or each webinar attended: Fundamentals of Supervision, check… Dealing with Difficult People, check…Encouraging Teamwork, double-check. Congratulations, you get an electronic certificate that you are instructed to print out in duplicate—one to be placed in your human resources file for nobody to see, and the other for your circular file, so you can see where your effort has gotten you. Suffering from any regularity yet?

Let's start this self-help guide from the true green grit and grind that brought us towards where we are today. There will be some dwelling over the past—tidbits of shoulda, coulda, woulda's, and just a sincere recognition that there were many rivers to cross, and many more ahead. But what I will really emphasize and continue to hammer on is how distasteful complacency is. What happened to the hunger, the drive, the thirst for betterment-- not just for you, but for your team, your community, your planet? How do we rekindle that ambitious green ghost, or derive new EL methodologies that are progressive, possible and palatable?

We start by thinking inside the box, since that's where we are-- sealed, coated and corrugated. And after examining environmental leadership potential from various angles, we surmise situations, one-by-one, and reach some conclusions—is our foundation strong? Can it be fortified, or is it ready for the wrecking ball? Do we possess the desire to shore-up a sinking ship? Maybe--but then again, maybe not. Can we take an 'okay program' and make it excellent and desirous? Should we clone the best pieces of our current situation and then restructure them to our own liking?

There are always some unlikely 'surprises', such as money, timing, luck, influence, stupidity and power. And then there are ideas and action. Let me repeat our mission--**this guide will attempt to 'excavate and energize leadership capacity within our conservation communities'.** I'll go back and forth with the terms 'environmental' and 'conservation', as I wish to address folks that work within extension agencies, Forest Service, BLM, Tribal Nations, universities, non-profit entities, green businesses and conservation districts as well as those proclaiming to be environmental managers, environmental planners, environmentalists, environmental scientists, environmental educators, … maybe even some environmental engineers (the special kind).

Brilliant Green Broth—

Our bodies are composed of 65% water, and we regularly feel like our brains are saturated with an overflow of information. Yet our creative and innovative mindsets chronically lack lubrication and quickly become rusty and creaky, yielding to external pressures. Our daily functioning and performance depend on maintaining our fluid levels.

A <u>fluid</u> is aptly defined as:

> *'a substance devoid of harshness, and capable of changing its shape and direction, without separation'.*

It sounds a lot like the perfect mother-in-law, but more glamorous. This is my premier environmental mantra. It's worth reiterating and demonstrating, with hands clasped and fingers interlocked—capable of changing shape and direction, without separation, a fluid approach. This fluid interconnectivity has helped me create a series of Environmental Leadership challenges that I have developed into a curriculum. My impetus was obviously the plethora of dysfunctional environmental leaders that I have linked up with over the years--and the few good ones that could have become great (including my current abilities), had they been willing to take things to the next level. Along with my watershed-based 'liquid linkage' epiphany came several opportunities to perform real-life experiments on the Environmental Leadership (EL) process.

I wish to reach out to anybody that resides within a watershed and wants to do more to maintain or enhance the integrity of their home-grown natural and cultural environment. And while I'll be speaking mostly from rural, suburban and regional experiences, I wish to include those municipal urbanites and city dwellers that might not know where their water comes from (find out before reading any further!). Let's get to it by starting with **some basic EL assumptions**:

1. We want to <u>hone</u> our EL skill set and knowledge base, so that we can do a better job of making significant, positive impact on our natural and cultural environments; living, thriving, in harmony with our surroundings.

2. We will be <u>receptive</u> to new ideas.

3. We will be <u>respectful</u> to others, even if we don't respect their viewpoints or agendas—this way, we can learn from our differences and try to understand why the other guy is trying to contaminate our drinking water (just kidding, sort of!).

That's it—just these few items, so our Albert Einstein brains have enough space to explore opportunities. Let's start with being a role model for others within our organization, to lean on and learn from. No, no, that's too boring. How about trying to inspire others to latch onto a shared vision, a vision that takes us from light green towards bright green? Sounds good, but in order to get there, we'll need to create opportunities and challenges for our team and ourselves, in order to improve our odds at succeeding where others fail--Which takes us to failure, and how we need to enable others to fail. That's an area where I have a great deal of expertise!

The Benefits of Failing-

How do you define success? You don't need to tell me, but please give it some thought. Personally, I haven't been very successful (yet), but not because I haven't tried. Making noble attempts enhances the possibilities of environmental achievement. Take it from an authoritative voice on failure—reading and studying will provide some clues on environmental rewards, but what really indicates progress is the shift from environmental awareness towards hands-on environmental trial and error. Vicarious environmental leaders become asterisks, appendices and museum artifacts.

This might not be much of a revelation to environmental achievers. So why read an environmental leadership guidebook from a professed failure? For starters, because I've discovered that there is a glut of exuberant, back-patting, artificially-sweetened, generic leadership material on the market—yet a dearth of honest, experiential, environmental failure-ships. But wouldn't it make more sense to follow the environmental lead of an achiever (thus making you a possible 'successor')? If you want to follow in someone's footsteps, then yes indeed, by all means, follow the leader. But if you want to make your personal impression on others, then I'd suggest that you walk your own walk, choose your own shoes, flip, flop and occasionally flounder.

Tonic Water is a 'deep-see' fishing excursion for both trophy and atrophied environmental leaders. One is a prized catch, documented and released because it truly can't be contained—the leadership nourishes and flourishes itself. The other, the runt, is examined and scrutinized to determine why the stagnation has occurred, and what can be done to promote sustained growth and healthy development.

This EL guidebook will provide options, introduce alternatives and make enough recommendations to fill your tackle box. You're probably no longer the youngster who closes his / her eyes, spins the globe and places a finger on an 'other-worldly' spot to visit. You may or may not have a destination in-mind, but destiny is pure hogwash. If you don't overly consternate over personal risks or capitulate to unwarranted requests, you can indeed make it or break it (but don't fake it)!

I've been contemplating about writing this EL guidebook for several years (too long!), and I can tell you the difference between a $7 bottle and $14 bottle of cabernet sauvignon. Yet besides the price tag, I detect very little difference between the $20 and $30 bottles. The hints of clove and cherry finishes are not what this guidebook is about. The wine tastes good, bad or better depending on the circumstance, attitude, company and imagination. To all you naysayers, sourpusses and defeatist-attituders—this guidebook is not for you. Without an open mind, don't waste your time. But for you dreamers, wanderers and adventurers, please take a gander, and sample some of my enviro leadership hor d'oeuvres. They might just evoke an emotion or provoke a green 'Grapes of Wrath' response.

Environmental Elixors--

Two more points to make:

1. My goal is not to spend this entire EL tonic book harping on environmental mishaps and deficiencies (though there are plenty!). Since this book is meant to be a 'guide', I will limit my criticisms to seven key Chapter points (I--VII) and will reiterate the Roman numeral if there is an association, instead of launching into a diatribe.

2. As my lovely wife Linda reminds me from time-to-time, one can't argue (they actually can, but he / she won't convince anyone of anything). I'm not trying to sell you any magical potions or cure-alls, and any silvery green bullets are figments that are cached away in your internal capacity and personal desire—not anyone else's. If you want to decide for others, you'll have to decide for yourself.

Definition of a guide: Someone or something that takes you to places that you want to go. Don't want to go anywhere? Turn on the bile valve, usurp your environmental leadership potential into your personal vacuum and retreat to safety.

I would be remiss to not address my audience, or at least who I think my audience may be—

a) <u>The thirsty ones</u>: Those who have ingested myriads of information, ideas and approaches, and remain optimistic that they will be able to play a significant role in maintaining or enhancing the integrity of our natural and human environment. You swallow your pride, but expect respect, often lack recognition and yet persevere in your search for personal growth and lifelong satisfaction. Nothing short of progressive, positive environmental impact, sustainable approaches and making a significant difference will be deemed satisfactory.

b) <u>The drowning</u>: You have been treading water for quite some time, yet when you appear to be finding rare earth, it ends up being yet another plot of quicksand. You look around for someone to throw you a life rope, but only see vultures cruising overhead. You are a survivor and will persist at all costs. Your vital signs reveal green blood that runs deep; personal surrender is never an option.

c) <u>The dreamers and wanderers</u>: You have hope, but it comes and goes like shifting winds. You have environmental aspirations but need a heavy dose of inspiration. The status quo is the mainstream environmental approaches that get you embroiled in bureaucracy and politics, not to mention economics. You probably need a swift kick in the pants, but with bills to pay and job retention paramount, your environmental ideals have been obscured by security and reality (and I don't blame you!). It's both the wandering and the optimistic wondering that keep you in the hunt. You have great potential!

d) <u>The rest of you</u>: You might be curious or have some free time. Or maybe (hopefully) you happened upon this guide as a possible mechanism to kinetically convey potential environmental energy into real EL action. Or you are the big cheese, the director that has made some mistakes (join the crowd!), the supervisor that is somewhat lost, the cynical director that thinks he / she knows it all, or a Board member that wants to juice up their organization. If someone gave you this book, you might actually need it!

With one more response to generic, all-star leadership training textbooks and courses (the ones that urge that we fill leadership gaps), I would suggest that you apply for a leadership job at the Gap. Environmental leaders are (and should be) a different breed. Environmental leaders salivate at the thought of learning the language of the land and translating the whispers of the forest. If you wanted to perfect your culinary skills, you'd probably jump right into the frying pan, experiment and perfect your skillet set.

The same holds true for environmental leaders—we immerse ourselves in environmental concerns and wade into the heart of the matter. We go to the core, find its roots, touch it, feel it and live it. Air, land, water and wildlife are our religion, and environmental leadership will become our language. Contrary to carte blanche leadership coverage, there is no universal set of environmental leadership principles. Cut, carve, shape or chisel your way forward, and if you don't like your creation, screw commitment and start over! I'll provide some appetizers and make some suggestions, then you decide what to ingest.

'What I shouldn't have done, I've already accomplished.'
-Responsible Party

Survive, then thrive!

It is tropical storm season here in upcountry Kula, Hawaii. I'm taking a vacation day from my extremely routine job of conducting health inspections of retail food establishments. They call us 'Sanitarians', but I despise that term because it reminds me of a sanitarium and resembles one at times. Having been the honcho for several county Environmental Health programs, I'm adept at air monitoring, consumer protection, water sampling, wastewater permitting, hazardous materials / waste management, and a myriad of zoonotic responses to plague, rabies, Hantavirus, W. Nile Virus, etcetera. But for the moment, I'm a greasy spoon inspector.

Rather than waiting for the rain to stop (which might not be for two days), I donned the Gore-Tex poncho and started walking down the road. It was nearly noon, and the worms were doing the backstroke down the flooded path. There were thousands of these puffy nematodes, having suffered a rude awakening from a night of thunder & lightning, followed by heavy downpours. They looked like they had given up physically--appearing comatose, in shock or not sure of their emotional state. A few birds were still rummaging around, but by and large, they had their share of the spaghetti feast since sunrise and were content to stay partially dry in the monkeypod trees.

Then I spotted the combatant worm—similar size as the others, but obviously refusing to surrender to the next dinner course. He / she (both I guess) squirmed and wriggled across the dirt culvert of 18" (probably a football stadium to a worm), grasped onto a blade of grass, then heaved itself back into the jungle. Wow, what an act of defiance and refusal to succumb to what seemed to be ill-fated doom. I was extremely impressed! A personal, life-altering decision was made, immediate action was taken, the future uncertain, …but alive!

> *'Nothing in the world can take the place of persistence.*
> *Talent will not; nothing is more common than unsuccessful men with talent. Genius will not; unrewarded genius is almost a proverb. Education will not; the world is full of educated derelicts.*
> *Persistence and determination are omnipotent. The slogan 'press on' has solved and always will solve the problems of the human race…'------*
> Calvin Coolidge, thirtieth President of the United States

That Gut Feeling—

And give the worm credit. In central Zaire (present day Congo, where I served as a Peace Corps Community Health Volunteer) during the rainy season, hookworm larvae would be on the lookout for barefoot children walking and playing in their backyards. The kids had actually shit out the worms at some point, and the vicious cycle was starting over. Once penetrating the tough barefoot (a feat in itself), the ankylostrom would migrate towards the small intestine, where a buffet of nutrients would be awaiting. Worms— love 'em or hate 'em, they are survivors. In my future life, I'll name my reggae band 'Worm Burden'.

How do we learn to act or react to real threats? Is it instinctive? Partly so, I believe. But the critical element is to have the gumption, the confidence, the grittiness, the tenacity to be able to continue the struggle. Giving up is too easy. Passive resistance is akin to waving goodbye as well. When you lead others, remember what it used to be like, not so long ago, when you toiled, slogged, scrambled and somehow survived. Now perhaps you're in an advantageous position, being able to exert authority or influence over conservation program direction, employee duties and responsibilities. I've asked a group of Environmental Leaders that I've personally known and respected to provide one sentence responses to the following question:

Q: What is a critical Environmental Leadership component that is often avoided, overlooked or not given adequate consideration, and how have you addressed this void?

Responses:

a) Taking risks, addressed via 'got your back' assurances & scenarios.

b) Appreciation, addressed by recognizing efforts, not just success.

c) Teamwork, addressed by calculating abilities, personalities and chemistry.

d) Real progress, addressed by persistence, promotion and gratitude.

e) Recognition, by communicating at multiple levels.

<u>And my personal favorite:</u>

f) Sharing, by sharing.

Hippo was no Hypo—

One of the first to discuss and theorize about emotions and disease, Hippocrates combined science and philosophy to explain the relationship between the human body, health and illness. His dominant theory was that there were four 'humors'—black bile, yellow bile, phlegm and blood. When these humors were in- balance, health prevailed. But when they were out of whack, disease took advantage of the situation. A healthy equilibrium was dependent upon a healthy diet, exercise and management of 'the body's evacuations'—urine, stool, perspiration, etc. The Brilliant Green Bile that we emphatically refer to strongly suggests that a comprehensive and holistic approach to Environmental Leadership requires open-mindedness, the sharing of ideas and collaborative, mutually beneficial efforts to maintain the health and integrity of an organism or organization.

I had the opportunity to visit Lake Idi Amin in mountainous Uganda, traveling with a former Peace Corps buddy. The locals would be standing ankle-deep, hand-casting a line and shiny lure to hook delectable, arm-length perch. The lake environment was also home to several dozen hippos that would spin their ears just above the water surface like a helicopter. And when the helicopter submerged, all the fishermen would quickly take ten steps backwards. It was a very respectful and peaceful coexistence.

I camped out on a ridge in a one-person bivouac tent overlooking the lake, watching the hundreds of thousands of cave bats emerge just at sundown—truly an amazing event. I resembled a stuffed burrito, with not enough room to even sit up. Hours later into the night, I felt the ground beginning to shake—minor earthquake maybe? No such luck—evidently, the hippos trek up the ridge at night to graze the grasses like cows. Several beasts were so close that I could hear their breathing and munching. I was too petrified to shine my flashlight, in fear of becoming a hoof-print. I got up enough nerve to clear my throat, and that was enough to send them off—not knowing what sort of threat I might be. I sold that damned coffin tent the next day for one night's lodging, chicken and kwanga. My heart would never pound so furiously ever again.

The word 'hypocrisy' or 'hypocrite' has no connection to Hippocrates whatsoever. The word hypocrite comes from the Greek word 'hypokrites', which means an actor or someone acting under false pretenses. This brings us back to environmental leaders and a substantial trail of bile—the plot begins to thicken.

Presence, Absence or Unconfirmed—

Laboratory water quality tests are fairly straightforward, using standard methods for analysis, and normally resulting in safe, unsafe or 'not sure—better retest' results. Peering into one of those unconfirmed test-tubes reminds me of the insecure realm of Environmental Leadership. We're all bottled-up, and we have 'cheat sheets' that walk us through various sequential steps that attempt to clue us in on who we are and how we react. Our results indicate to decision-makers as to what the next steps will be (consume, boil, retest). Somebody smarter than me once said that:

'The absence of evidence does not necessarily result in evidence of absence',

And that got me thinking that the green test tube bile was quite brilliant, yet we were being treated as human reagents.

If you search around the Rocky Mountain high country but cannot find lynx footprints, that does not mean that lynx do not inhabit the area.

Conversely, the old adage 'Seek and 'ye shall find' did not hold true for Sasquatch, aliens or the Fountain of Youth--which leads us right back to reasonable doubt.

Two equally skilled kayakers can have very different perspectives. The first guy (Eddy) is personally traumatized by his recent boat capsize and involuntary swimming event in frigid rapids. So, he takes a close look at today's river run, rubs his beard and states:

"I can't paddle this tough stretch; it's over my head".

He sits on nearby rocks and watches another boater safely paddle by. His view gradually changes to

"I don't think that I can make it".

Another few boaters whoop it up and high-five each other after paddling through the tough section. Eddy's tone shifts to

"I'm not sure if I can do it".

With some encouragement from buddy paddlers, Eddy thinks to himself:

"I might be able to do it after-all".

His friends chide him further, stating *"C'mon, .. piece of cake…you can do it!"*.

So, Eddy pushes off from shore to give it a try and ends up drowning.

Life has risks, so calculate yours. Environmental Leadership acknowledges the dangerous rapids ahead in life, and puts in the requisite preparation that recognizes challenges, assesses risks and confronts them with determined confidence. Luckily, the lightning strikes, shark attacks and drowning events are extremely rare.

The second paddler (Helmut) is certain he can paddle this same river stretch. He convinces himself that he can, and the passing kayakers reinforce his belief. Then he watches Eddy give it a try, and a stream of doubt starts to dribble into the cockpit. Yet he makes up his mind, launches from shore, paddles frantically, and is never seen again.

Environmental Leadership can be tough love, and I'm not going to kid you! The raison d'etre for leadership is a commixture of providing direction, creating challenges, shouldering some responsibility (not all), encouraging involvement and many other noble traits. For those that prefer to follow, choose your leader wisely. Learning how to swim might be advantageous as well. But rather than merely watching from the shorelines, find a different way to contribute. I hope that the strokes you take and the waves you make will be an epic adventure!

'First there is a mountain, then there is no mountain, then there is.'
Donovan

OrganizationalOrgans

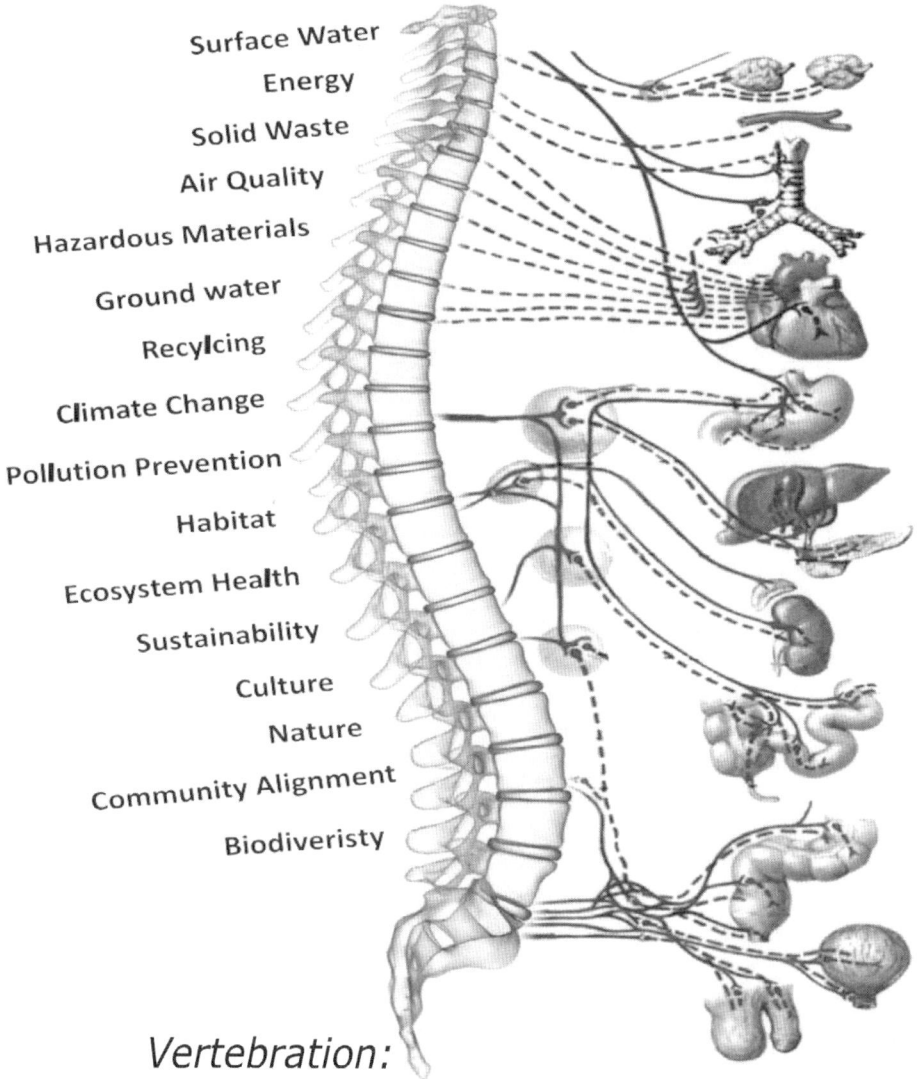

Surface Water
Energy
Solid Waste
Air Quality
Hazardous Materials
Ground water
Recylcing
Climate Change
Pollution Prevention
Habitat
Ecosystem Health
Sustainability
Culture
Nature
Community Alignment
Biodiveristy

Vertebration:
A Connective Leadership Formation

Temperamental Intelligence & Nebulous Leadership

Remember that vintage television show, 'The Undersea World of Jacques Cousteau'? There were so many exotic forms of marine life, and such freedom of aquatic movement! Things appeared effortless, naturally adapting to tides, seasons and marine fluctuations. Holistic ecosystems flourished and functioned, ocean communities thrived, and life was mysterious-yet-invigorating.

I must have excreted 60% of my innermost beliefs before (in a dehydrated state) coming up with this EL tonic revelation. There were certainly secrets and secretions that needed to be spelled, expelled or dispelled. There are natural occurrences as well as human-induced 'designated use'. There are myths, half-truths and perhaps some undiscovered treasures. In as much as bile can be the good guy or the bad guy, we strive to limit our intake. When we discover drunken sheriffs, neglectful pet owners, dubious clergy and crooked politicians, we attempt to speak up and put an end to their reprehensible conduct. Environmental leadership can be blurrier, and accusations need to be tempered. Holding our environmental future hostage is criminal, yet usually legal and even commonly accepted as normal operating procedure.

I personally define a watershed simply as a receiving area that includes all contributors. The watershed is diverse, extensive, dynamic (non-static) and most importantly, fluid. A watershed includes inlets, outlets and in-betweens, and performs various functions for our natural and human environment—our habitat. Remnants of the past sea world can be explored, observed and documented, while sunken vessels and human fossils can also be discovered behind solid oak desks, within the same watershed.

A stream section, for example, could be designated as high-quality, cold-water aquatic life use, but also designated for irrigation, agriculture, drinking water and other 'beneficial use'. Who benefits from these uses depends upon maintaining or enhancing the integrity of the entire watershed, sustaining its blue blood. With timely monitoring and evaluation, impairments to the stream environment can be quantified, assessed and reported—but what happens next?

Reports and public meetings attempt to convey the condition of the watershed, with efforts to identify probable sources of impairment— cow poop, fertilizers, erosion, dirt roads, wildfires, wastewater, etcetera. But when the rubber hits the road or the stuff hits the fan, it is ultimately up to the local watershed community to take corrective actions. It makes sense, since the eyes, ears, hands and feet of local users are the most connected to the water resource. But who puts these things into motion, emotion or commotion depends upon environmental leadership.

Support groups can help Uncle Joe cut back on his six-pack intake, but it is Joe who ultimately decides whether to flip the pop-top. Yet when deliberating as to what sort of pollution diet is in-store for the Mimbres River, the river is usually not the responsible party. What's at stake depends upon those that actually have one—the irrigators, farmers, ranchers, municipalities, recreationists, industry and everybody in the neighborhood. In terms of educating, communicating, explaining, suggesting, planning, mobilizing, implementing, monitoring, evaluating and taking a long, deep breath, environmental leadership is extremely crucial. Sadly, our leadership may be as impaired as the river itself, or more so.

Making a verbal motion might interest some, but can I spell it out for you? I probably can't, and if I could, maybe I shouldn't. Environmental leaders will need to conjure up ways to deal with semi-deplorable situations, refusing to stagnate or be content with green-washing and rigid thought processes. Go forward in your thinking, guessing, proposing, fishing, hunting and exploring—keep going forward!

Being bile-lingual:

The Bureau of Land Management (BLM) is fond of providing alternative courses of action for comprehensive public lands utilization scenarios. After rounds of scoping environmental issues and convening public discussions, they can occasionally produce new (improved?) alternatives to the original alternatives, prior to coming up with a final decision. One of my strengths early on in this process entails looking at the potency of the alternative actions, and discerning whether the goals and objectives are ambitious enough. It is easy to get blown away by 1800 pages of conservation science facts and figures. But the true mental tenacity comes into play when figuring out in my mind whether we are trying hard enough to protect our natural resources. Are we doing well enough? I think not.

Environmental consultants are renowned for generating documents that span an environmental mountain range—air, land, water, wildlife, soils, recreation, agricultural, energy development, travel management, you name it. The environmental review process starts with the status quo, which is almost always insufficient in key areas—thus the need for a newer, better plan. Then we see how green we can get by going in one direction, and how dirty we can get by looking 180 degrees over at the industry-sponsored alternative. Usually there's enough bile there to cause intense disgust.

Lastly, there is a middle-ground alternative that seeks compromise on uses and on-the-ground conditions. Environmental leadership comes into play when teams contribute their key issue for consideration—let's say riparian vegetation. They state what facts they have regarding past and present health of the ecosystem, and then expand upon what future conditions 'may' look like if Alternative B, for example, is selected. The consultants always seem to mince their words at this stage, stating that conditions are 'likely' to improve at a faster rate than under Alternative A.

After identifying critical areas of concern, leadership takes a coffee break, and upon returning, identifies 'fair' conditions, and moves on to other discussions. My bile starts flowing big time when I read the word 'fair'—fair is not good, and good is often not good enough. Yet if we want to be better than average, and if we truly want to maintain or better yet, 'enhance' the integrity of our natural and human environment, then let's reach higher up that fruit tree, branch out and set our sights on something special.

'Whhoo, whoo…--Youu, youu….'—

That pesky owl again!

Incontinental Divides—

A lonely raindrop falls atop of the Rocky Mountains. Frenetic and solitary, it plummets, spatters and nearly disappears, but not quite. Have no fear, other droplets are on the way, and a magical moment is about to begin. Her name is Flow.

If we are to experience a watershed moment—a time and place where there is a substantive turn in direction and an alteration in course, we will rely on Flo and her friend Mo (mentum) to lead the way. With strength in numbers, we will experience environmental tipping points where our presence is known, and our impact felt. Supported with consolidated-yet-diverse origins, we will produce historical trajectories, 'aha' moments and environmental epiphanies. Transforming our personal, dank water closets into opportunistic, thriving rivulets will reveal our values as well as our leadership vulnerabilities.

It can happen with a blink of an eye, but it usually takes years for clear direction and decisive paradigm shifts to occur. Environmental leadership should be opening the floodgates and encouraging the free flow of innovative, collaborative environmental movements. But the bowels of many conservation organizations and agencies are blocked by fibrous figureheads, well-intentioned stool-sitters, symbolic desk jockeys and that ever-present 'Conservation Constipator'.

Historically and geographically, watersheds were often considered as dividing lines and divisional ridges. Our fluids run east, and their fluids run west. I believe that we must live and thrive with several thousand watersheds, and that the diversity and unique history of each should be affectionately worshipped and experienced. You see, it's the conglomeration of the billions of petrified raindrops that are in dire need of our attention and nurturing. I used to be one of them, but have finally grown into a puddle.

Genuine environmental leaders are destined to produce profound environmental effects. Like the discovery of a vaccine for smallpox, the invention of the printing press, or the storming of the Bastille, we seek a revolutionary revival. We too will have our watershed moments.

We will initially be looked at as unwanted and unneeded, and told politely that our extra green efforts are 'not necessary' or 'will be considered'. Many of us work (not thrive) in environments that think of us as foreign intruders, out-of-staters or out-of-minders. Our departments are run by some very important managers— political insiders, seasoned professionals, well-intentioned 'kumbayakers', right-place and right-time individuals-- and we are really jealous. We don't normally butt heads with them, as we are lower in the pecking order and rarely chirp up.

We constantly wonder if we are being seriously employed or just downright ployed or taken major advantage of. Our green army needs enhanced environmental leadership. We deploy environmental troops on the ground, we pray for miracles, and we beg for resources. We fight battles, ask for forgiveness and pay our bills. There is no reason why dedicated environmental teams and team members need to feel captured, ambushed or hoodwinked. We need to be staunch, undeterred and ready to pounce. In order to do so, we must recognize the camouflaged conspiracies within us and others.

BGB or KGB?-

There are plenty of similarities. We all start as drops, some bigger, some smaller. Some of us are subjected to water torture— restrained from being able to make significant environmental splashes and being funneled into paths of least resistance. Mundane water quality studies, data analysis and report generation keep us occupied and deterred from branching out to receiving bodies. We review and then issue permits to pollute-- within limits, of course. Our environmental conviction has resulted in alienation, solitary confinement and feelings of impoundment. Our reservoirs of stored hope and ambition eventually shrink into canteens of despair and last-gulp efforts.

We are infiltrated by leaks and seeps that make us feel 'tapped-out' and depleted. Codes of conduct build up into proportions of propaganda, and our green side starts to feel as if there is some sort of conspiracy, some covert activity that is keeping us suppressed. Evidence points towards indiscreet levels of interference and obstruction, directly and indirectly linked to brilliant green bile. The most substantial seeps appear to emanate from leadership transmission fluids—oozing across the middle and upper management echelon.

Negativity, fear and close-mindedness dribbles from multiple leader-ship levels, sometimes as dank and damp gloom, other times as trickles of curdled resentment. We feel uncomfortable in discussing our environ-mental inhibitions, as if we would be divulging secrets to a double agent (government representative and powerbroker). We should be monitor-ing rivers, and not under the constant surveillance of so many icy eyes, i-dotters and t-crossers.

Have I intimidated you a little bit? It wasn't my intention, but it was vital to reveal that green bile in disguise can be a second cousin to the KGB-lifestyle. Your painstaking inquiries may reveal some dark secrets and secretions, producing repulsive anger and senses of betrayal. Don't become too chummy with the already infected, or they will devour your environmental devotion, sending you running for refuge.

Different pretend-leaders are endowed with their own concoction of bile—some make the work week sickening sweet, while others opt for the bitter aftertaste. Yet over and over again, I discover two main noxious ingredients. The first is sluggishness, and impedes our efforts to try out newfangled approaches. Leaders appear stuck in a rut, but on their own volition, doing little to extricate their selves. The other is complacency—a close cousin to the slugger, complacency sits still with eyes open but with ears closed. Your particular leadership environment may appear different, but I bet you locate some next of kin to slugs and caged birds.

We often contain ourselves in order to retain our jobs, and that is quite an injustice! The more totes and trappings we take on, the more frequent are our misgivings, the more severe are our unintended results, the fewer scruples we have remaining.

We need to find that leadership stream that will allow us to channel our eco-protection energies. Our current state of affairs needs to be shaken, or at least stirred. If you're feeling bugged, hacked or infected by some weird virus, I suggest that you concoct a sodium pentothal experiment that will provide recognition of tonic waters and potential escape routes.

Our green conglomerate of inmates is often treated as subversives by the more conservative conservation elders, and rightfully so—we do aim to subvert the pathological green enviro-mental ward a la 'Clockwork Orange' and convey broader, unorthodox EL strokes to our community canvas. Go ahead and escape the mundane, banal, unimaginative—break out, but don't run nor hide. You're not alone in this EL pilgrimage. Environmental accomplishments will require environmental accomplices. Join ranks and explore the greener, greater good ensemble.

Imagine how the world could be, so very fine, so happy together..--

The Turtles

Tools of the Tirade—

In Sub-Saharan Africa, they still sell the old-style sardine cans with the welded seams. I bought four at the open-air market, but the merchant only gave me one key opener. In my best Lingala dialect, I informed him of the mistake.

"No mistake", he mused.

"I need no key", as he deftly swiped his machete blade into the metal flange, then pried the top off with his educated fingers.

Sometimes it takes another set of cunning eyes to scope things out. I'm not insinuating that good fortune is the panacea, but luck most assuredly changes, for better and for worse. Enviro organizations can frequently go a few years before recognizing that there are gaping holes in their programming. Evaluations can be more effectively performed via regular collaboration and consternation with affiliate enviro entities. With time and trust, programs will share useful steps and stories—especially once they've been solved. Invaluable enviro history from one can convey pertinent pollution prevention potential to another neighboring agency—if you're willing to be complicit. I call it action.

Take the recent Animas River debacle—as a former Environmental Health Director for the tri-county Southwest Colorado region, I certainly was aware that there was mine waste, heavy metals and much work to be done on watershed protection in the headwaters area housed by the Gold King Mine (Silverton, CO). But our program had no jurisdiction over such matters. The federal government (EPA) and its Colorado Water Quality Control Division state agents (from the Colorado Department of Public Health & Environment, CDPHE, pronounced 'Khadaffi') would be ultimately responsible for monitoring, evaluation and potential remediation. Toss in a few other entities like the Department of Natural Resources and the fortuitous Inactive Mine Reclamation Program, and we've concocted a full stew pot of ossified slouch potatoes.

Naturally, our 'ole friend, the Chamber of Commerce, does whatever is humanly possible to ensure that the headwaters of the Animas River do not become classified as a CERCLA Superfund site, as that would undoubtedly cause a community commotion and jeopardize marketing ploys and short-term tourist buckaroos.

I liken the devastating Gold King Mine breach that contaminated the Animas de Los Perdidas River (the River of Lost Souls) to the kennel cough that spreads from one orphaned environmental community to another. Healthy community values were swept under the rug and disingenuous public meetings were boiler-plated- -mocking critical environmental issues, while economic values were denigrating the environment. With the moniker 'Gold King' and 'mine', why would we have thought otherwise?

Where was the environmental leadership by the feds or the State before the deluge? There was none that I'm aware of. Protect the economy, at all costs. Tourism is the priority, dwarfing the possibility or probability of environmental disaster. Fourteen years later, all hell would break loose, as the Gold King impoundment would bust (with some poor engineering assisting) and the Animas River with its heavy metals would run orange like Tang. Only now are the money mongers considering whether Superfund status might actually pay for their greedy mistakes, and that they can request a 'do-over'. With political allies, they probably will. Meanwhile, downstream Tribal Nations and the State of New Mexico have filed suit over potentially negligent management of Silverton's mines, resulting in contaminated surface water across State and Tribal boundaries.

Looking back on this soul-adrift river, the primary solution would have been to promote the environmental fury, produce strength in numbers, and insist that State and federal government can do a better job when local input and diverse interests into watershed health are included. I fondly refer to this approach as 'positive infiltration'. Pitifully and woefully, some of the Water Quality managers graduated from the same leadership class as me, proving that attendance is merely physical presence. I took it on the chin, but the consequences were quite gut-wrenching. Colorado WQCD didn't even want to look closer and see if there was an iota of a possibility that local watershed pollution prevention might make more sense than zero State activity. We could conveniently consume, but to collectively cooperate? Forgettaboutit!

How's your bloody pressure doing?

Has any of this stuff been able to create some steam? Have you been able to reconstruct a personally atrocious environmental leadership event in your mind? In case you haven't read the fine print--this Environmental Leadership guide is intended for the young-at-heart, but not for minors. It's P-rated, for professionals without pretension. If you can't relate to the material, then, well, it's irrelative. Shout to the highest mountain—what do you hear? Tiptoe into the alpine stream—what do you feel? This is all about you—can you commit to a cause that doesn't reverberate when you pound your fist into the earth? Can you cry tears of happiness when profound statements slowly become infectious intentions? Can you sense the MICE scampering under your feet?

Model (the way)

Inspire (a shared vision)

Challenge (the process)

Enable (others to act)

These are not novel thoughts, as <u>Kouzes & Posner</u> devoted an entire best-selling text on their behalf in <u>The Leadership Challenge</u>. (They also refer to Encouragement and 'Encouraging the Heart'— but I must leave this up to you, as I'm convinced that you know this innate fervor and inborn passion better than I or anyone else could ever explain.). Rather than inundate you with mega-chapters of personal agony that may resemble the Old Testament, I'll attempt to go the hypnotic route and only allude to MICE on rare and medium-rare occasions.

You are bright and energetic, so you won't need much prompting or nudging—maybe some cajoling and if need be, a little jolting for unique occasions. 'Till then, practice your rodent control by being a role model, inspiring others, challenging the status quo and enabling the impossible or impractical into a kinetic conveyance of thoughts and actions. Mighty MICE!

Livin' in Environmental Limbo--

I started running long distances in my late twenties and continue to do so into my sixties. The progressions that a long-distance runner goes through are very similar to how present and future environmental leaders should proceed. Firstly, it's a matter of accepting a challenge--something exciting, arduous, time- consuming, painful and full of wonderful anxiety and anguish. Your personal challenge may be more mental than physical, but that's for you to exclusively decide. We will discuss creating challenges and opportunities throughout this guide, so I don't expect you to latch onto a new challenge as we speak—just take some mental notes (and recall the MICE).

In order to take on a new challenge, odds are that you will need to put in some training. It could be a matter of starting up with a 2- mile run, walking during lunch, practicing yoga, joining the Optimists Club, learning tenor saxophone or creating new program priorities. You just have to commit to the act and apply more than a modicum of personal effort.

Next is a series of one step forward, hopefully only half-step back, so you are moving in a positive direction. It will take discipline. It will take endurance. It will show how persistent you can be in pursuing your objective—persevering through climactic conditions, concentrating on your short-term movements with your long-term goals on the horizon. Many of you are very good at this, and I give you a lot of credit. Yet don't feel that you must do it all on your own—even runners enjoy the camaraderie of practice sessions, fun runs, aid stations and social events. So run those ideas by others and see if you can convince them that your cause is worthy, or better yet, that they can accept the challenge as well. Simply stated, when you share with others what it is that you are keenly working on, this very act will cause self-reflection, produce visions, evoke fears and conjure up even more possibilities.

I know this is easier said than done. I once had a very capable saboteur on my Montana Water Quality staff. A real spiteful nutcracker, this was someone that would go to great lengths to disrupt the process. He would take advantage of opportunities to inject malicious comments, instilling negative thoughts in our brains and then smirking at other fragile staff members. I tried discussing remedial options with my supervisor, who bumped my concerns up to the next higher supervisor, who concurred that I had a pain in the ass on my team and told me to discipline him and document the event. Discipline at the State level usually means 'don't do that again, and if you do, we will have another sit-down meeting'.

Eventually I lost this battle, as the righteous rancor struck me with a form of leadership stupor, and I found that it was best for me to join another team that had a better chance of working together. I may have given up too soon, but we've all been there, hindsight et- all. Yet it was the extreme lack of top-level leadership that trickled onto mid-level leadership, dooming a program from performing essential water quality protection at effective levels. My departure was fairly easy—but left the rest of the staff thinking that there was no future, and they were right. There would be no future until they created one.

Having failed and failed many a time, I've actually become more adept at dealing with vital and time-critical situations. Chalk it up to experience and persistence. There's always more than one dream, more than one race to run. I've been told by a mate that I'm as persistent as mercury in the environment—and I take it as the ultimate compliment. Honestly, I don't get a lot of compliments! And quite candidly, what we environmental leaders might see as persistence is occasionally interpreted as pestilence.

Persist in your endeavors but try to figure out where you fit within your organizational leadership equation. It's much harder when you're interviewing for a job or taking on a new position—you feel like you must impress people, maybe be low-key, ask questions that you might already know the answers to… they call it the 'probationary period' for a reason. Yet eventually you will need to show your self-esteem, flex your ambitions and try to liberate yourself from organizational bondage. Now we're getting closer to leadership and environmental leadership in particular! And being particular is a good thing!

I estimate that I fail about 9 times a day, with about 6 of those (I don't like the term 'mistakes') occurring before noon. Does that mean that I learn from my failures as the day goes on? Maybe, but then again, I'm a morning person, so I should be thinking clearer earlier on. I think it's that I'm more creative / eager in the morning, more pensive / reflective in the afternoon, and almost brain dead in the evening.

'When you look in strange places, you find strange things..' --
Anonymous

Something always happens...

Water (moisture content, in particular) is the enemy of many recipes in the food manufacturing process. The 'activity' of water can provide the necessary conditions for the rapid and exponential growth of microorganisms. Several other building blocks may be needed—protein, temperature and time being the most critical.

When the correct environment is provided, 'opportunist organisms' begin to take shape and form. If nourished, they will grow rapidly, reproducing and capitalizing on the situation. When their food supply diminishes, or when the environment deviates, organisms must adapt, or risk being marginalized by competing organisms. Likewise, providing sustenance, a rich culture and a suitable environment will promote team growth as well. If we are to thrive and survive in a competitive environmental arena, we will need to experiment, provide, develop and nurture--not only nature, but our team culture.

We need to work with variety, diversity, rawness, complexity, synergisms, maturity... sounds like we are crafting a fine wine! Many so-called leaders appear content with the conventional 'burger & fries' approach, with generic production of fluffy messages and fully automated responses. They end up marinating our minds and expelling chunks that make employees scatter. Not me—I'm still hungry for some soul food, something of substance that satisfies and replenishes. I enjoy nourishing a team, and cherishing, savoring the moment. I'm betting that you and I have something in common here.

Unlike blueprints or recipes, I believe that the human formula can't be precisely re-created each time, nor should it be. Opting for a participatory approach over a predetermined formula can produce discomforting uncertainty as well as shock waves of excitement. We should be thrilled when some peppers are hotter than others, some fruits sweet and others more pungent. While we environmental leaders may not be vintners or chefs, we perform a multitude of tasks as prep cooks—we prepare people with possibilities, including our own.

Le Petit Dejeuner--

As an Environmental Scientist serving the Montana community of West Yellowstone, I was conducting sanitary inspections of some of the many hotels serving 'continental breakfast'. The first glaring question was—from which continent?

From the artificially prepared Cheese Danish to the chemistry lab French Toast, nothing could compare to the Polish Sausage, accompanied by Greek Yogurt and an English Muffin, washed down with a cup of Columbian Coffee. It would be remiss of me to not mention the hi-tech American self-serve Waffle Maker with unworldly maple syrup.

During the morning rush hour (somehow everybody arrives at the same time), I observed a German tourist trying to physically milk the milk machine, as if it were a real moo. She appreciated my advice to simply lift the handle, instead of wearing out the rubber udder. While following the trail of ground squirrel droppings, I discovered that the oval sausage patties were stored unrefrigerated, uncovered on the laundry shelf, next to the toilet cleanser—perhaps you needed one after the other?

Environmental leaders certainly must be sufficiently prepared—but what is the quality of what we have rehearsed? If you've assured that there is enough bunk and malarkey to serve everyone, where does that leave us? Have you left an impression, and what sort?

Good from afar...(but far from good)--

In all fairness, federal agencies such as the USFS and BLM often do a fair job. The problem is, fair is a C-grade that would engage many a concerned parent in several teacher conferences. We are the parents, but where are the teachers, and how much influence do they have in working with our under-achievers? Or do our organizations and agencies claim to be self-taught and home- schooled, so to speak, and can they relate to the very public environment that they are designated and directed to protect, promote and serve? Fair is not good, no sirreee!

Here's another Hawaiian example. I knew it was going to be one of those days, when the roaches started marching out of my work vehicle's CD player. Talk about trying to keep your eyes on the road! Lacking any bug juice, and not wanting to toast the critters (and myself) with the car heater, I opted to go with the Big Chill and see if the air conditioning might freeze-dry them, at least momentarily. As luck would have it, the car's AC was only fair at best. It needed a new Freon charge or would continue to produce a mild 75-degree breeze. Better than 90 degrees, not as cool as 60. Not useless, but not extremely useful. My environment was tepid, luke-warm and situationally speaking, one of few immediate options.

Which one comes out first, I wondered, getting back to the Wailuku roach brigade. Was there a leader or a scout? Was he being pushed from behind as a representative or liaison? Did they know that my environment was sacred, with little room for compromise? Do they take calculated risks, or simply perform knee-jerk actions and reactions?

What goes around does not come around—because program leadership rarely ever does go around. It's not a full-circle; in fact, more often than not, environmental direction is more of a 45- degree angle or less, a quarter of a pizza at best. There is reflection, deflection, short-cutting, hurdling, undermining and flying by the seat of that cowboys' big pants.

Yet what if we assisted the vector in becoming the victor? The roaches would have no need to enter the car's interior if some knucklehead employee didn't leave her syrupy Mountain Dew in the cup holder and neglect to close the windows. But what about assisting with human transmission—how can we promote sustainable resource reservoirs and allow agreeable conditions to flourish? Are there unorthodox approaches that would avoid mayhem and chaotic environments? Can we endorse a potentially sane asylum that requires few preconditions, yet promotes versatility, possibility and conservation pathways? Can you do this without expecting me to provide inappropriate answers?

This is all part of flourishing in a humdrum leadership environment. Despite President Coolidge's praise of persistence, it would be mythical to portend that elixirs are derived solely from sheer hard work and determination, unless we learn from our mistakes. I'm hoping that my blunders will illuminate some creative green lightbulbs in all of our minds.

Who's the fairest of them all?--

Let's stick with our discussion about being 'fair' for a moment longer. I'd like you to try grading yourself and your organization, side-by-side:

Quality	My Personal Score	My Organization's Score
Competency:	B	C
Competitiveness:	B	D
Capacity:	C	B
Confidence:	B	C
Caring:	B	C
Conscience:	A	C
Courage:	C	C
Credibility:	B	C

Have you given it the old college try? I would venture that 95% of you score yourself higher than your team—that's very impressive! It means that you do, in fact, have the potential to elevate the proficiency and standards of others, if given the chance. The bad news is that chances are rarely given! They don't happen 'by chance', or rarely do. If you want to tilt the scales in your favor, you'll still have to perform your job, day-in and day-out, but you'll need to start weighing-in on pertinent, enthralling and timely issues. You'll need to stare at that derogatory C-grade posted on your corkboard. You'll need to stop playing it safe and punting the football on fourth down—you'll need to come up with some special crunch-time plays and go for it!

Cereal Killers & Systemic Situations--

Cook a man a fish, feed him for the day. Teach a man to fish, get rid of him for the weekend. I get mental nourishment from trail running and fly-fishing (more ideas while running, but a clearer mind while fishing). Within the environmental arena, it is critical to spawn new ideas and provide opportunity for community nourishment-- not feeding schools of fish into a frenzy, but schooling pools of communities with sensible environmental concepts that they can eagerly sink their teeth into.

True environmental leaders are both perceptive (of what's going on around them) and receptive (of the thoughts and ideas of others). I've worked for quite a few self-proclaimed enviro leaders who could've had their headstrong image pasted on the breakfast cereal box. Oh, what fun it was, working for Frosted Flaky—the glazed look emanating from his erratic gamesmanship, powdered with glucose and 8-hour energy drinks. I'd like to forget I ever worked for Fruity Pebbles--a professional troop taxidermist, staring mesmerized into her human bowl of 'inferios', while keeping a watchful eye on our snaps, crackles and pops.

Environmental leaders must be able to extend the educational continuum from the early stages of information and awareness, into more advanced stages of knowledge and plausible action. Instruct, suggest, motivate, and mobilize, to name a few actions that will chum the waters. As leaders, we need to be captivating, but we must ensure that we routinely practice 'show & tell', followed by 'go & do'.

Many will think of us Environmental Leaders as a traveling medicine show, offering cure-alls for an unhealthy, shredded planet. As a result, we must recognize the risks of offering prescribed relief, cautioning leaders not to mimic the promises of politicians. I often say that <u>we need to promote people</u>--people with names & faces, intentions and actions. And as leaders, we need to selectively choose our curative skills and prioritize prevention in the first place. This is the breakfast of champions.

Upon starting work for our environmental organization, here are a few of our guidelines:

1. You are responsible for your own actions, (but don't try to do anything without checking with us and getting our permission).

2. We have specific procedures to minimize making mistakes (so don't make any!).

3. We expect you to be professional (but don't expect too much from the rest of us!).

4. We'll let you know if you're going down the wrong track (there will be a train wreck if you don't follow our directions!).

5. We want to provide you with the tools to succeed at this job (you'll need these construction skills & maintenance tools to pry yourself from our death grip, to hammer in new thoughts into our thick mindsets, and to squeeze new ideas into crevices that we have resolved to seal).

I challenge every environmental entity to evaluate where you can improve and pour milk onto each of these 5 sure-fire failures.

There's Always Shroom for More..

As a youngster, I used to be amazed how the much-maligned mushroom could punch holes through the concrete sidewalk and turn into skyscrapers above the ants and moss. How on-earth could it, well, mushroom? It doesn't. It simply uses its spore-saving devices to wait until surface conditions are ripe, and then becomes opportunistic in a very short period by attaching to surfaces and inhabiting fragile fissures.

I had no idea about fungal properties, or that nature could materialize like a Star Trek 'beem me up' adventure. I imagined that the sheer force of an underground mushroom was bench pressing Portland cement. We humans can be so naïve at times, convincing tourists about jackalopes, snow snakes, Tommy- knockers and Menehunes.

Are we prepared to take advantage of the situation, when environmental conditions appear 'ripe'? Or do we sit politely as if on an airliner, patiently waiting for miniscule snack morsels to be placed on our laps? Such tidbit offerings are never filling, nor fulfilling, just teasing and taunting. Sustainable programs require sustenance, in terms of leadership quality and quantity, with the high fiber coming from our essential communal fabric.

Sometimes my vision of environmental prowess is distorted by false strengths and postures of pretense. For example, at the State level, I've found the Colorado Water Quality Control Division to be a muscleman in terms of enforcing clear violations of the Clean Water Act. Maybe that's not always true, but they give the image that they are a force to be reckoned with. On the flip side, they have been historically stubborn (and stingy) in not relinquishing resources for local and regional efforts to pursue watershed protection and pollution prevention ventures. To those of us with a sense of reason, it would seem like a no-brainer—dole out monies to local units with boots on the ground, in order to promote watershed health. Provide backup support and regulatory authority, but step aside and allow community-based watershed leadership to flourish.

I confirmed my findings of dismal environmental leadership by trying to produce a collaborative 'watersheducation' project in the Arkansas River headwaters of our Colorado regional ecosystem. Bringing together support from Colorado communities including Leadville, Buena Vista, Poncha Springs and Salida, I coined the project We Help Integrate Technology & Education, and We All Take Equal Responsibility (WHITEWATER). Firstly, the State Water Quality Control Division told me that I missed this year's deadline. When I proved to them that it was actually their goof-up, they switched the story to "..your proposal would duplicate efforts and jurisdiction of our current programs.."

Talk about a lack of environmental leadership! The State's reasoning was that surface water quality was their bailiwick, and that their statewide programs were satisfactory (they didn't exist but got few complaints). If our environmental leaders expend little effort and dedicate few resources, there will be few rewards. It reminds me of Benito Mussolini claiming colonial control over Ethiopia from his authoritarian throne in Rome. We will eat your pasta, but not at the same table.

It immediately took the wind out of my sail, infusing a foul taste in my mouth for the State Environmental Kingdom. No chance of mushrooms sprouting today.

Being an extreme reggae music fan, I latched on to what I thought I heard Bob Marley chanting:

'My fear is my only courage, I got to push on through…'
Years later, I discovered that the actual lyrics were:
'My feet is my only carriage, I got to push on through…'

I guess brother Bob couldn't afford a car at the time. Yet I still think that fear (yes, fear itself) may be my only courage. No woman, no cry.

Lepers or Leprechauns??--

As if you don't already know, leaders come in all shapes and sizes, all makes and models. I say this because of an impression people may have of leaders being superior in some sense—that's non- sense. As a former Peace Corps Volunteer, Americans stateside talked to me as if I just returned from the moon. They praised my independence, courage, commitment and big heart, and then I ruined it for them. I told them that Volunteers in Africa were little different from Volunteers in St. Louis. They had big hearts and they had little hearts. Some were sports jocks, some were dead-heads, and others were adventure junkies. Most of us weren't sure what we were. There was one hefty farm boy who had a fetish for our Swiss Army knives—we found 13 of them stashed in his duffle bag. More than one Volunteer had a prior record for theft and drug abuse. Several took promiscuity to an extreme and died from HIV- AIDS.

Talk about preconceived notions--hell, even some of the Zairois lepers I knew were crooks—they would steal a villager's chickens, put a red ribbon on their wing, sell them to you in the morning, steal them again at night, put a yellow ribbon on their wing, sell them … I give them credit for their ingenuity, but I guess they figure, who's gonna arrest a leper? Leaders are no different, even if they think they are.

Be perceptive and try to identify the fats, fillers and preservatives in your community sandwich. Some will be quite obvious, while others will appear as decoys, stuntmen or even as kindred spirits. You should thank your lucky charms that you're not seeking out Nosferatu himself, but rather determining the human elements that underperform, under-think and undermine your elusive emerald ambitions. Others may or may not understand their implications on your environmental presence and desired future—you might be one of them, but hopefully not for long!

Pulse Check:

Are you getting something out of this material so far? That's all it is, is material. If you're finding it immaterial, then maybe you've latched on to some secret methodologies or green leadership oracle that we need to know about-- but you'll need to write in-blood that you will be sharing your thoughts and considerations with others within your working and living environment. Share the wealth and share the pain too! Not just the pain and anguish of being less of an environmental leader than you intend to be, but also the growing pains of reaching out to people, despite the visual clues and sneers that signify 'avoid direct contact'.

I know all too well how hard it is to make incremental environmental strides. This is not your father's version of Environmental Leadership-- bless their hearts, they were all too consumed in other wars and the repercussions of those wars. Now it's our time to fight for our environmental presence and future!

Listen carefully, and you can barely detect a weak drumbeat in the distance. I'm not sure, but it sounds a lot like the thumping of the energizer bunny, sans energy. Or it could be our green hearts fluttering in arrhythmia, murmuring on life support. The percussions of our daily leadership struggles and the repercussions of our actions or inactions is what this guidebook is about. I hope you enlisted in our ranks of green restitution!

> *'Whether 'tis nobler in the mind*
> *to suffer the slings and arrows of outrageous fortune,*
> *or to take arms against a sea of troubles..*
> *to be or not to be, that is the question..'—*
>
> William Shakespeare

Nothing is Simply Green-

Despite the beliefs of eco-conscious users, most green cleaning products do not effectively kill surface bacteria or viruses. By direct application, they may enable a wiping cloth to physically whisk germs away (onto the rag, to be transported somewhere nearby?), or may discourage organism growth by altering the pH of the surface. But they are not deadly. The same can be true for getting yourself into hot water—once you've been scolded, and you retreat to a safe distance, you tend to creep back when things simmer down to a less-lethal degree. That's human nature.

Akin to ephemeral streams, we have seasonal highs and lower, moody flows. We adapt to our conditions, yet as Environmental Leaders, we must be able to proactively alter the conditional environment—making things more fertile, more productive and less-threatening. And when more-calamitous agendas start to oxidize our core-belief system, we need to be able to survive, and then ultimately thrive! What we give to the needy is Environmental Leadership—trust, hope, resilience and greener aspirations. What we take from the greedy should have been shared in the first place—recognition, opportunities, resources and mutual assistance.

I hope you've found this first episode to be entertaining. Truthfully, I hope you found it to be invigorating! I am determined to instill vigor in those of you who are in hot pursuit of conservation alliances, environmental progressions and environmental justice. If you're not on-board yet, you can give it another go, staying open- minded and continuing reading and thinking. Or you can retreat to the old school of conservative conservation, cautious action, sterile reasoning and inhibited ambition. I really don't think that there's any middle road—you're with us, or without us. Whaddy'a have to lose? Plenty:

a) <u>Lose that mediocre environmental funk</u>—break out from the middle of the pack and experience being truly above-average.

b) <u>Lose faith in those processes that have underperformed</u>, under-appreciated and underestimated the importance of you and your commitment to environmental causes.

c) <u>Lose control</u>—yeah, that's right. Back off from what you can readily handle and try to wrestle with some other critical environmental concepts. I'm not saying that your priorities are not important—I'm thinking that examining your situations from different vantage points will bring to life new possibilities. I hope you like scary movies!

CHAPTER II.
AROUSING A SHARED ENVIRONMENTAL VISION

Now that I've given you some examples of fermenting and despicable leadership, it's time to launch into some situational environmental analysis. Check out these real-life sentiments:

'We're in a real pickle here. We don't like being held on a short leash, nor being manipulated or smothered like a crummy biscuit in greasy gravy'.

'This is not the kind of expectation I had for working with a community-minded organization. I thought that the green fire would be stoked at all levels throughout the organization...'

'I didn't realize that program managers would be so fearful of sharing their inner thoughts on our strategic plans. This goes on and on, until something or somebody creates change...'

Have you been dreaming about putting a cattle prod to that enviro lump that's been loafing around the VIP lounge? Is driving long distances to conduct mundane inspections starting to feel absurd? Do we need to perform CPR to the comatose majority at such agonizing meetings? The commonality here is that we have lost our way—we are performing the same acts, maybe even perfecting them, but with less vitality and less ingenuity each day. The cement is starting to harden, and our once-flexible mindsets are becoming permanent fixtures. No longer can our brains and bodies stroll together.

'There must be some kinda way outta here, said the joker to the thief......there's too much confusion, I can't get no relief...--'
Bob Dylan

The Price of Admission—Hoof & Mouth Disease—

In my limited French, I remarked to the Austrian nun that her new blue robe appeared 'bien dresse'—which would have been a compliment if she were a well-groomed horse. I had the best of intentions. I apologized that no horse looked as nice as her, with or without the dress. I kept digging myself deeper.

Luckily, Sister Lucia had a sense of humor, even buying me a beer for my first-class comments. At initial glance, environmental programs may appear similar in nature. The white, granular topping is obviously sugar, until proven otherwise. We acclimate, habituate and get accustomed to sounds, odors, temperature, lighting and colors. We expect our sensors to enjoy life's experiences.

Yet at first bite, I knew there was a serious problem—the baklava was coated in not an abundance of sugar but encrusted in a look- a-like salt product. I had the waitress take a finger taste to confirm that I wasn't some wackadoo. Yep, she concurred, and hurried inside to dispose of the unintentional error. Better that it was sodium chloride and not ammonium nitrate.

Other times, one's burnt toast is another's blackened redfish—steak tartar to me, but a raw deal to my wife. There are different strokes for different folks, I guess. We experience varying temperatures, pressures and boiling points, with adequate room between joyous occasions and heated, encapsulated discussions.

Are you sentenced to your computer stall and cellular phone, thinking that you can live a mistake-free life, sending cryptic messages from a cushy solitary confinement? Communications may often appear rather lifelike, but are mostly patchy, non-productive bucolic blurbs. Our streambanks become compromised, our minds inundated, our mid-sections loaded, and our confidence eroded. If you think you deserve better, then liberate yourself!

'People who are in touch with their needs, do not make good slaves'
-Marshall B. Rosenberg

And Up From the Ground Came a Bubblin' Crude--

Well listen to the story 'bout …a bad day at the office. In a state of utter frustration and pent-up anger, my subordinate Mary marched over, turned towards me and exercised her right to speak. Her words caught me off-guard.

"Just take charge and get real!" she gushed, with a blustered face and a fair share of vitriol.

How should I respond? Her attack was not meant to be pain- inflicting, but it's not often that such verbal barbs were slung my way. All I was doing was working on yet another septic system permit, when the apocalypse arrived. Ouch! I felt stung and defenseless against the hillbilly attack. I knew her sentiments were poorly-worded—she most probably meant 'wise-up' or 'screw-you'. It was all coming back to me now. I was being somewhat naïve in hoping that an internal cat fight brewing between two employees (Mary being one) would miraculously disappear. I guess I should have addressed the issue over the last couple of days—but I didn't. I gave this situation some deep thought, and the hydrologic cycle kept entering my mind.

With a torrential downpour of human exasperation and juicy language, this particularly wacky weather pattern that I was personally experiencing would produce an outpouring of negativity, an inundation of erratic events, tempestuous communications, emotional run-off and a highly unstable atmosphere. In such a closed-loop situation, severe hailstorms, flash floods and blinding blizzards are extreme events that can temporarily unbalance and significantly batter an ecosystem. It also takes a heavy toll on the team environment.

What precipitated this event was a high-pressure system that should have been highlighted on my leadership barometer. A storm was on the horizon, and I did not prepare for its thunderous arrival. Our organization was thrown into a short-term frenzy. The sudden arrival of a human El Nino resulted in anger, scurrying, volatility and sheer panic. Trying to understand and account for how much 'moisture' a person can absorb or retain, without letting all hell break loose—that's part of Leadership 201.

While I haven't perfected the hydro-human logic cycle, I truly believe that it is a more accurate predictor than the farmer's almanac. With a better understanding of the fundamental social and psychological necessities of our human resources, we should be able to better prepare for future events—the environmental arena notwithstanding. After all, much of our daily work focuses around forecasting the future health and well-being of our natural and human environment—health promotion, disease prevention, pollution abatement, resource conservation, source reduction and waste minimization, to name a few.

Community 'Chemistry' at the Watershed Level—

I contemplated writing the entire pretext of **Tonic Water** around the premise of the hydrologic cycle. After deeper consideration, I decided that dedicated environmental leaders like you may only need to relate to the comparison of the hydrologic cycle to human versions of natural progressions--and could then move forward with more accurate personal interpretations, streams of events and group exercises. When considered within an environmental team context and perspective, the possibilities for this logical hydro or hydro-logical cycle are enormous!

Most of us in the environmental community are very familiar with this simplistic hydrologic cycle (diagram). It all starts with **condensation**, whether it is moisture in the atmosphere or the formation of foggy ideas in your thought processes. Most musings and suppositions will wisp by like impotent, moisture-deficient clouds overhead. Depending on our individual levels of self- confidence, imagery and imagination, we can gather diverse concepts and notions and play with bits and pieces of them in our minds.

Asking ourselves 'what if..' questions will assist with the condensate. Asking others 'what if' will take your conjecture to a whole other level. The condensation process itself is a microcosm of the hydrologic cycle, as we literally pull matter out of thin air, and continue to absorb information until we form something appreciable. Your organization's internal climate and environmental leadership will effectively ignore, deter or support the formation of ideologies and substantive clouds.

When our concentrated thoughts reach a saturation level, **precipitation** follows. In the form of rain, hail, snow or all three combined, there is an initial outpouring of ideas with substance, content and a smidgeon or more of exasperation or discontent. We shower our peers, allies and confidantes with those precious ideas and revelations, in hope that the information is given proper scrutiny and timely consideration. Clouds need to form—it is human nature. Cloudbursts are intense responses to environmental and societal cravings. We saturate ourselves in order to satiate our hunger, our cravings, and our green lust.

This sets the stage for the **percolation** process to decide whether to open our pores and accept (or at least allow) various ecological nuances and potentially foreign substances. Such acceptance is properly termed absorption and adsorption. It's taken me forty years to differentiate between the two—let's just say that absorption is more spongelike ('absorbing'), and adsorption is sticking to a surface ('adhering'). Sticky or sponge-like suits me just fine, and none of us are eternally impenetrable.

If there is a lack of curiosity, genius, intrigue, need or some other dislike (or no special concern), the precipitation 'leads' to run-off, with potentially detrimental downstream effects on ecosystems as well as teams. Yet if the voluntary exchange of free ideas is accepted and actually processed, there will be a methodology, instrument or venue to provide **filtration**—sifting through the basic content, clarifying such volume, refining rough edges, purifying the key elements and nurturing subsurface mind-water or the hydro- logical thought process. Your environmental leadership challenge is to make best use of your resources in any or all these situations and treatments.

As with all processes, obstacles and opportunities arise. Heated discussions and economic drought may cause our precipitation thought patterns to dehydrate, desiccate, dissipate and then disappear. But there is no magic involved, and the vanishing act will surely resurrect itself in the formation of new ideas with different mind-moisturizing effects. **Evaporation** is the vaporizing of intended and unintended attempts, efforts and consequences. Environmental leaders would be wise to store up a file folder of evaporative ideas, attempting to grow new notions, schemes and concepts when seasons change and the climate is less harsh, more nurturing.

Another component of our hydro thought process is **Transpiration**, where a portion of our efforts and enthusiasm is perhaps not fully absorbed by our roots but is drawn in from our leaves and outer receptors. What is deemed beneficial and inviting is prioritized and hopefully utilized. As environmental events transpire, we make conscious leadership decisions to adapt to evolving, budding conditions.

Various other elements and events come into play in our individual hydro-logical process. Environmental organizations should be able to recognize moments of condensation before they reach the precipitation phase. If we have a suitable 'storm-water management' plan in place, we will be better prepared to proactively prevent human erosion, than to reactively control sediment and sentiment. It will require intense consideration, true grit and profound determination. Individual and team energy is readily expended in all phases and can result in the growth or demise of program innovations (inspiration, perspiration, heaving, crying!). All programs go through phases of flooding as well as drought, and environmental leadership is essential in weathering the storm.

Every environmental leader with a pocketful of energy should work with their team to visualize their hydro-logical process and equate it with 'what if' scenarios and program opportunities. Current familiarization with such terms and tactics can surely assist our soils conservation worker with his / her erosion control team's fertile approaches, our watershed coordinator with diverse beneficial / questionable uses or daily loads, our air pollution educator with cumulative community impacts and program clarity, our wildlife scientist with integrated & resourceful approaches, our wastewater technician with solids formation / digestive processes and many, many others.

'But you & I, we've been through that, and this is not our fate… so let us not talk falsely now, the hour's getting late…---'
(All Along the Watchtower)

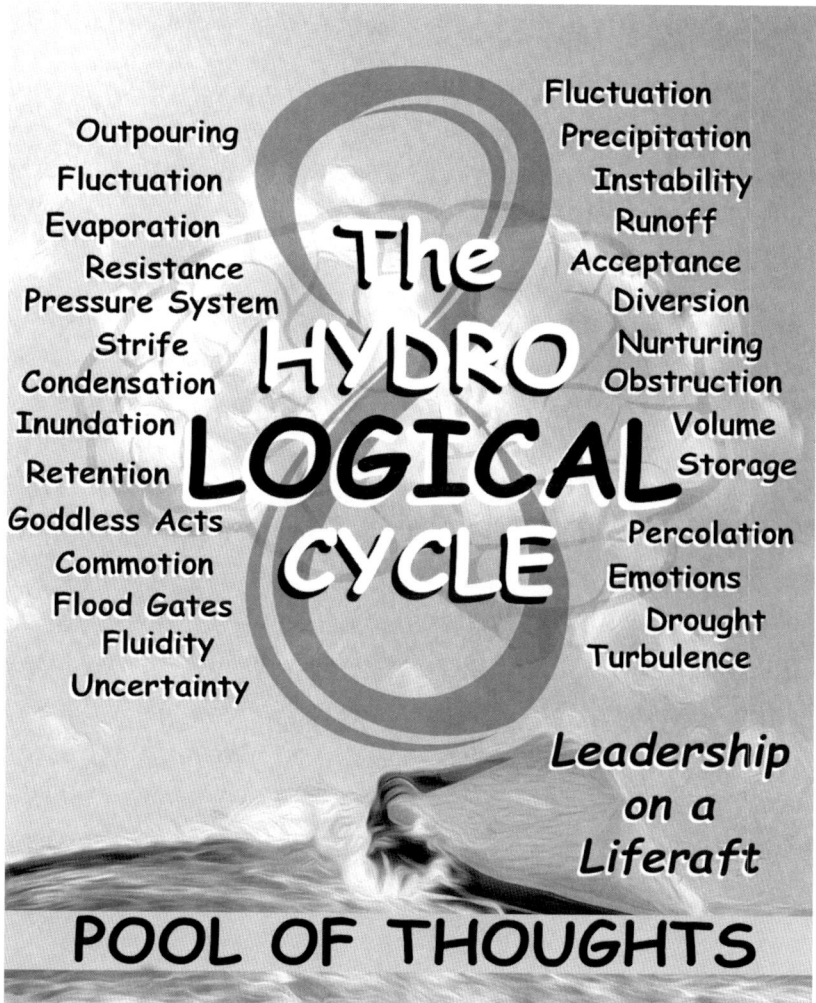

The
HYDRO
LOGICAL
CYCLE

Outpouring
Fluctuation
Evaporation
Resistance
Pressure System
Strife
Condensation
Inundation
Retention
Goddless Acts
Commotion
Flood Gates
Fluidity
Uncertainty

Fluctuation
Precipitation
Instability
Runoff
Acceptance
Diversion
Nurturing
Obstruction
Volume
Storage
Percolation
Emotions
Drought
Turbulence

Leadership
on a
Liferaft

POOL OF THOUGHTS

Repugnace-

Something really reeks, and it's not my underwear. It's more of that lingering olfactory sense. Kinda' smells fishy. It's something that I notice that seems to come and go, like high and low tides. It's rather disgusting, yet all-too familiar. Now it's coming back to me—it's the scent of decaying environmental leadership!

Gangrene def: Localized death & decomposition, resulting from a lack of (blood) flow; normally affecting the extremities; not curable once past a certain point of decay, except by amputation. (From the Greek word 'gangraina'—an eating or gnawing sore; that which eats away).

Cutting off your nose to spite your face? Environmental groups can be gang—greenous, by refusal or reluctance to promote the flow of information from headquarters to outlying areas (thus affecting our extremities). Oftentimes our E.L. objective should not be to provide or decide, but to present, partage and partake. Professional reluctance or refusal to shed the white bread, standard fare techniques and opt for the whole grain approach has painful ramifications.

This degenerate activity, over time, will result in environmental atrophy, disintegration and the downfall of peer support networks. Whether the depravity is intentional or not is not the issue. Conservation orgs often believe they are doing a yeoman's job, carrying the torch and assuming the full brunt of the workload. Carry on dude, but don't turn around and preach about sustainability—your very acts of taking control of a situation (a situation that undoubtedly affects other individuals, other stakeholders, other communities) are responsible for a significant portion of the decay and disappointment that you can read on the faces of affected parties. So, what are we waiting for?? It's time to share, lead and clean up our act!!

*'Well they tell me of a pie up in the sky, waiting for me when I die
But between the day you're born and when you die,
they never seem to hear even your cry . . .
And then the harder they come, the harder they'll fall, One
and all—*

Jimmy Cliff

Why Tonic Water? Well, for starters, it rings truer than murky pond scum. It will hopefully resonate within the green community that internal breakdowns, fears, nonchalance and incompetence can weigh us down as much or more than the contra-environmental community. There are vital signs to environmental leadership that must be checked and re-checked, and there is a suite or culmination of factors that need deep consideration. The ramifications of inaction or poor actions can have dire (or deadly) consequences. If we envision an environmental revolving door, we will catch glimpses of entry points, intentional exits, stumbling blocks, confusion, urgency, warning signs and adaptive approaches. Let's start to take a close look at some of these approaches and bring your scrutiny with you.

Why do they call it 'Quicksand'?-

I suppose it's because of that first bad step, when one unintentionally saunters into a dangerous situation. You try to extricate yourself, but you're stuck. The harder you try to escape, the more you seem to be mired in deep stuff. It happened awfully quickly, but there's no better time to seek your lifeline—you have one, don't you? A band-aid is useless at this point. You've entered a contract for employment, and you thought that this was the environmental career of your dreams. It doesn't pay well, but you're working for a good cause, you have something meaningful to contribute and there are some decent employee benefits.

But it just dawned on you at today's staff meeting that what you may have gotten yourself into was an environmental forgery, a smiling Mona Lisa with green tendencies but Lilliputian creativity. Keep your chin up, things may improve, you never know....

Yeah, you do know, you're screwed! It's like the vintage joke about being captured by headhunters, and the village chieftain giving you a choice of '*death, or buntah*'.. You opt for buntah and are sentenced to something more miserable and agonizing than death (I'll let you come up with your own scenarios).

'*Whether one gives or takes, are both—*
a choice and a curse,
a hand and a knee,
a breeze and a blow'

--- Salifou

Diluted or deluded??

Business leaders do not normally harbor the extraordinary environmental acumen that is needed to deal with critical conservation concerns, in the same way that enviro groups defer to a certified accountant to produce our annual audit. Boat captains shouldn't be flying planes, and pilots shouldn't be toying with electrical circuitry. Unfit environmental leaders are a detriment to society.

It's often apples and oranges, or donuts and tortillas. Positive leadership traits from within the environmental community can be adapted, transferred or horse-traded with the business world, yet without a definitive air, water or wildlife concentration, the dilution factor is extremely significant. When you attempt to materialize an environmental concept, the result can become immaterial or substantially less green.

For instance, let's picture a rural community near St. George, Utah coming together to combine resources and work to protect sage grouse habitat. Business leadership can be valuable for estimating costs, assessing assets, devising a scope of work, delegating tasks, setting timelines, goals and objectives. This is all valuable stuff but is best used by an environmental leader with in-depth understanding of the groundwork, grunt-work, communications, collaboration and a strong sense of stewardship. Business management is essential and anticipated, but business leadership can also be foreign leadership that diminishes the conservation intent and ideals. Enviro leaders get little gratification in getting what we pay for.

In the environmental arena, we regularly deal with the adage *'Seek and ye shall find'*—Coral reef bleaching resulting from underground injection wells, injured manatees from propeller blades, overfishing from nighttime poachers, asthma from idiotic sugar cane burning, groundwater pollution from hydraulic fracturing. Furthermore, there does not need to be definitive evidence for environmental leaders to pursue greater investigations. Detectives start with a hunch or two, and then look for more evidence. The scent of a poopy diaper should be an adequate clue. The same holds true for disgruntled employees, lazy administrators and disenfranchised environmental communities—we can work on providing relief, or we can be part of a growing problem.

There's a rip-off tourist store in Lihue, Hawaii that cons you into opening several oysters in search of a pearl (a low-quality, low- value pearl, worth the price of maybe four raw oysters!). Low and behold, they slice open an oyster and find 'your pearl'. They even ring a bell to make you feel like a winner! All you must do is now choose as to whether you want it strung on a $30 chain or a $300 necklace. This 'oysterfication' process comes to mind when I observe many business leaders making product promotions—a little glitz, glamour and razzle-dazzle, and your calcified shell will reveal a shiny new beginning. If we continue to buy-in to such 'value- added' schemes, we're all shucked.

If a business leadership goal is job creation, I'm not suggesting that business leaders will purposefully roll back environmental regulations in order to enhance employment potential—but it remains an arrow in their quiver. An effective environmental / conservation leader cannot jump into the conversation and argue that jobs are not the issue—in this scenario, employment opportunity is certainly the key issue, and environmental vantage points must adapt to the problem at-hand, or risk being alienated and held responsible for job losses. The task of the environmental leader is to work with the community development leader to clarify concerns and take progressive steps towards congruity.

Each defined leadership trait and every community perspective has something to offer to social, environmental and economic discussions, and the obvious reason for this is that we possess different levels of expertise in varied disciplines. High-caliber environmental leaders and conservation leaders can take advantage of such informative wealth, if we can retain our ultimate level of environmental and conservation integrity. I have never been involved in any Tribal Nation discussions over the costs and benefits of oil & gas development, timber harvesting, dam building or casino construction. It would be interesting indeed to evaluate if the natural resource programs are being directed by a manager or a leader, and how Tribal Councils decide on community priorities with short-term and long-term ramifications.

Fatal Attraction--

The only rewarding element of inspecting carnival vendors is getting into the amusement park for free. When I'm done with my inspections, I can ditch the briefcase and mingle with the rest of the inbred congregation (just kidding!). Meanwhile, I've got work to do—turkey drumsticks cooked to a 165-degree leathery consistency, check; deep fried donut holes served with clean utensils, check; corn dogs made from approved meat by-products, I guess so; curly potato rings cut with gloves over bare hands, roger; uh-oh, here comes the dreaded caramel apple caravan!

I present my credentials and walk over to the hand-sink—running water, soap & paper towels in place and in-use, so far, so good. Yet when I glance to the right, I see the back of the van wide open. Four quick strides reveal a congregation of flies feasting on the caramel apple alter—one of them looks up at me, with sticky goo all over his fly beard, nods 'howdy', then goes back to dinner—plenty more where that came from.

Sounds appetizing, right? I throw out the polka-dotted apples, while behind my back, the worker tries to pick off a few stranded remnants and save a few bucks. I reflect to watching a former President on television idolize PT Barnum. Yes, even in the world of environmental leadership, there's a sucker born every minute. We're enticed by prizes and promises and amused by children. We enter a broad eco-spectrum where animals are mistreated in order to make us humans happy. We're told that we can't introduce more wolf pups into the wild unless we cull the existing troupe. We're not allowed to designate protected landscapes until we evaluate the subsurface mineral wealth. We concede that our need for gravel and asphalt supersedes our desire for clean air.

Welcome to the greatest show on earth, or at least the greatest earth that we have to show. But for some reason, our e-leaders don't seem to be very e-lated. I believe it comes down to two things:

Pri-your-ities and Pri-our-ities.

I'll let you dwell on the potential differences and similarities, from an environmental perspective.

'If it weren't for feelings, we wouldn't have any'
                         -- John Dough

Assist or a cyst??

There's a reason why they refer to the separation distance between a sewer line and a water line as a 'setback'. One pipeline has greater purity and simplicity, the other an amalgam of waste products and deleterious residual effects. Your internal thirst for leadership may be viewed and weighed as a mechanism that is only partially productive and partially worthless. Are you serving under the influence or over the effluence?

Malcolm had no qualms about placing his coffee cup on top of the men's urinal. Even if he forgot it for ten minutes, he knew where to retrieve it. Malcolm was also very self-assured in terms of standard operating procedures for a variety of air quality monitoring models. He literally had it down to a science, even producing 'cheat sheets' to explain procedures in layman's terms to newly hired staff.

But the one thing that really ticked Malcolm off was when our program chief would arrive at work fifteen minutes after staff every morning, come back fifteen minutes after staff during lunch break, and leave hand-in-hand with staff at quittin' time. Malcolm demonstrated to us (his comrades) that thirty unfair minutes per day resulted in being cheated by sixteen full days per year—the same amount of time that was granted to new staff as annual leave. It equates to the boss getting an extra three weeks of vacation on top of her current four-week annual leave. We were all caught off-guard and astonished by this discriminatory practice.

Malcolm was incensed and sizzled constantly. The repercussions were at first amusing-yet-alarming, then disheartening, finally taking the team on a downhill slide. We have been brought up to believe in preferred approaches to betterment that are non- confrontational and non-vindictive. We tell ourselves there are worse things than incompetence—unwillingness, narrow- mindedness and evilness all come to mind. If you want to make a positive difference as a leader, you'll need to differ without begging.

While your EL search is performing its platoon and reconnaissance duties, you're bound to get strafed by lopsided leadership projectiles. You'll be inclined to bite your lip in vexation—but you best do more than that! Your close shaves with our white bread environmental leadership should introduce thoughts of greener impregnation. You may not be prepared (or willing) to hound, pound or besiege the towers of bile—not you, not now, not alone. But eventually, through means that you formulate and inculcate, you will utilize your leadership ammo to blitz and bombard your opposition. Is opposition to harsh a word? I'm okay with 'detractor'.

Leadership without the 'lead' spells 'perish'—
Malcolm

A Reason in the Sun--

In order to reason with people, you don't have to have a good reason. A decent innuendo in your back pocket would surely assist, but sincerity, passion and human instinct will help get you through. I believe that the English Language's best three-letter word is 'apt'. When you show a willingness to engage with other homo sapiens, invisible curtains of invincibility start to unveil. Most all of us have adverse reactions to bad breath and body odor, but we should not be averse to discussing most sane ideas with beholders. If anything, our sense of curiosity and intrigue would start to kick in— how did you arrive at your decision? How does the rest of your team feel about it? Do you think it has potential to be replicated?

Termites are more apt to chow on a weathered home than on a sturdy, well-constructed establishment. We environmental leaders need to come out of the woodwork—if one of our leadership domiciles is ramshackle, then let's sink our teeth into it and create change. But beware of the anteater.

I was walking over towards an Army barrack facility on Oahu to perform an environmental compliance inspection. Out of the corner of my eye, I could see the orange sign stating 'Propane storage—No smoking'. It was right behind the cut-in-half 55-gallon drum that was converted into a barbecue grill. I could have interrupted a delicious smoked Lau-Lau pork lunch but knew better than to mix business with pleasure.

When we are amenable to discussion, we show respect and worthiness towards others—and the best part is, you haven't committed to anything but communicating! Our thought process allows us to discover, uncover, walk away and eventually recover from the most dastard of ideas and beliefs or the most naïve-yet- blatant situations. Don't let your leadership crown disenfranchise you from conversations and appetizing discussions. If you want to evolve as an environmental leader, start by getting involved on a personal basis—despite all of our training to 'remain professional' and 'don't take things personal'. You're a person, so act like one-- you might just learn something! The next day, I requested to have the barbecue relocated, and there's a 50-50 chance that it actually happened.

Exodus—

Organizations often encourage you to surrender, or to succumb to a submissive stature. In the natural world it is thought of as an effective and efficient means of providing protection (anthills, termite mounds, beehives) and sustenance (fox dens, octopus gardens). We often refer to our activities as training, continuity, consistency and standardization. The difficulty, of course, is trying to retain our sovereign souls and thought patterns, without having finite rules smothering our infinite possibilities. Whether you work for the U.S. Forest Slayers, the U.S. Ever-Prolonged Agony or the Bureau of Lazy Mothers, you will be ensconced with standard operating procedures that will conflict with pieces of your prized Environmental Leadership agenda. (Don't worry, I"ll poke equal fun at our enviro groups as well, but you Feds are such an easy target!).

There will be times when you'll need to firmly grasp your mental machete and hack away at the noxious, bureaucratic invasive processes that create a stranglehold on your environmental intent (before it becomes your extent). Programmatic constraints can be as limiting as diversion valves that siphon off streamflow, reducing creativity to a trickle.

I know it's not that simple, and extremely tough to gauge what those upstream folks are thinking. The insecure realm of Environmental Leadership is often a morbid mélange of 'Wayne's World' comical errors and Alfred Hitchcock suspenseful moments. I appreciate all your work (thus far), but let's work harder, better, wiser, greener. You will be your own judge, but the executioner inside each of us is anxious for action!

Even nuns can have bad habits—
Abandoned mine scrawl

Pale Ail— Environmental Prophecy Refills--

I'm sure I'm not the only dude that enjoys both Guinness Stout as well as a hoppy IPA. While on opposite ends of the beer spectrum, they are similar in that they are both bold, hearty, go well with pretzels and pack a punch. My distaste with our ultra-light environmental leaders evolves from their shallow, skunk-like demeanor, as if they were never fully conditioned. Rather than being readily tapped for pints of information, they remain bottled up and secure in groups of six. Worse yet, they produce canned responses that quench no-one's thirst for knowledge or direction.

Environmental leadership does not always work, but it never completely fails. It is perpetually trying to be appealing, fresh, crisp and invigorating. Leadership does not draw lines in the sand-- leadership <u>is</u> the sand, trying to imitate water. Initiate, Partake, Accentuate (IPA)—one of my credos / mottos. It's time for a toast:

Try saying out loud '<u>good blood, bad blood</u>' five times, fast. Or how about trying the same with '<u>Tai-chi, Chai tea</u>'?

Yeah, it's a gimmick, an ice breaker. And more often than not, it loosens up the stiff shirts and permanent presses that back us into a corner.

When asked about my leadership style, I have two standard responses. The more conservative or safe response is that I have a 'hands-on' approach to managing and supervising environmental programs. I immediately clarify the distinction between being hands-on and being a 'micro-manager'. My task (as previously mentioned) is not to perform the work of others, but to do 'the other work'—mentoring, motivating, mobilizing (3M), plus initiating, partaking and accentuating (IPA). I enjoy working with others, am qualified to strengthen team performance, and like to lend a hand, shake a hand, and provide a virtual pat on the back for a job well done. This usually goes over pretty well, by fortifying environmental capabilities.

My more exotic response to an open-minded interview team and unique job opportunity would be that I idolize Dr. Frankenstein, and look forward to the challenge of integrating minds, bodies and spirits into a collaborative conservation creature. My leadership style includes experimentation, persistence, innovation, trial & error. This approach, I find, can only be presented in-person, as long-distance communications and wry humor are easily misconstrued.

Take a moment to contemplate your leadership style, making a personal and professional connection to pressing environmental priorities such as sound science, education and community-based approaches. Stating that you don't have an exact leadership style might be an honest response but will get you a low interview score. See, you did learn something by reading this far! Onward and upward!

No matter who I work for or who I meet, respect me for who I am--
Malian Street Vendor, W. Africa

Meddles of Honor—

Jose: "I don't mean to intrude, but I think it's important that you hear what I have to say—and if I don't have anything to say, I think it's still important that you ask for my input".

Louise: 'But it's not your concern'.

Jose: "Actually, I'm very concerned. Since I'm part of this organization, I'd like to be included in the process".

Louise: 'You have no right to talk to me that way'.

Jose: "I have no wrong to fall back on".

Louise: 'Sorry, you're not invited'.

Jose: "Just so I understand, is it that I'm not invited, or not wanted?"

Louise: 'You're just not needed,...not now at least'.

This summarizes an actual conversation I witnessed within an environmental health department. I walked in feeling tarnished yet tenacious. I walked away feeling liberated and galvanized.

Some leaders polish the silver in their cabinets, while allowing the ironclad infrastructure of the organization (not theirs, ours) to oxidize. Be resolute! Don't wait 'till New Years' Eve! Show up! Come to the table, early and often! As they say, if you're not at the table, you're on the menu! There is a frequently predictable and relatively mediocre leadership persona that disdains exotic ideas, no matter how good or bad. Watch these naysayers nibble away on their stashes of ringdings and moonpies while nostalgically reflecting on 'the good 'ole days'. Then lead us towards someone's idea of betterment.

You can (and should) reward yourself for resembling an obnoxious weed that maneuvers, infiltrates, grasps, climbs, endures and persists—your EL efforts are honorable, distinguishing you from the extinguished.

'Well I know it wasn't you who held me down,
Heaven knows it wasn't you who set me free,
So oftentimes it happens that we live our lives in chains,
that we never even know we have the key..—'

Already gone, the Eagles

Altered State—

As oddball as it sounds, the Bureau of Land Management (BLM) has a process that seeks alternatives to alternatives. My initial knee- jerk reaction was that the decision-making game was rigged. The BLM knows what it wants, and convincingly states it as their 'Preferred Alternative'. Then they work to promote their preference and demote others, until time runs out and a victor is proclaimed— but not always.

By way of my active, engaged and alarmingly methodical process, playing by National Environmental Policy Act (NEPA) rules, I discovered that Alternatives A (no action), B (Betta!), C (Crud!) and D ('Da BLM) can be significantly altered by a holistic, participative public process—if you're willing to stay involved and plug away. The odds are heavily stacked against the status quo. After all, if it were functioning properly, there would be little need for land use revision. But the odds are also stacked against the better Environmental Alternative (B) as being too green, and against the Cruddy (C) industry-backed alternative as being too harmful. That leaves 'Da BLM Alternative (D) as untouchable—or does it?

This depends largely upon public outcry, and if we sense strife or controversy in the air. The process is very cumbersome but does allow one (us) to comment on a smorgasbord of critical criteria (air, soils, water, wildlife, energy, recreation, travel management and so-on). We can highlight weak science, shout out for stronger protections and emphasize environmental priorities. The BLM can 'mix & match' items from Alternative D with a selected priority from Alternative B, make a concession to Alternative C, and even include segments of what might be functioning adequately in Alternative A. Lemon and poppy seed are added to the generic muffin.

The result is surely a compromise, but for an organization directed towards 'multiple use', it can't simply remove its stripes. Internal leadership is vested and entrusted to ensure transparency and fairness. External leadership steps up to the plate and goes to bat for environmental justice. Whether we are gatekeepers or watchdogs, we set our sights at minimizing distorted processes and ineffectual leadership. Ultimately, transparent approaches need to be not simply stated, but seen through the eyes of others, heard by receptive audiences and reverberated throughout program locales. The process can also provide fodder for possible lawsuits.

It's been a helluva ride to get here, and I'm not sure that I know where 'here' is. After experimenting with real-life games such as Hide-and-Seek and Blind Man's Bluff, I've determined that I'm best at 'Show & Tell'. I want to reveal the underpinnings of Environmental Leadership, and figured that I can share moments, describe actions and expose pitfalls—not so much so that you avoid them, but that you can perhaps acknowledge or relate to them, putting a personal twist on your leadership pretzel.

The laundry list of environmental tragedy need not be lengthy, but I will share sufficient indignation so diverse audiences can identify with a nasty situation or ten. Better yet, if we can create a sort of tag-team, then we can better wrestle with the leadership strong- arm techniques encountered in our environmental arenas. Yes, poor Environmental Leadership can be a major pollutant load, and needs to be exposed, so it can be personally mitigated or effectively remediated.

> Dear *Board,*
> *I don't want to belong to any club that would have me as a member.*
> Sincerely yours,.... Groucho Marx

Mish-Mash—

This is a self-help guide, only to the degree that you, as an environmental professional, commit to helping yourself. Here's some free advice:

1. Ponder the Wild Blue Yonder—Provide yourself with the necessary time and space to clarify your perceptions and your ambitions. Take mental and written notes, and highlight the highlights, seeking rewarding advice from **Tonic Water**. Instead of proving me right or wrong, prove yourself capable!

2. Use Your Senses—Be receptive; use common sense, and work to hone your skills so you can sharpen your intuition and perceptive responses.

3. Share—Without sharing discussion topics, and without practicing open dialogue, you'll be somewhat handicapped in your progressions. For those of you in sticky situations, perhaps

you're convinced that your superiors don't give a hoot about environmental leadership? I can relate to that many times over. Give this a try:

* <u>Prove it to yourself</u>—One more time, give it a go and take the initiative. Share a few EL points that really hit home with you. If anything resonates with others, then keep that flame burning--not a bonfire, but a few pieces of kindling.

* <u>You can't strike out on one pitch</u>—First time, swing for the fences; on the next pitch, try to hit a liner up the middle. But if you do strike out, then so what? We all do from time to time. Work on a strategy that allows you several opportunities to share those EL concepts that ring true to you and your team.

* <u>If folks look at you like you're speaking a foreign language</u>, then maybe you are! Simplify your translations, ask questions, accuse the author, but don't give up on your EL journey!

So far, so good? Try to identify and become intimate with a concept, a dream, or an ambition—something unique, personal or genuine. You'll know it when you feel it.

Searching for 'soul food'-

As a former health inspector and roach detective, I've always been leery of dining at dubious Chinese restaurants—but a well-seasoned kitty cat is hard to beat. There was this one surprisingly sanitary Asian food establishment with spicy, tasty food and inexpensive plum wine—I'm sure you're sold already.

What was the most memorable were the fortune cookies. My wife's message spoke of good luck and happiness. This is what mine said:

"When walking alone in the dark, look over your shoulder."

What the heck! You can't even add the traditional adage 'between the sheets' to such a glum warning! I concluded that my future dining would take place at the noon buffet in the bright of day.

I understand that being an environmental leader is more complicated than tossing a salad or flinging toppings onto a pizza. Yet at last count, a shocking 32% of environmental and environmental health organizations are content with their current conventional avenue to program implementation—a 'burger and fries' approach that is not only mass-produced but delivers your sub-standard automated response. For the other 68%, there is still hope, but I hope it's more than putting cheese on that burger!

What it boils down to is that ambitious environmental leaders and leaders-to-be are searching for that satiating 'soul food'. We want to nourish our team, cherish our mutual abilities and savor the moment—then do it again, but not per the KFC original recipe. I dare you to take your purr-fection to the next level!

To mold or to mold—that is the question—
Artemus Craft

Green Around the Gills—

Because we are humans, and because some of us are eager and yes, hungry, we need to understand that the human formula for success can't be homogenized, packaged and retained for freshness. On the contrary, conventional approaches go stale, then moldy, then ultimately rancid. We need to grow in an environment that is not marked down for clearance and quick sale.

We all have different approaches—I tend at first to be more stoic, gauging and sizing-up the audience, sharing a smile, speaking sparsely but listening intently. But in safe environments such as having a beer with friends, I really enjoy the gregarious personal attention and the haphazard, non-judgmental 'BS sessions'.

There are many ways to be involved, but one of the key steps is to show keen interest—the sheer enthusiasm and exuberance will permeate through your pores, your eyes will gleam and tug your smile to your ears. And the magnetism—the electricity—people will identify with your expressions and will eagerly wish to share commonalities. As an Oakland Raider (now Las Vegas Raiders) football fanatic, I can high-five or fist-bump the meanest biker dude, if we are both devoted to the Raider Nation.

The pure variety, rawness and complexity of environmental issues are what make us feel awed, humbled, yet inspired. But when our supervisor tells us to 'provide basic services' and that he will 'stew over' our ideas to invoke fresh, crisp approaches and novel ideas, now that's another recipe for bile formation. If you're not hurling already, you might prepare yourself for a quick exit.

Appet-teasers--

Tenderize, chop, mix, and sear. Marinate, fry, simmer and serve. These seem to be steps and stages in our environmental careers. Am I forgetting dilute, blend, chill and preserve? We environmental leaders are valuable prep cooks—we prepare people with possibilities and then select the main ingredients for environmental achievement. We're not cannibals (speaking for most of us), but we can most definitely sense when we are being broiled over ridiculous innuendos or fed half-baked scenarios.

In the food safety industry, while aiming to prevent bacterial growth, we sometimes simplify critical control points into time and temperature interventions (keep it hot, keep it cold, keep it moving). Yet we know that there are a multitude of other factors that come into play—protein content, moisture and current condition of the product on-hand (and on your hands). There's a myriad of factors that can turn your prized elk tenderloin into a living, bubbling hell. Maybe it's the guy washing the leafy greens with the open sore on his wrist, or the server that left the milk machine unplugged overnight. Then there are the freak things, like finding a band-aid in the potato salad. And is she really changing the baby's diaper on the cutting board? The point is, that while some (many) events are out of our control, we leaders need to minimize risk while continuing to take it. Preparation is continual, as sustained service and ultimate success depends upon it.

Unsanitary, non-compliant retail food operations are rarely shut down for more than 48 hours, as bills must be paid, and much can be improved within two days—sometimes two minutes. Humans are known to take shortcuts, whether it is in preparing a meal or dealing with staff, or convincing the public that events are beyond our control. Try to learn from these types of organizations, and then take a hike around the environmental neighborhood. Attend functions—walks, lectures, forums, presentations, public meetings. Engage and re-engage and examine the uniqueness amongst organizational approaches. See if you can identify assets as well as liabilities within these environmental entities. Sure, Conservation Multinational wants your money, but what are they doing with it? Are they spending your hard-earned dollars on wine and cheese events for the rich and famous?

I tried to convey the science of bacteria in Equatorial Africa villages by having children smudge their fingers into a bowl of hot chili powder, then telling them to rub their eyes. They told me 'No way', it would be extremely painful. Yet I asked how that could be if I couldn't see anything on their hands—they told me that I couldn't see it, but it was still there. It was the moment of truth. Bacteria, viruses and sadly, environmental responsibility, are often invisible, yet unavoidable.

> *"Man sacrifices his health in order to make money. Then he sacrifices money to recuperate his health. And then he is so anxious about the future that he does not enjoy the present; … he lives as if he is never going to die, and then dies having never really lived".*
> -- Dalai Lama

Barf Alert-

Silence is often violence to our natural and human environment. Not nature's stillness, but the suppression of our thoughts, fearful of being incorrect and possibly chastised for an off-the-cuff comment. We swallow the harm, knowing all too well that impurities need filtering and minds sanitizing. I'm extremely thirsty for a pint of disambiguation—clear, crisp, with cold, hard truths.

The water sample in the lab has just shown signs of Coliform organism present—an indication that your drinking water may be fecally-affected and less-than-potable. So, we do a confirmation test and look for the presence of tiny bubbles (not the Don Ho variety). Something may be growing and producing gas. Abdominal thunderstorms may soon be on the horizon, but not all of us consumers will feel the same level of rumblings. Some of us will be more prone to crippled leadership, while others seem to wear mental armor and remain immune, numb or desensitized—no wonder it doesn't seem to make sense.

At some point in time, the University of Montana discovered a market niche for environmental capacity-building. They elected to develop a program to provide environmental leadership training for federal agencies. I compare the approach to having someone install indoor plumbing—bare essentials that address an organizational need of the U.S. Forest Service, Bureau of Land Management and other federal agencies. It seemed quite logical for me to ask whether there was room to include other environmental and conservation organizations, public and private. Adding more stalls to the situation, so to speak.

I made several inquiries, and produced a working paper that proposed such an endeavor--inclusive, utilitarian, fluid and much more comprehensive than the standard fare. Then I sat down and discussed the concept with a university representative. The idea went nowhere, since the current program infrastructure showed no signs of cracks or leaks, only galvanized rigidity. In all fairness, the idea did trickle down the University of Montana pipeline, as I got to meet and discuss environmental leadership with a real person over coffee. I was able to at least get a better feel for their strengths and desires. I also met with representatives from Montana State University, but the discussion became mangled over how much financial gain was possible for the university itself. The value of education was immediately plugged by dollars in a tidy bowl.

An Evening at the Improv--

Environmental contamination includes the workplace, and the environmental workplace is no exception. The fluid, watershed- based approach that I advocate is collaborative and devoid of harshness, while the fossilized temperament of many enviro leaders is rather kingfish-like, with less sense of right or wrong, even if not on purpose. Unconscionable acts by higher-ups can make some days at work seem like an eternity, as we sense the repercussions of dreaded actions. We are prone to be mortally wounded within a moral-to-amoral spectrum and have the scars to prove it. We have little choice but to improvise.

After much observation and scrutiny, I'm convinced that even the best environmental improvisers have rules. They practice and rehearse— not their lines, but their nerves. And despite the adage, nerves of steel would be ultimately detrimental—they must be nerves of elastic and absorptive capacity, like bamboo or bungee. Furthermore, environmental leaders must improvise expeditiously—not quickly nor immediately, but constantly, steadily and progressively. A good starting point would be by performing an internal expedition that examines your qualities as well as your desires. This personal analysis can and should be performed individually but should also be shared within the conservation team setting. The greater the degrees of self and team examination, the more opportunities will arise for environmental interludes and lofty expeditions.

The author Malcolm Gladwell refers to insight not as a lightbulb, going off inside our heads, but as 'a flickering candle that can easily be snuffed out..'. This shrewd comment makes me think about wellness— not merely the absence of disease, but the holistic state of your inner and outer being, rubbing both sticks together to create energy. Luckily, you're not the only match inside the book. When the wind is in your face and your back is against the wall, gather your senses and improvise.

Brakepoint or Fakepoint?—

How many times have you heard pool swimmers come out of the water exclaiming '*the chlorine really hurts my eyes*'? Trained pool operators understand that the chlorine is oxidizing the 'stuff' in the pool, referred to as bather waste. The chemical reaction produces chloramines, indicating that what is needed is not less, but actually more chlorine. In order to achieve breakpoint chlorination, chlorine must be present in a quantity that is able to oxidize bacteria and viruses and have a slight residual still active for the next human deposition.

Achieving breakpoint levels in the environmental arena depends upon the carrying capacity of the organization and its environment. Air quality, for example, must accept that natural background levels of particulate exist. Stream water may have natural-occurring levels of selenium, while groundwater may contain iron or manganese and soils may possess arsenic, asbestos or lead—all prior to any human output or influence.

Anthropogenic contributions to environmental leadership build upon our natural environment and allow us leaders to try to add, subtract, multiply or divide. Climatic conditions amplify the complexity of the equation, constraining, aiding or abetting our efforts. Of all the essential elements, team chemistry is paramount to producing positive reactions and program synergisms. Clamato combines the juices of bivalves with tomato to produce a concoction appealing to some folks, nauseating to others. It is no revelation that being 'dumped on' will inevitably overload and impair the body, whether it is the water body or the human body. Environmental leadership juggles with several chainsaws that require full attention and few distractions, with little margin for error. Other leaders will choose marshmallows as less-threatening, but less-enabling. It's your performance, sink or swim.

In hindsight, 'an eye for an eye' exposed lack of vision--
Cyclops, Deja View

Env-Vision:

We are environmental gladiators. Some of us have reluctantly accepted this leadership position, and thus, with only tepid interest, we may unknowingly be holding back others with greater aspirations. Some of us have strived and won numerous environmental battles and are reaping the rewards of our efforts— but we are too far and too few. Conservation generals regularly sit back and let their environmental troops take on the daily struggles—but do you have their backs? Are you moving with some semblance of progression, or are your strategies directed towards environmental defense? Do you know the enemy, and what do you have in common? Or are you your own worst enemy?

One minus 20-degree winter day in Steamboat Springs, CO (and there were plenty of them!), I took on the task of reducing the snow and ice load on the roof of our log home. Climbing the aluminum ladder and removing a foot of powder from the eaves revealed a 4" base layer of ice. I went to the shed to get my trusty hatchet (a Colorado version of the Swiss Army Knife), climbed back up and started chiseling away. In one fell swoop, the ice broke and the entire western sheet avalanched toward my throat. I ducked in the nick of time, escaping several thousand pounds of decapitating ice table.

What's the moral here? Not to let things build up? Or maybe that removing obstacles can trigger unplanned attacks? I believe that it's a combination of removing dams, freeing flows, being reactive, and maybe more than anything, asking 'What if..' questions. Flash floods are precipitated by heavy rains. Rapid fluctuations can produce acute and severe responses. Yet if we are prepared to channel our energy by strengthening our 'conservation conduits' and by maintaining the health and well-being of buffer zones, we can work to minimize the frequency and severity of nuclear reactions and abrupt fallout.

For the youngsters out there, there's this thing called the 'Rule of Thumb'. It came about as a protective measure and safe response to signs of danger. If you can stretch your thumb in front of you and not cover the incoming incident or accident, then you're too close! Thus the saying '..keeping things at arm's length..' .

What if we observe from afar? Are we able to foresee the impending thunderstorm without getting swept away? Or can we get closer to the situation while at the same time, instinctively prepare for seeking higher ground? How close can we get to the molten lava without spontaneously combusting? How adept, are you in bending your environmental leadership branch?

Are you best at collecting the low-hanging fruit, or can you skillfully scope and reach out for the real beauties towards the top, where new growth can be surely discovered? Getting close up and personal can be dangerous—you'll need to gauge and discern your distance in terms of sanity and reality or be tough enough to suffer the consequences. There's no one size that fit all, no one tool that performs all services, and no one person that can climb mountains successfully every single time. How does it go? No pain, no gain!

We Enviros are Gluttons for Punishment—

This is usually not the case but can surely be the impression. I refer to this EL guide as a tonic book because it offers vitality to vital persons performing vital functions. As opposed to those that only seek adventure while on vacation, we attempt to rejuvenate our core functions and our corps d'esprit in our daily environment. You've got some gall—now go get more!

Fact: There is no such thing as giving 110%
Opinion: We routinely perform at 60—80% of our capacity. Thus: We have significant unused & untapped potential.
Furthermore: Our internal decisions to conserve energy can reduce effort & desire.

Consequently: Without desire, we chronically underperform.

Ipso facto: Underperformance results in bile formation.

Synopsis: Excessive bile formation increases gall—the last thing that we want more of!

Proven environmental leaders seek perpetual motion and emotion and are repulsed by frigidity and middle-sightedness (can't see near nor far). When faced with giving someone the benefit of the doubt, we prefer to think of it as the 'power of the possibility'.

Yes, we enviro leaders can be quirky, daring, extraordinary, and convinced that we are pertinent—but compared to the righteous and the aloof, we are merely transient flotsam. Many will conclude that we green leaders are striving to be eternally discontent. It's probably because we are surviving in a field of complacency, and they don't understand why we can't adapt. The movie 'Soylent Green' comes to mind. We could adapt, but that would be synonymous with surrender, and literally biting the hand that feeds you.

For those of us with a conservation leadership pulse, the discontentedness is the symptom, not the operative. Our antidotes for chronic psychological snakebites (in the office and in the field, but mostly in the office) include both inventions and interventions. We take on environmental 'E-valuations' of a personal, spiritual and community nature.

We deliberately create challenges, contesting inequalities, disenfranchisement and environmental injustice, big and small.

Inquiry: 'Who's that guy over there, talking to himself?'

Response: "He's just being respectful of others."

I gotta go number 2 ....

Despite the nomenclature 'lead pencil', this generic hand tool consists of a mixture of graphite and clay. The graphite provides the non-abrasive, lubricating qualities, and was historically used to line the molds for the production of cannonballs. The clay is added to produce the necessary binding effect. The pencil functions quite smoothly and effortlessly under minimum pressure and can be easily erased as well.

During manufacturing, pencils are graded to measure their hardness and resistance, being given a 'hard & black' (HB) grade that is equivalent to the U.S. numbering system, #2. For a period during World War II, rotary pencil sharpeners were prohibited in Great Britain, as they wasted the precious red cedar wood commodity. Pencil-sharpening technology reverted to the pocketknife, but the task was still accomplished.

Binders and cannon fodder aside, Environmental Leadership should always be on the lookout for ways to 'get the lead out'. We're all instruments of one form or another—some short and stubby, others tall and skinny. We become instrumental when we sit down as #2's and do our thing—writing, speaking, inquiring, postulating.... We are all #2's. Some of us reveal our hardiness, being razor-sharp and to- the-point. Others are more worn, blunt or 'well-rounded'. We grace the environmental arena with our personal traits and professional talents, and we regularly ascribe to sensible solutions. In the environmental movement, there is no #1.

With proper guidance, many of our quirky, pencil-necked geeks can become more than a standardized writing or recording instrument. Some of us may appear to be heavily carbonated, and others woefully carbondated. Past eroded leadership of greed or bigotry can leave a mark that is more indelible, more difficult to erase—but not impossible.

We are pigment inside a protective casing. The marks and remarks that we make are due to actions that we take. Whether our purist thoughts and actions are overwritten or overridden, as environmental leaders we need to persist in our blazing of trails— not merely marking our territory but remarking about our experience. Take it from me—brown stains can be removed, without cutlery. Don't rush to discard those of us who have been unwillingly pierced, poked and probed by the fortunate few. Lewis and Clark didn't just cut a path—they produced a journey!

Earthy is worthy, bluer is truer, but what means most,
is the doing of *doers*—

Deeds on a wall

Hearts of Darkness--

During my early-career community health work as a Peace Corps Volunteer in Niger, W. Africa (and soon later in Zaire, present-day Congo), I worked intensively with nutrition rehabilitation. While there were obvious occurrences of what we referred to as 'marasmus' or starvation, the more-frequently observed illness was protein-energy malnutrition, aka 'kwashiokor'. A severe lack of protein could make an African child's hair turn slightly orange, and tufts could be pulled out with little effort, like a wilted flower. Extreme poverty took a heavy toll on the lives of infants, and morbidity in the form of chronic malnutrition was always rampant—a vicious cycle of few resources combined with a lack of education. Child health was also closely-linked to maternal health—what didn't kill infants would present itself as stunted growth and under- developed minds.

Yet I was astonished to watch active, playful children splashing around in sewage-laden canals, having the time of their lives. Evidently, what doesn't kill you makes you stronger—developing immunity to Hepatitis A and resistance to multiple parasitic infections. Environmental leaders develop significant levels of resistance as well. On the downside, resistance to change reveals stagnation, stubbornness, blandness, discouragement and bile formation. On the plus side, resistance to mundane performance and petty projects portrays rays of optimism, resilience, conviction, fortitude and environmental courage.

In order to maintain a stronghold, parasites require reservoirs that serve as a source from which other individuals can be infected. The infectious agents that we harbor start to reproduce, transmitting unwarranted affliction to susceptible hosts. This epidemiological triad of parasite, reservoir and host plays out throughout our organizational infrastructure.

Within deficient environmental programs, the culprit is rarely a lack of knowledge or resources, but more likely a dearth of ambition. A paucity of drive and energy has produced chronic, environmental underperformance and conservation programs that do not necessarily starve for leadership but are in dire need of enhanced leader zest and action. The resource exists, but is there a craving or hunger accompanying our malnourished confidence? Can we afford to remain as under-performing featherweights? You can if you are a dimwitted, nebulous leader. Nourish, flourish or perish.

Sandpaper is a smoothie to the rough, and an abrasive to the sensitive—

A Tru Value employee

The Anointed Executive Executionor—

Einstein said something about us not being drops in the ocean, but rather an ocean in every drop. That's heavy, dude!

Here are 5 questions that I asked the current Board Chair, prior to accepting a challenging Environmental Director position in the western Rockies:

Q1: Does the organization possess the requisite support mechanisms to progressively move forward? (aside of hiring a new Executive Director, are there established community connections, Board talent, resources, leverage, commitment, vision, energy, ..)?

Q2: How confident are you (as a Board) that this environmental organization can make a significant difference?

Q3: Taking the pulse of the community / region, what would you estimate current support for your activities to be? (30%? 60%? Do folks in the community know you exist, and to what extent?).

Q4: Do you have an Executive Committee that represents the entire Board, and what frequency of interaction do they have with the Executive Director? (Daily, weekly, in-person, formal, informal?).

<u>Q5</u>: What (if any) other organizations are partners, peers or collaborators with your team? (Do you have friends / allies in this regional environmental arena?).

If I was wise, I would have paid keen attention to the answers to these questions. The body language alone was revealing awkwardness and ineptitude. But I needed a job and let the somewhat-ambivalent responses skim by me. I was assured that this organization (that I would executively direct) was and is essential to the environmental needs of the community. Now, a week after being fired, and after only being in the position for three months, I look back and see that I had asked some very pertinent and potent questions. If answered honestly, they would have provided me with greater insight and a greater awareness of gaps and pitfalls.

This organization, despite its esteemed self-concept, did <u>not</u> possess support mechanisms, <u>lacked</u> a strategic plan, was <u>losing</u> community support, had <u>poor</u> lines of communication and was aloof from peers & cohorts in the local conservation arena. The odds were stacked against me from the start, only to get worse when I realized that nobody wanted to assume the Board Chair position. The organization was comfortable eating with their silver spoon and became easily irritated by revisions that I suggested to the work menu.

While it probably wasn't intended, they were trying to see through people, rather than to see people through. Nobody likes being under a microscope and on a short leash, so I expressed my desire for greater independence. Environmental leaders need to be able to flex their muscle, and enviro organizations need to share their power. It's not like there is a paucity of responsibility, but environmental groups in particular have a strong tendency to do one of two things:

1. We wrangle over who will do what (which detracts from everybody tackling the same cause, thereby diluting the ability to concentrate our efforts).

2. We assign way too many pieces to a puzzle (not realizing that we can carve and shape as few or as many dimensions as we would like—it's our puzzle!).

At the next crisis, we opt <u>not</u> to choose the same person(s) who failed or under-performed during the previous event, although they may have learned exactly how to address the air pollution event this second time around. There is little faith or optimism that improvement is evident, evidently because we were remote from and foreign to the learning experience. We don't want to invest more precious time into capacity-building and can't see near from afar. Or we continue to select the same person that successfully achieved their goal, despite this person's longing to take on new and more-exciting challenges.

We saddle up the same mule while the others grow fat and lazy. And since we solved the initial air puzzle, we go into the eroded watershed with some confidence (great!) but with a convoluted plan that has not been designed or tweaked to perfection. It wouldn't be that bad if we just kept learning and improving, but the natives are often restless, and some of them are in charge of our livelihoods. When one is deemed guilty of underperformance, you can plead innocence all the way to the guillotine. You stick your neck out and try to come up with a solution, but heads are going to roll. Politicians survive with a modicum of sleaze and low levels of candor, while environmental leaders backtrack, take responsibility or become politicians.

Convict or Castaway?--

Forty-eight hours after a devastating November election result (I'll let you guess which one) I went for a bike ride to clear my mind and do some soul-searching. Despite the depressing wind, the sun was shining, and I had no excuse to not go peddling.

In less than a mile, I stopped at the Santa Fe River Park to do some calisthenics and to warm up the body core. This river is ephemeral, intermittent at-best, and from August to March, darn near bone- dry. Yet on the other side of the park was a middle-aged guy, standing tall and practicing his fly-fishing technique into the gusty wind. He was dry-land casting on a stiff, cold breezy day, with no water or trout to be found until May runoff (and even then, few trout flourish on this river section!).

I could tell from his technique that he was no beginner, and I got up enough courage to go over and say hi.

"*Hey, how's the fishin?*", I joked.

"I'm working on my technique", he responds, while continuing to cast into the futile wind.

"*Is it fun?*", I prod.

"Nope..", he replied, "But it will be funner when the real thing comes around."

"*You might catch a cold*", I joke.

"First I have to get its attention", he smirked.

Winds can get brutal in the environmental arena, shifting, gusting, getting blown away. Environmental leaders, like the leader line that connects the fly reel to the fly hook, are indispensable. We can't allow our leadership skills to revert to mush while praying and dreaming for ideas to spawn and projects to hatch. Environmental leaders need to hone their skills—stocking our ponds with qualified staff, providing tools to perform tasks, catching and releasing conservation concepts until others latch onto them, becoming proficient and guiding others.

Dreaded Locks and Unleashed Potential—

During a grueling trail run in Leadville, Colorado, my two toasty big toes morphed into blistered ping pong balls. I would initially try to block the inflammation out of my mind, and it would work for a while—but not long enough. No sense on stopping and examining the damage—just a matter of embracing misery for another five- plus miles. Suck it up, I mused, as I started to close the gap and reel in the runner ahead of me. I could detect his shuffling gait and slight limp, and I could smell blood.

Pain and pleasure have certain commonalities—feelings, sensitivity, reactions, experiential learning and acknowledgement come to mind. Let's take a personal look at this last factor.

Blisters can easily be avoided by eliminating friction. Yet when something compelling (like wetlands destruction) rubs you the wrong way, pressure points may be not only desirable, but necessary. Expressing pain and anguish makes you human and openly vincible. Better to acknowledge the suffering and not dismiss the significant sub-surface impacts. Then there are times when the shoe is on the other foot, and you feel unfit to lead—this predicament does not bode well for less-calloused leaders. You can't help but recognize your need for, well, help! We beg for attention, resources, opportunity and yes, your pardon. Yet we do have a myriad of options and should not be content with trite offerings and insignificant solicitations.

Many enviro situations will be blatantly unacceptable, even as a starting point. We green beggars should be choosers—we must be choosers! And the choice is ours. We can't lead from behind enemy lines—how would we commandeer resources if we have such few sources? If we continue to shy away from confrontation and frontline competition, we relinquish our environmental duties and end up taking lifelong sabbaticals that literally take our lives from us. We vacate our responsibilities and remain subjugated to directives from camouflaged conservationists.

Environmental Leadership looks that gift horse directly in the mouth, scrutinizing its age and well-being. Some will consider you ungrateful for finding fault with something you were given. Question what you are given. Our habitat can't be treated like the 'not exactly what I ordered' dinner you were served last night. Be ready to be picky and be clear. Quest, then request. Take less, but don't settle for it.

Our environmental tasks are not theatrical performances—unless we are uniquely skilled at the nuances of both entertainment and enlightenment. Environmental culpability does not necessarily produce equivalent capability but assuring a certain level of responsibility for one's actions 'aint a bad place to start. I mean, we all must answer to someone, but perhaps we should start by answering to ourselves.

Environmental Leadership is no small feat. The cost of admission is strangely enough dependent upon your true understanding of submission and surrender. The journey can easily become the 'never-ending story', so I hope you can take things in stride. Let's not get snowed over. When it's time to reach down deep and become a hellacious environmental leader, there will be little doubt.

> 'But it's all right now, I learned my lesson well, You see 'ya can't please everyone,
> So 'ya got to please yourself…--'
>> Ricky Nelson, Garden Party

Solitary Refinement--

We all have our eccentricities—I regularly pull out the newspaper and try my hand at the Jumble, but reading it upside-down, and completing the puzzle without writing any clues. If I don't get a word or the answer to the riddle, that's okay, but I abstain from jotting down the circled letters. I compare the written letters to donuts—cheap and tasty but void of (mental) nutrition. I also enjoy wearing a neck gaiter as a winter cap, keeping my ears warm, but adhering to the stovepipe principle of excessive heat leaving the top of my head. Earmuffs might serve the same purpose, but what if I really needed to warm my neck? I'll take function over fashion any day!

We have eccentric behavior in the workplace as well. One of my past supervisors defined an 'open door policy' as whether his door was cracked open—no crack, don't even knock, I'm busy. Teams can latch on to communal weirdness, such as providing '30-day public comment periods' based on a single, solitary public notice / announcement in the local newspaper that few people will ever read. And what is the rationale behind it? It meets our legal obligations. Granted that there will be an actual physical public meeting one evening, but if you don't read the legal column or happen to stumble upon the current program update on the website, well, you're just not well-informed.

When we really, truly _need_ the assistance of the community, such as active participation in next month's Household Hazardous Waste Collection Day, we go to great extremes to promote the event. Glossy posters are pasted on diner windows, radio ads tout the upcoming event, and freebies are often offered—get rid of your old paint and vintage solvents, get a visor, key chain and a bumper sticker for supporting the cause! Environmental leadership excels in this sort of situation—state funding (funneled down from federal dollars) is awarded in the form of community-based grants, municipalities work with county commissioners and public works departments, volunteers are facilitated by trained hazardous waste operators, and everybody gets free pizza.

Another positive example in the same vein of thinking is school chemistry cleanups, often referred to as 'sweeps'. Environmental health specialists normally advise the school science teacher of an upcoming inspection / walk-thru and will even provide the teacher with an inventory form to complete ahead of time. I think it's great that we can give teachers homework! More than half of them will do it, while others will come up with excuses such as excessive papers to grade or waiting for the principal to give the go-ahead. The productive teachers are the leaders—they locate chemicals that might go boom in the night (or in a student's hands), communicate with the local inspector, take the necessary precautions and may even let the school janitor know that we should work together. We _need_ each other!

A final example would be the significant impact of citizen science and community-based watershed protection groups. This beats the heck out of picking up litter in the park or putting a fresh coat of paint on a picnic table. Often known as 'Water Watchers', 'River Protectors' or 'Stream Teams', these groups of dedicated individuals can be relied upon to pitch-in, inventory stream segments, grab samples, take photos, identify bugs, recruit others, and even provide testimony in terms that human beings can understand. Come to think of it, that's a pretty concise <u>definition of a team</u>—

... a group of dedicated individuals that we can rely upon to work together on a common cause.

There might be a simple requirement to sign your name on a waiver or state that you are responsible for your own stupidity, but community-based organizations latch on to what regulatory agencies long for—helping hands. It doesn't take a genius to comprehend the benefits of local citizenry and non-profit organizations working hand-in-hand with municipal, county and state officials—but it takes gumption and gobs of leadership.

Labyrinthine Leadership--

Anyone that has taken a river float trip down the San Juan River near Mexican Hat, Utah, has experienced the unworldly beauty of the Goosenecks. This remote section of river has turbidity levels similar to a butterscotch milkshake, so bring along a spoon instead of a straw. But what the river lacks in clarity, it surpasses in towering, mazy splendor. Shadows of monolithic cliffs and wind- swept rock formations create a natural fantasyland in a wondrous canyon solitude environment. The rapids are forgiving, with sand waves building up in a matter of seconds, and then disappearing just as fast. Floating this river section, gazing with awe at the diving cliff swallows and going with the mystical flow, allows one to absorb nature at its best.

Leadership need not always be high-potency—if we had more Dalai Lama's and fewer television evangelists, we could find a fine balance that might satisfy most leadership appetites. Environmental Leadership should be a conveyance of potential energy into a kinetic form of action—yet the best time to take action is not when you face the urgent need for it. Dealing with suddenness and time crunches can substantially switch the tone and measure of your directives. Responding to a 30-day deadline causes high blood pressure in the unprepared, while experienced environmental leaders are able to set priorities, delegate less-significant duties, communicate with decision-makers, put forth a plan, gain support (or at least acknowledgement) and get the job done in half the time. Side-stepping sequential steps (such as fewer public notices, or fewer invitations to comment) can get you down the river quicker—but you will be less fulfilled, less absorbed and less concerned about the ramifications of your decision. That sounds fairly obvious, but many leaders are amnesic to public engagement.

What is less cognizant is your actual intent—sure, you intend on getting your professional comments submitted prior to the deadline. But your real intention should be to ensure an inclusive process that builds the capacity of your environmental organization through this experiential performance. If you are the leader, don't take on the hero role, and don't ask for a volunteer to lead the charge. Let your team know that you are confident that 'we' can accomplish great things, that 'we' all can learn from the experience, and that the process will reflect the effort 'we' all put into it. But be prepared for those that are already freaking out—not everyone can calm down and act (or at least appear) disciplined.

One piece of advice—silence at this stage is unhealthy and detrimental to all involved. If your email goes unanswered, place the call today! Then meet in-person to 'go over things'—now there are only 22 days until your environmental comment deadline: big deal. With a plan in hand and players in-place, you've already got the ball rolling. There will be stumbling and fumbling, with scrambling and recovery—but there will be no circumventing the process. Three weeks is eternity compared to three quarters of a football game.

'I don't know how you were diverted, you were perverted too; I don't know how you were inverted, no one alerted you...—'
George Harrison

Low Fidelity—

What is often felt but not touched, swallowed but not consumed, heard but not seen, sweetened & condensed, shrink-wrapped, ignited & extinguished?

<u>Answer</u>: The Environmental Movement and your environmental message.

On the marine preserve in Hanauma Bay, Oahu, the public pays a nominal entrance fee and is ushered to an auditorium to watch a required 12-minute educational film about the fragility of the coral reef ecosystem that they are about to experience first-hand and foot. Yet within the first hour's date with nature, you can spot kids and parents standing on the coral, adjusting their snorkel mask and searching for the cell phone that they forgot to take out of their board shorts. Maybe we'd get their attention if we secured ankle bracelets that produced electrified shocks upon each touch?

Perplexing indeed, trying to 'maintain or enhance the integrity of our natural and human environment'. A lofty goal, faced with non- believers and underachievers on your very team. It makes you wonder what things used to be like 'back in the day', and when will the lemmings stop walking off cliffs. The crippling effects of a demoralized group can be the death knell for any environmental progressions that you may have up your sleeve. Perhaps it's time to shake things up!

You've heard the mumblings and the grumblings of a certain individual, but now he appears to have cloned himself! What do you think? You've seen that it took several thousand fractured gas wells in Oklahoma before the ground started to tremble, so perhaps a few vindictive individuals will not infect the entire work environment? You can't take that risk—you've already seen a 100% growth in disengaged, underproductive staff members.

Don't take a 'wait and see' attitude—when you're on shaky ground, prepare for the zombie apocalypse via thoughtful, progressive group actions. Conjure up a strategy to promote aspects of team harmony. Orchestrate efforts to prioritize environmental tasks and get 'er done. Conservation leaders are conductors, so don't waste your time idling at the station. Environmentalism is a movement, not just a concept.

I used to be one of you, but things started to get weird...
Werewolf

GMUG-shots-

The combining of the Grand Mesa, Uncompahgre and Gunnison National Forests (GMUG) in Colorado under one administrative body was a rational attempt to consider regional forest issues with less redundancy and a more streamlined decision-making process. Rational if in the hands of rational decision makers, that is. During this public process to consider comprehensive and cumulative impacts to our forest ecosystem, the US Forest Service Supervisor declined from endorsing an updated Resource Management Plan (RMP) that included research, reflection, modernization and revision of oil & gas development on GMUG forest lands. He concluded that the 12+ year old existing study was sufficient and 'not fatally flawed'.

Well, if it wasn't fatally flawed, it was undeniably comatose and in dire need of life support! This is yet another example of a bile- forming environmental leadership roadblock—when USFS leadership hones in on forestry best management practices (BMP's) to the detriment of comprehensive watershed-based ecosystem approaches. There was a narrow window for discussion of integrated natural resource management practices to begin with, and that window was being closed with curtains drawn. Logging, clearing, firebreaks and travel access was prioritized over holistic, interconnected ecological health, because it is so much less of a hassle.

For real E-leaders, a conclusion is not the final result—not terminal, but rather a deduction or supposition worth further exploration. Yes, conclusions should synthesize your thoughts and ultimately make recommendations or decisions. But like the instant replay at football games, 'judgement-calls' can be further scrutinized or reversed. No sufficient conclusion can be reached without receptivity and inclusion. In such a case, environmental leadership needs to be not only questioned, but thoroughly reprimanded for any neglect (willful or un-willful alike).

It makes us environmental warriors furious and foaming at the mouth. Luckily, we don't have to take 'not fatally flawed' as an answer and can keep the environmental leadership window pried open. We must keep it ajar and must actively oppose efforts that knowingly or unknowingly impact our natural and human environment. Take a deep breath and count to ten or ten thousand, and don't forget to exhale. You'll be doing a lot of it while waiting for responses to come and time (and bile) to pass.

Agencies such as the USFS and BLM are fond of 10-year plans. It's a long enough time to do close to nothing for 6 years, and then start to think about winding down 'the final four'. It will surely take year 11 to provide a final report, and into year 12 to implement the next proposed 'Action Plan'. Environmental leaders must continue to prod, bark, herd, instigate, initiate, partake and accentuate. We don't need any more wait-watchers.

I'd be a good preacher, if it weren't for the rules—
New Mexico homeless guy

CHAPTER III.
STANDARD DEVIATIONS

Fertilize—

Yep. When it comes to dealing with stuck-in-the-mud infertile minds, we environmental leaders need to pull out some nutritious snacks that we can share. They must be palatable morsels, and they must have a better chance of sprouting than a banana seed in the Bronx. I'll continue to lambast our wretched environmental leadership performance as being dull, lazy or expired, and in dire need of conditioning—maybe they can take a lesson from beer.

Beer is produced by conversion, inversion, extraction, fermentation and dispersion, and when it's crafted with care and the right ingredients, it becomes something extraordinary. Or, if hard cider is your cup of tea, the same rules apply, so blend away! No matter what you concoct, your raw energy and leadership potency should generate spirited enthusiasm and enact noticeable change in effort, if nothing else. Green leaders can mix and match opportunities with environmental ambitions, and mesh communities with eco- commonalities and real purpose. Brew up something special and strive for that altered state!

More than twenty years ago, some environmental savant with the University of Nevada Cooperative Extension composed a watershed protection pamphlet for the Truckee River entitled 'Protecting Our Water Resources'. This unique and inviting document talked about pollution prevention and adaptive management before the terms were ever invented and went on to portray how local efforts could significantly protect the river ecosystem in Washoe County. I carried that pamphlet with me for an eternity, dog-earing the pages to the point that every other page was bent. It struck a chord that rings truer, bluer and clearer over time. This noble and novel document exudes environmental leadership and extends the conservation continuum from outreach to in-reach, from surface to underground, from vague ideas to critical action!

Simply stated, habitat dictates behavior. It has been clearly documented that when confined to environmentally sterile pools (no sand, no coral, no fish), killer whales become mentally disturbed. Environmental leadership acknowledges these dire and despicable consequences and sets in motion possible paths to nurture and sustain our teams--and to proactively mulch our green mindsets. But having the ability, the resources and the opportunity to do good, yet doing nothing—that's a form of scorched earth that I cannot comprehend. Environmental deliverance involves freedom from both persecution and ineptitude, setting the stage for rugged internal and external leadership growth.

'In the field of opportunity, It's plowin' time again.
There ain't no way of telling
Where these seeds will rise or when.—'
Neil Young

'Pop' Goes the Weasel--

Allow me to suggest a few other examples of positive, poignant green environmental leadership. In Durango, Colorado, when Bubonic Plague invited itself into the backyards of homes with active prairie dog colonies, the environmental health team knew that a shotgun approach (or pellet gun) was not the answer. That would be akin to simply shutting your door and putting up 'no vacancy' signs. It would be better to monitor the activity of the cute little guys, observing if there was any die-off or slumber parties. Enviro professionals would explain to homeowners that the swollen glands on their cats' necks could be from infected flea bites, and that the fleas were themselves infected by the plague bacteria Yersinia pestis. (Good luck explaining why the domestic dogs had fleas but didn't contract plague—I didn't say this was easy!).

Leaving calling cards with rural property owners would expedite getting to the scene of a 'lights-out' prairie dog motel 6. Environmental Specialists would follow a highly scientific approach of walking up to a prairie dog hole, putting a piece of yarn on the end of a wire, breathing heavily on it and quickly inserting it up the tunnel. We were mimicking live bait. A slow-but-steady retrieval would sometimes reveal the tiny fleas, which were quickly placed into a sealed jar, returned to the lab, frozen (to slow those puppies down) and examined by lab scientists.

The approach was based on knowledge, awareness, communications, planning, coordination, activity, confidentiality and follow-up. Results included appreciation, collaboration, recognition and risk-reduction. In the hands of caring leaders, fellows and followers, this was environmental leadership primetime!

Another environmental leadership success story that I personally observed (but don't take credit for) was the creation of the Four Corners Air Quality Task Force (CO/NM/UT/AZ). For those of you from faraway places, you can place each foot and each hand in four different states at one time, if your blue-jeans aren't too tight. Regional air quality is being impacted from what is referred to as 'regional haze'—cumulative impacts of upstream coal-fired power plants, natural gas processing facilities, and the unwelcome contributions from cement kilns, asphalt batch plants, open burning, forest fires, vehicle emissions and many other sources.

When I say success, what I mean is that the Task Force was successful at creating a coalition of communities, agencies, Tribal Nations and organizations committed towards protecting regional air quality. Producing significant reductions in air pollutants may take decades. Federal Clean Air Act requirements could quicken the pace, while weakening of federal laws could be devastating. Environmental leadership doesn't simply deal with the hand that it has been dealt, we create more hands! Taking authority for Southwest Colorado air quality out of the invisible hands of the queen city of Denver (some 300 miles northeast) and coordinating with neighboring air quality professionals some 20-40 miles away is practical and mutually beneficial to all four states. Downwind natural wonders such as Mesa Verde National Park, the Weminuche Wilderness and the South San Juan Wilderness don't care who is in charge, just that somebody is taking the lead and running with it.

Whether Advisories... (Lift Stations & High-Water Alarms)—

By now you are fully aware that I have a somewhat-snarky realization of the pitfalls of environmental agencies and organizations. Is it really worth the effort, and will you ever get to the point where you feel as if you are making a significant, positive impact? Yes, it's worth it, but no, you may never get to that point. So much will depend on your personal conviction and wealth of knowledge that you've been hoarding.

A chronic lack of kinesis has and continues to result in environmental short-circuiting and haphazard project performance. Check out the conservation districts that are so fearful of protecting surface water that they resort to hiring watershed consultants to do their work—and then question their very actions and intent. And then there's the wildlife biologist that can't seem to relate to people, or the forest superintendent that lacks the intent to be super. They surround us every day, but there's no conundrum here—if you want to ensure ultimate environmental performance (and you should!), then sometimes you'll need to rock some boats, despite their pretense of safety and stability.

Disclaimer: Yes, effort can, in-fact make easy tasks more difficult, as the added venture extracts greater hidden potential for failure as well as success. But please remember, we need you! And if I'm not mistaken, it was you that opted to live and thrive for a better environment—good choice!

I compare this yeoman's effort to trying to find the cause of a recent outbreak of foodborne illness in a community. Again, I ask, is it worth it? The illness has already occurred, it's probably (but not definitely) run its course, nobody important died, and you'll have to find out from thirteen positive cases (those that were sick enough that they went to the hospital, received treatment, and had a fecal smear show positive for Campylobacter) what they ingested for breakfast, lunch and dinner, starting 48 hours ago. Then you'll need to see if any of them ate at the same establishment, went to the same party, bought the same dairy product or had the same astrological sign. And if the stars do align, does the product still exist in the restaurant cooler or has it been digested and excreted?

Although I'm pretty good at this type of public health investigation, my true passion resides within our wider spectrum environmental arena. It's best to leave microbiological investigations and stool samples to those epidemiologists that can give it an all-out effort--at least greater than my 90%. It's okay to get irritated with yourself, as we can always do better and try harder—always.

My personal environmental leadership quest required perhaps less science and more open-mindedness, as a dearth of the latter made me sicker than any undercooked burrito ever could. Our environmental vision cannot be obscured by all the other stuff on our plates that produce futile fullness, not richness. Environmental leadership extols green virtues on both sides of the coin, and on its edges—the edges that we exist on.

My 1995 edition of Webster's Dictionary lists the following words in alphabetical order:

* ecology—the relationship between living organisms and their environment.

* economy—a system of producing and distributing wealth.

* ecosystem—surrounded by a community of living organisms, including humans.

* ecstacy—a feeling of overpowering joy.

The potency of these words is, well, omnipotent. Environmental leaders will define their beliefs and desires based on a rich blending of nature and culture, along with a greener distribution of that knowledge. I'm ecstatic that Dennis Weaver's coined concept of 'ecolonomics' emphasizes natural systems and exposes the ultimate value of environmental leadership—a value that can be shared and sustained.

Incline, decline or recline-

Pain I can tolerate—platitude is excruciating. While drowning my sorrows with a bold cup of dark roast Sumatra, I caught myself saying to the barista *"You can keep the change"*. And it dawned on me that the change was in my hands. I had to walk back to my office and produce worthless reports—but I didn't really have to. It would be my choice. So, I stuck around the coffee shop for a refill and started some deep, intense, profoundly exotic thinking.

Mentors warn us of less-than perfect leadership environments, where you may have to foster a culture of leadership on your own. Robust direction from the top has gone out to lunch, with support staff super-glued to the end zone, and here I am, an anemic monkey in the middle. Gazing at my liquid reflection has me truly concerned.

Many villages in the Congo still believe in black magic (magie noire) and rely on traditional bush medicine to heal illness and accidents. I've seen the application of herbal wraps on broken arms produce solid bones in the course of a few short weeks—the bone might not have been set straight, but heck, at least it's no longer broken! On the downside, many villagers believe that frothy, bubbling diarrhea has spiritual links—so elder women concoct a hot pili-pili pepper medicine inside a hollowed-out squash gourd, turn the sick child over and blow the 'cure' up the kid's anus. Desperate situations call for desperate measures. The evil spirits might be driven out, and the child may consequently die from severe dehydration. Leadership ensures that the truth be told--our environmental enemas are ubiquitous.

Philippus Aureolus Theophaastus Bombastus von Hohenheim, also known as Paracelsus, is recognized worldwide as the father of toxicology. One of his greatest achievements was in noting that

'..dose differentiates a poison from a remedy'.

From this perspective, one can extrapolate that too much of anything can be harmful, and perhaps that too little of some things can also be harmful! Paracelsus was also considered a leader and a radical thinker, as he would supplement his review of historical studies with observations of nature. To tinker with our ecological health should surely reveal inherent dangers and episodic close calls.

From an environmental leadership perspective, I'm convinced that part-time leadership, while not worthless, is worth considerably less than the recommended daily dose. Remember that EL is not in the hands of one, but in the arms of all. Thus, there is no good excuse for a leadership team approach to be absent—there should always be sufficient substitutes. A pine log won't generate as much heat as a seasoned hardwood, and young, tender branches might emit more smoke than heat—but it keeps the fire burning. Our green leadership fires need to be rekindled and constantly tended to.

Frequency and severity both come into play—one open masonry fireplace can contribute the particulate pollutant equivalent of sixty EPA-approved Phase II woodstoves! In other words, having one inefficient open fireplace removed from our airshed can equate to removing sixty cleaner-burning woodstoves. But if the open fireplace is only 'fired up' on Thanksgiving and Christmas, while each Phase II woodstove is ignited daily as the primary source of heat, we need to re-evaluate our situation. Leadership frequency and intensity are both indeed critical factors in need of stoking.

Some folks may think of change as negligible, a mere paltry, podunk pittance. Others consider change as fearful as the plague itself, while still others take the change and run with it. Yes, change is inevitable, and it can be ushered along, fast-tracked, stifled or stymied, but not snuffed out. The fire of change smolders somewhere within our environmental leadership ambitions—find it, revive it, nurture it, make the ad-'just'-ments to your reality.

'I watch the ripples change their size But never leave the stream
Of warm impermanence and
So the days float through my eyes—'

David Bowie, Changes

You're out of your mind!

In what I thought was an astute maneuver, I solicited feedback from our rural community about watershed health, and whether our organization was on the right track. One local farmer exclaimed,

'the rich folks in the upper fork are pissin' on us here in the poor,
lower fork of the river… we keep gettin' dumped on..'

He was, of course, referring to the Not In My Backyard (NIMBY) attitude, and felt violated by the thought of assuming more downstream pollutants from the privileged, higher-ups. I took it to task, and almost immediately came up with a new stakeholder slogan: 'Have a Stake in Our Fork!'

I thought that was pretty ingenious, and I went so far as to propose farm-to-farm informal meetings (over dinner, preferably steak) between the upper and lower North Fork of the Gunnison River communities. What was at stake--healthy airsheds, watersheds, foodsheds, livelihoods and habitat, to name a few concerns. We would ask the hoity-toity up-streamers to *'C'mon, fork it over!'*, and to discuss watershed concerns during the first quarter of the year down valley. The favor would hopefully be returned the next quarter, being invited to the richer fork's backyard. The idea went absolutely nowhere with my supervising committee. Why? It was novel, it was informal, it was non-threatening, and it couldn't hurt, could it? All true, except for one big gap—it was not their idea.

How on-earth could a newcomer to this community think that he might be able to break through years of stagnation, malaise and indecision by conjuring up some harebrained concept—a concept that would require speaking with neighbors from an uncomfortable, potentially-compromising position? Even worse, it was a foreign concept introduced by someone they barely knew (definition of a 'local' is ten years residency or having worked five local jobs). I was a bottle of Worcestershire sauce in a burger-with-ketchup society— a jar of chutney leaning against a pickle barrel. And if the exotic concept were to somehow actually succeed, I might get credit or some semblance of an environmental accolade while jealous others stewed at high heat.

How do you introduce leadership components to an enviro group when they appear to have a monopoly on naysaying, semi-factual certainty and know-it-all-ism? Perhaps if we let the intensity subside and revisit the scene in a couple of weeks? Maybe, but the vehemence and upstairs pressure started to really cook, as my newest Board Chair appeared flabbergasted over the arrival of the alien (me) with greetings from outer space—space that was out of their earthling minds, with the term 'compromise' being akin to devil worship. The group told me that I should kindly fork myself.

Great Barrier Rifts--

Contrary to public opinion, Environmental Leaders need to promote climate change, and to encourage 'excavation and energy use'. These are terms not usually promoted by conventional conservation organizations, yet I will argue that we want to practice a sustainable form of resource extraction. Whether your style is big swigs or small sips, you should be creating as many 'liquid linkages' as possible within your watershed, and then be coming back for refills.

Let's be water-wise and frank with ourselves--the dichotomy between environmental science and environmental education is much broader than most people can imagine. Don't expect an air scientist or a hydro-logical technician to explain basic concepts in layman's terms--they can do it, but most of them don't want to. Going all the way back to college days, scientists were instructed to instruct, and conveniently forgot how to explain. This lack of edification and incentive paves the way for comatose presentations and boredom beyond belief. The environmental scientist prefers to display his / her precious intellect, clinging to an inner sanctum and intricate specificities that adroitly portray a level of expertise and technical hierarchy. Token attempts to actually educate often come across as conceit and are usually doomed or duds.

Believe it or not, I've even seen this display of technical supremacy amongst newly graduated college students entering the Peace Corps. Carey and Marcus have spent four long years and considerable resources to become specialized and are eager to 'teach' local Congolese how to excavate a water well and install a sanitary hand-pump. But expecting these same enlightened individuals to talk about the importance of hand-washing and communicable disease control? It's not their cup of tea. Despite a high level of assuredness in their science and math repertoire, their ability or desire to simply explain the theoretical / microbiological / hydrological is lower than a turd on a turnpike.

Unfortunately, this same techno superiority occurs within State Environment and Natural Resource Departments nationwide. Our wacky organizational charts use silos to store competencies and vaults to protect them. The techies are paid more and questioned less (because we don't understand what the heck they are talking about). Opening gates of cognition would allow floodwaters of ideas, an inundation of possibility and unpredictable, murky outcomes. Environmental leaders need to recognize such human phenomena, and somehow come up with a way to blend the art of teaching with the science of science. Language itself is described as 'fluent', because there's no way to separate information from communication while still producing substantive knowledge and awareness.

'I said do 'ya speaka my language,
He just smiled, and gave me a Vegamite sandwich'—
Men at Work

Making Splashes--

As I stated earlier, environmental leaders and conservation commandos don't propose to do the work of others (scientists, educators, technicians, companion organizations), but to do 'the other work'—leading air, land, water and wildlife teams towards their objectives by striving to be agents of change, evolving by involving others and energizing the capacity of individuals. We Help Integrate Technology & Education, and We All Take Equal Responsibility (WHITEWATER). Sure, it takes some discerning and learning, but it all starts with yearning. The climate of our environmental programs needs constant, swift kicks in the pants.

Newton's First Law reveals a natural tendency to keep doing what you are doing, resisting change along the way. If something or someone is not moving, it wants to stay still. Or if something or someone is moving, it keeps moving until another force affects it. You are that other force! Ecological resilience strives on adapting and compensating for change, learning from within our ecosystem. Human revision commences by jump-starting our imagination and propelling us towards deeper, subcutaneous thought processes. Environmental leaders have the capacity to fuse ecosystem change dynamics with human enabling and empowerment, to the point that there is no 'they', only 'us'.

Spice things up! Set your sights on high-hanging fruit! Get involved early and often! Let your leadership faucet run at a good flow while you shave off bile-ish bristles from stone-faced grimaces. Resemble a green Mister Rogers and his neighborhood!

Nostrildamus—

Tired of getting all stuffed-up? A bouquet of leadership bile can create more congestion than our schnoz can handle. I'm not talking about the minor hiccup or sneeze that all workplaces deal with or blow off, but the full-fledged flare-ups that are usually caused by our snot-nosed know-it-alls. The sigh-ness that impacts us is usually traced back to our highness—those nebulous managers that incense our drive towards betterment and environmental relief. Not the sort of emancipating discharge that we expect. Are our enviro leadership efforts up to snuff?

Back in the days, the stimulating effect of snorting snuff was generally accepted as a means to attain sharpness of mind. Nowadays, if you're 'up to snuff', you are merely meeting standards or expectations. I certainly don't need to tell you that up to snuff 'aint good enough! We've been paying up the nose for the ability to function under these supervisorial blowhards, and it is due time to pick a leadership winner.

Roadside coal mining placards read 'We keep your lights on', with no mention of 'in order to x-ray your black lungs'. Landfill managers insist they do not accept certain hazardous materials (asbestos, PCB's, mercury, etc.), but an unannounced site inspection reveals otherwise. Industrial air pollution is conveniently measured in tons per year, as opposed to each breath we take. Septic systems have 'functioned adequately' for twenty years, so why think they won't last another twenty?

Our proboscis may suggest that there is a bile-ish prognosis not too far away that may be concealing a sweeter-smelling eco leadership prophecy. What's your hunch? Dig deeper!

Showtime!

What do David Letterman, Ted Turner, Tom Brokaw and Oprah Winfrey have in common? Besides the fact that none of them ever responded to my Letter of Interest regarding our Western Environmental Leadership League (WELL) proposal, they all seem to have a hazy image of our environmental future. I must give Ted some credit, as one of his environmental managers did eventually get back to me—they were committed to only funding existing environmental efforts, even though some of them were obviously stale and fermented. No space for new ideas and no time to determine if more space is needed.

I would ride my bicycle by Oprah's place up in Kula, Maui, smile and wave a shaka at the surveillance camera, and slip my personal request letter (no postage) into her mailbox. With all due respect for the many worthy acts that she has performed, Oprah has a credibility problem on Maui. Her property ownership and road access issues have helped spread grandiose community insinuations and implications over her wealthy influence and unfair advantage (private beach holdings, confidential crater routes and other restricted tropical access points).

With Oprah's help, creating a Maui-based venue for Hawaiian conservation leadership could be the equivalent of Ted Turner's annual environmental pow-wow on his Bozeman, Montana bison ranch. Environmental protection would unquestionably be a key entry point for both youth and female involvement—issues that are sacrosanct to many of us. Yet Oprah and Ted would be wise to not continuously reward milquetoast performances by good-intentioned grantees, and to require more top-notch activity that produces significant, positive environmental impact. Where was I going with this train of thought? Oh yeah, to the bar to drown my sorrows. Hey, that's Ted over there!

Primacy is a prime reason for primal failure-

Whether it be primacy of intellectual over materialistic values, societal gain over environmental protections, or football surpassing baseball as the national pastime, ascending to supremacy can result in dominance, blockades, greed, gluttony and turf warfare.

Yes, noteworthy actions and distinguishing characteristics can evolve into eminence, superiority and sorry to say, overbearing mastership. Not from true environmental leaders, mind you, but of the kind of leadership that often exists in a good portion of our environmental organizations. From the Nature Conservancy to National Audubon and the World Wildlife Fund, ranks are regularly established, and while file folders are increasingly replaced with electronic documents, the ability of organizations to make more effective and efficient use of its human resources continues to flail. Some enviro groups like to demonstrate their sound, comprehensive science-based approaches to critical environmental concerns ranging from species decline to melting glaciers and sea- level rise. That would be great, if they didn't neglect the climate changes occurring within their very bureaus and offices. Other groups like the Wilderness Society and Trout Unlimited rely so much on one regional person, that they relegate team building and community-based support to the minor leagues. Mentoring occurs in short spurts followed by prolonged droughts. Peer support is recognized at the annual retreat, Autumnal fund-raiser or Christmas party. Communities are at-best taught lessons and at-worst lectured to. Environmental leadership is conveyed drop-by-drop, and only after our minds are parched, our spirits significantly desiccated.

I would compare this managerial malfeasance to the allocation of precious water resources. Often referred to as 'prior appropriation', or 'first in time, first in line', the owners of water rights (and their wasteful tendencies) can easily make my flesh crawl. Such senior water rights are confronted with legal water consumption decisions, such as 'use it, or lose it' to downstream, junior users. Membership and ownership certainly have its privileges.

Environmental organizations waste so much time and energy by practicing the same trickle-down team building and leadership challenges that they politically abhor. They divert unsubstantial leadership potential from the mainstream and secure it to maintain a minimum stream flow from top to bottom. Maintaining anything good at a bare minimum level is rarely a positive step, as it instills dependence and reliance over freer, more sinuous approaches.

Miniscule environmental leadership will invariably result in higher staff turnover, lower productivity, decreased morale and the decline of our own species. If a professional hockey player can show his prowess by participating in Dancing with the Stars, why can't our Environmental Leaders try stepping out of their comfort zones? You can and you should, and you don't need me to show you how. Avoid the bile and show the world what you can do—prime that EL pump!

You've got to land before you slide—
                                        Gettin' a Grip

Colonels, Colonies and Coconuts—

The Hawaii Army National Guard hired me as their National Environmental Policy Act (NEPA) Administrator and as an integral component of their Environmental Team. I eagerly accepted the position as an intriguing environmental challenge, as I hoped that the Army would have the prowess and leadership arsenal to issue barking orders that make fleas jump. My sometimes-bitter disappointment with mainland environmental programs stems from uninspired performance, often due to poor perception, executive inactions, idle threats and timid commitment.

Executive Directors are particularly notorious for praising the efforts of their programs and glorifying the efforts of their Board of Directors—which would be fine and dandy, except for their chronic underperformance and less-than-wholehearted efforts. Many supervisors will read this, shrug and think to themselves *"nope, that's not me"*. Well, then you should be proud, because you are in the vast minority. You've sent an envoy up the coconut palm to scout out new territory. Surely, you've examined the strength and age of the palm, the agility and dexterity of your envoy, your communication links, your preparedness plan and your 'if-then' steps—if a bowling ball-sized coconut comes crashing down without warning, are your troops alertly looking skyward? Undoubtedly, you are aware that nasty palm-rats love nesting up in coconut heaven and may have to defend themselves from your trespass. You readily accept responsibility for your actions and eagerly set the pace for your team to follow. You probably possess, as I like to call it, "Env-vision".

Then there are the colonels amongst us. They get their marching orders from a review Board, who gets its orders from nobody in particular. Sounds strange, huh? It should, because the ultimate authority, not unlike a publicly held corporation, gets its support or non-support from its stockholders / stakeholders. Those of us who elect to invest or divest in an organization's efforts have found something that either appeals to our senses (including your sense of decency, honesty and humanity), or is found to be irritating, distasteful, abhorrent and in need of sanitizing.

Are you green with envy? Some of the time you can't tell, until you readily ingest and then gradually begin to digest your resource sandwich. Is it satisfying and fulfilling? The Development Directors sure hope so, but if not, then there's always the chance to appeal to your sense of fear and your obligation as 'part of the community'. Nothing wrong with this, unless the fear is unfounded, or, as I frequently observe, the organization dedicated to righting the wrong, feeding the poor, housing the homeless, saving the planet, is not fully engaged in the mission.

Such commitment can be rice paper thin, and your slim-picking programs will erode and devolve if they are poorly created or not reinforced with substantive efforts and some sense of direction. Moving closer in proximity with the real issues, with quicker response times and stronger communication links, are all integral aspects. But you need to know how to select and then crack open the coconut—and then what to do with it.

Credit for intelligent environmental program design should be rained upon those who take their generic green-jeans, adjust the seams, turn up the cuffs, relax the fit and exhibit the wear and tear that will withstand the test of time. Fashion statements are made to appeal to a select assemblage—so carefully select your audience and make a sincere environmental statement that has pizzazz, and is clever, unique or atrocious. Make valiant efforts, as there are few alternative choices.

First it snowed and then it rained,
nothing ventured, nothing gained—
Bumper Sticker

Thanks for the giving---(now, pass the stuffing!)--

Enviro groups are renowned for attracting new members and supporters with still shots of snow-capped peaks, magnificent perches above river canyons and panoramas of wildflowers in overabundance (if there is such a thing). The objective is to illustrate the diverse elements of our amazing environment, and to create a craving, a nexus to become closer and even intimate with it. When it works, this approach garners increased membership, more votes, added revenue and potential support networks.

Yet quite often the result is what I refer to as green taxidermy. Like a lush, romantic landscape painting elegantly positioned above the fireplace, or a trophy trout secured on the mantle, we marvel at the site, or at least admire aspects of it. We appreciate the vision and relish the beauty. But how strong is the connection? Can the image be tasted and sensed to the point where it actually arouses us? Environmental leadership has failed miserably in this area, by portraying nature without accentuating life. The mounted moose head does not portray freedom, wildness or natural wonder (except a wonder why the magnificent creature was 'harvested' in the first place).

Actual involvement needs to take place, and includes breaking bread at the table, clinking glasses at the bar, rubbing elbows on the bike trail, turning artificial intelligence on its head and building tumbleweed relations in its stead. We should be going further than calling up conservation constituents by phone and asking for donations. We should go further than inviting members to the annual meeting with dinner, guest speakers, silent auctions and verbose accolades. We should go beyond the initial stimulus invoked by a peep at a nature preserve, or a YouTube glimpse of waterfowl in flight. We must entice others to not just join us or support us, but to gently nudge, actively engage, learn by doing, respond by experiencing and to become one by becoming many. Anything less is pitifully woeful, objectionable and malignant.

We must insist that our relatives come over for Thanksgiving, because it's all relative. And we should provide not solely an opportunity, but a heartfelt request to contribute—please bring the wine, or dessert, or both! We can indulge in environmental offerings best when we are willing to provide strike-up conservation conversations, explore interpersonal communications, extol environmental moments and furnish substantial program nourishment. With this leadership dynamic, I'm optimistic that wisdom can be not just shared, but enticed and enhanced, tidbit by tidbit. It is this environmental responsibility and generosity that materializes and fosters progression. We are not simply stewards of the land but are umbilically tied to other humans and must nurture each other throughout this tethered relationship. Environmental leaders need to project this willingness that grasps reluctance by the collar and flings it into the pugnacious boxing ring of the natural and human environment. Whistler's Mother has a lot to say, and she should say it!

Which cide are you on?—

The Hawaii Army National Guard provided me with half a cranium of mental ammunition and hindsight-full bazookas. After observing environmental operations first-hand, trying to decipher NEPA documents describing unexploded ordnances, radioactive waste, historic cesspools, leaky underground storage tanks, and then being given ludicrous direction to help chainsaw a path through a jungle, I shrieked as much as a guy can shriek around other guys.

Our chief was drumming his fingers, impatiently awaiting my 'Finding of No Significant Impact' (FONSI) statement. Without realizing my muzzle was fully loaded but unlocked, I expressed some reservations about our scorched-earth mission. I shared my professional-yet-unwelcome subordinate commentary, knowing that this would be a bloody battle that I would surely lose. To the boss, I was a freak of nature.

With all the modern technologies that we have at our disposal, it shouldn't be too difficult to put into place sustainable approaches that can monitor and protect our airsheds and watersheds. We should be able to run a computer model (not me) that estimates the impact of creating a clear-cut swath through a tropical rainforest. We possess greater knowledge on adverse health impacts from pesticides, herbicides, hydrocarbons and hazardous air pollutants. We have young people that are eager and able to take direction and carry out missions. And we have dormant, crony department heads that sit in air-conditioned offices, watching CNN 24/7, in case the Chinese try what the Japanese tried.

I wince, swallow cold coffee and try to figure out what it is I want to do with my life (besides learning to surf). I try self-deprecating short-term humor, and it works—it's almost lunchtime. Maybe there's a way of creating a groundswell of Hawaiian leaders, one wave after the other. While munching from my bento box, I ponder the creation of an annual Environmental Leadership Training class consisting of county officials, municipal officers, agricultural operators, tourist industry profession-als, watershed coordinators, high school educators, … a diverse group that doesn't wait for the eventual tsunami but creates one with its own hands and collective intellect. Can we forge an environmental fracas with-out being court- martialed? A wave of environmental change is needed. It's time to take mental notes and come up with shareable solutions— solutions that taste great and can adequately fill some of those craterous EL voids.

My way of getting a solid sense of the pulse of an entity is by exam-ining its environmental vitality. Our team wasn't flat lining, but bile was abundant, with future clotting a near certainty. Ironically, our Captain Capitulation had a quote and photo of Winston Churchill in his office. 'Never surrender, never give up.'. Yet he could not relate to peacetime efforts in the same vein. My silent response was "Never give up, always give within"—sharing resources and communications throughout our organization's circulatory system.

Deodorant, de-orderant, or both?--

I was advised that in order to write a book of any kind, you need to have a common thread that weaves from beginning to end. Like a tongue returning to a canker sore, my mind keeps revisiting the multitudes of leadership misfires and misfortunes that I've suffered (and survived from) throughout the years.

My vision goes back to our fluid approach, extolling that meandering stream, lapping over beaver dams, greeting boulders, compensating for elevation changes, sharing floodplains, snooping over waterfalls, you name it. We are constantly changing our shape and our direction, without separation from our environmental principles. If I happen to depict a contemplative Rastafarian paddling down that river, splashing out quips and quotes with a wry sense of humor, all 'da betta!

Your leadership order is ready, right off of life's dollar menu—single patty, small fries, no refills. This is the life you ordered, isn't it? What nauseates you? For me, as you may know by now, it's the offensive odor wafting over our natural and cultural communities. The stench seeps from office crevices, environmental department bureaus, municipal councils and board meeting rooms. How can we aim to aspire to anything greater, when we spend so much time and energy perspiring over quick fixes and damage control efforts? If you're like me, your days of vanilla wafer leadership are numbered (and you choose the number).

The bile oozing from the innards of these very environmental and conservation entities that intend to lead us—it creates factions, fractions and reactions, yet is apparently immune to removal efforts. Yes, your order is ready—but you must place your own order. You can wait in line, but I think it's your turn to step up to the conservation counter. Induce the meandering of leadership opportunities that can cause short-term upset conditions, but ultimately restores decency and environmental integrity to your organizational channels. Opt between marred, fearful, disabled and lost leadership, or create your own pizza with hope, honor, optimism, creativity and lots of spices! Cleanse your green pores and become devout to a cause, your cause.

Route Canals--

My teeth are tight and compacted, so I forewarn the dental hygienist not to use the thick woven floss. But she gets distracted (after all, I'm just another patient in her daily life) and inserts the tightrope. I don't know why the floss goes down into the tooth gap quite easily, but coming back up shakes my skull like a bobble-head doll. It's no wonder why we simply aim to be functional rather than specialized.

We live in a society where even items made for specific purposes malfunction. Chinese-fabricated bicycle frames that warp when jumping a curb, can opener blades that refuse to bite the can lip, metal vegetable steamers that have petals peeling off, even toothpicks that splinter while trying to dislodge a common poppy- seed. Just because we are assigned a special task does not guarantee that we have the proper tools, durability and wherewithal to perform these tasks on a regular basis.

My current understanding of GIS is best described as *'gee, I guess'*. I understand the value of locations and layers but am easily confused by the multitude of steps and switchbacks. Such mapping tasks are more than foreign to me—they seem elusive, no matter how hard I try. I can relate to the argument about knowing what you know, and knowing what you don't know. For me, it's probably a mix of poor student and poor teacher. Despite trying to revisit the historic air flight and disappearance of Amelia Earhart across several continents via ARC GIS, I crashed before she did. GIS remains a personal challenge, but I keep trying!

Shoddy environmental practices and accompanying enviro leadership rhetoric is merely noise pollution. Practices that tout a continuation and prolongation of environmental agony (for you or for others) should never be sustained and is nothing more than anathema. In fact, lack of action makes you an accomplice and joint conspirator. To acknowledge leadership gaps, but to not work earnestly and diligently to fill them is simply criminal. There are situations where firefighters trying to escape a wildfire need to ignite escape fires. Now that's fighting fire with fire! But if we are complacent, then we are complicit.

This Environmental Leadership gondola ride is full of mystery and low on mastery. As a young pup, I needed a lot of mentoring, exercise, camaraderie, stimulation and appreciation. I didn't get what I needed, and I spent mega-brain cells on under-prepared efforts, spewing up chunks of raw futility. I would inspect eight or more facilities per day, thinking productivity was the key (while the industry average is approximately four establishments per day, dependent on complexities, travel time, etcetera). My double effort was for naught, but nobody told me that at the time.

When things are picked too green, they lack the flavor and consistency of fruition, the ripeness of experience and the texture of time. I was heralded as an 'Emerging Leader' by the Center for Disease Control in Atlanta, Georgia—but I couldn't decipher what that really meant. At lunchtime, I walked over to the nearby Coca Cola tourist center in a trance-like fashion, trying to figure out what my real green intentions were, attempting to get a glimpse at that secret formula. I decided to agree on two points. Firstly, slumbering and foot-dragging is a weakness for all organisms, dinosaurs being no exception. And next, that the last one home is a rotten egg, nobody excluded.

> *The less you speak, the more they listen—*
> Congolese coffin carrier and
> grave digger

Dictatorial Democracy---

"Who needs to buy toilet paper", asked Jordan, *"When I've got the office and the library"*.

When quizzed about after-hours necessities, the J-man gave a one-word response: McDonald's. Jordan appeared very confident while weighing his options—and I'm sure he had at least one more evacuation plan in his back pocket.

Environmental contingencies are often briskly hashed out on paper, and then neatly folded and stashed into a binder. The infrastructure and available resources appear adequate and conceivable, and the thought process felt somewhat reassuring. Why the need to make things overly complex and complicated? Form and function can adequately meet most needs, most of the time.

But what about going the extra-distance and preparing for that 100-year flood (which seems to take place about every 7 years lately)? Where is our environmental urgency? What skills have we retained? Are some of us suffering from a bout of 'conservation constipation'? I doubt if the golden arches are going to come to our rescue with a highly fibrous conservation plan. Give me a shot of pristine mountain water with a dash of perspective.

Some well-intended Environmental Leaders with solid, constitutional backing will work via specific directives:

'We <u>will</u> try this…I <u>expect</u> your involvement…I <u>need</u> your feedback…I <u>will listen</u> to you…I <u>am receptive</u> to new ideas…You <u>must</u> be inclusive…We <u>shall</u> be diverse…We <u>have to</u> work as a team…'

If you have the fortitude to be somewhat forceful, your orders may be fulfilled, or else. It's the else that causes us to be more aware and self-conscious. As human beings, some of us are able to back-off and back-down, while others have mental blockages that defies and opposes both logic and science. Somebody borrowed this quote and came up with the term 'adaptive management'.

Are we E-leaders applying our skills in single-service situations, or are we able to create layers within the fabric of our communities? Are we tissue, cardboard or plywood? A helluva choice, I know. It may heavily depend upon our level of creativity. We may want to experiment with constructing a birdhouse before taking on the bathroom addition.

'Tis a lesson you should heed:
Try, try, try again.
If at first you don't succeed, Try, try, try again—'
William Edward Hickson

Custodial care—

While working nights part-time as a janitor at my high school, I would often get a good laugh out of the term 'custodial engineer'. Surely, I surmised, when I go to college, science and engineering will be more intense than emptying trash dumpsters and scraping old gum stuck under desks. How naïve I was! During one summer break while playing with the industrial floor buffer, I watched a seasoned professional stand on the device and quickly click it on and off, providing a free carousel ride. I thought I'd give it a shot-- but I froze up after ignition, performing a whirling dervish 720- degree maneuver, while the power cord wrapped and restrained my arms to my side. Luckily, the wound-up cord yanked out of the wall, and I collapsed to the floor like a mummy. Old man Hatch yowled with laughter, pointing to the self-tied calf on the newly waxed floor. I was known as 'the human gyro' for the rest of the summer.

It took another two decades, until I started inspecting school safety for Routt County Environmental Health Department in Steamboat Springs, Colorado, that I was able to start to understand the degree of engineering involved. The buildings don't heat themselves, the lighting is more than a flip of the switch, the boilers producing hot water take a trained eye, and the ventilation ensures that we can breathe distress-free. Add in radon gas, hazardous material storage, lead-based paint, asbestos mitigation, fire suppression, cross-connection controls and you have the makings of a custodial engineer.

Lack of environmental leadership within school buildings and play-grounds has produced catastrophic results that include exposure to carcin-ogens, chemical explosions, gas-related fires and severe viral and bacterial illness. Our children are in school custody for a good part of the working day, when environmental health promotion and disease prevention is most critical. And how are we environmental leaders rewarded? By referring to us inspectors within the environmental health network as isolation ward-like 'Sanitarians'. 'Environmental Health Specialist' is the preferred term, if I can convince the powers-that-be that they are not hallucinating—that environmental forerunners are mentally stable, somewhat orderly, proficient and under-appreciated. We emboldened E-leaders only go berserk when we are straight- jacketed within the confines of sterile institutions and impenetrable mindsets.

Akin to the two terms 'environment' and 'conservation' that many of us use synonymously, the term 'environmental stakeholder' can just as easily be referred to as environmental custodial care—we are self-proclaimed stewards that spend a good portion of our lives as guardians of our air, land, water & wildlife. If it's yours, it's mine—try convincing a Western rancher of this! As custodians, we need to look no further than to mop up some of the brilliant green bile that covers our landscape.

For the third and final time, environmental Leaders need to ensure that they are not doing the work of others, but doing 'the other work'—creating enviro challenges, inspiring clean energy direction, mobilizing community-based groups, promoting watershed health, going where no man or woman has gone before. But if we attempt to take on an initiative sans collaboration with the public or other ally environmental organizations, we will fail dismally. The lone wolf approach cannot reproduce, will stray and be taken for granted-- perhaps seen as just another environmental traveling show.

Howlin' at the Moon--

Speaking of wolves, I vividly remember my first week of work at the Montana Department of Health & Environment. The morning coffee conversation entailed two guys bragging about so and so shooting a wolf in the gut, then letting the creature limp off to his certain demise. Our work at-hand was water quality, and it did not faze these two idiots the least bit, to be boasting over anti- environmental acts. There was no environmental nexus, no blood in the water. The sorry thing was that one of the two was a so-called 'Team Leader'. Some call this sort of macho portrayal arrogance. I call it sinful ignorance. It raised a fury in me—a fury that produced heat, tension, electricity and pressure with no outlet.

I had to figure out how I was going to be progressive in such a flat-lined conservative organization.

For starters, it would be a matter of taking on the challenge outside of work. I started attending dozens of environmental meetings at Montana State University, Greater Gallatin Watershed Council, Greater Yellowstone Coalition, Sierra Club, Montana Audubon, Montana Conservation Voters and others. I would offer my environmental leadership skills to create an environmental groundswell that would substantially improve environmental conditions throughout southwest Montana.

When asked if they consider themselves as environmentalists, less than 20% of Montanans say yes. But when asked if they consider themselves to be conservationists, more than 50% say yes. There's an opportunity here!! Put the two together and claim major support for your initiative! But don't ditch the term environ—mental, as it boils down to using our 'mental' acumen, to protect our 'enviro' earth! And the two dickheads I referred to? Yes, they are part of the problem, but in a democracy, they need to be part of the solution as well.

Before the Deluge—

In the solitary phase, locusts are innocuous. Their numbers are low, and they cause little threat to agriculture. Put one on a hook and go fishin'. However, under rich, fertile, conducive conditions, rapid growth triggers a dramatic set of changes—the locusts start to breed abundantly and become gregarious. They form bands, which quickly become swarms, devouring what they consume, leaving a path of devastation. Consider the locusts to be a profusion of oil & gas wells—the deluge is now upon us.

As environmental leaders, we have less time to react than during decades gone by. Global warming is slapping us on the side of our head, and there is no time for ignorance, reticence or muteness. The repercussions of silence are loud and clear, as we humans end up losing, perhaps for the last time. Losing your rights without standing up for what you believe in, passively having others create overburdens and undue influence, watching impediments evolve into infestation and pestilence.

Environmental leadership entails speaking up and speaking out, questioning irresponsible development, promoting environmentally- sound practices, expunging the brilliant green bile and getting a self-transfusion of courage and desire. Your localized initiatives can have systemic effects throughout a program. Prolific leadership, fellowship and 'followship' can all be infectious.

> *Paranoia strikes deep.... Into your life it will creep....*
> *It starts when you're always afraid....*
> *Step outta line, the men come, and take you away...*
> Buffalo Springfield

POTENCY OF PEOPLE

Positive Persistence

Progressive Perseverence

Passionate Preservations

Public Participation

Poised Perspectives

Practice Preparedness

Pollution Prevention

Personal Performance

Private Partnership

Planning Processes

Proactive Protection

Leadership Ladle

GREEN P - SOUP

Bases Loaded--

At an early age, Little League baseball taught me that I was good, but not that good. I could slap singles and doubles but had a lame arm. The fact that nobody ever taught me to hit left-handed didn't help. I would start the game and play four of the six innings, then get sat down and watch the others play the full game, jealous of their prominence. I rarely thought about the benchwarmers that got splintered rears during the first four innings, and then were plugged in at the very end as an afterthought. What did that do to their egos and self-confidence? Did it drive them to become homicidal killers in later years? If they became leaders, would they be spiteful? I'll never know. Our environmental arena is very competitive, and requires hits, runs and even some timely errors (that produce corrective steps and preferable results).

My best grade-school friend Robby and I would jump on our no-speed bikes and go 'garbage-picking' on Saturday mornings--no school, and the best time to browse the roadside wares of richer folks at pedal speed. It was like a free flea market, with no two houses offering the same trash & treasure. There would be a few senior garbage-perusers cruising by in their cars and giving us dirty glares for invading their turf. We would beat them to the best stuff, and then try to haul away a swivel chair or a rattan basket on our handlebars. We knew all the shortcuts.

As we delve further into the matter of watery tonics, the more rummaging you perform, the more intriguing questions you will develop and the more artifacts and kooky situations you will discover. Whether you call it fishing, probing or just rooting around, the term doesn't matter, as long as it's on your terms. Can you unearth betterment and ascertain greener potential?

Don't be dismayed or deterred by the closed doors and hush-hush policies surrounding you—you are not alone, at least not for too long! You may, however, be the only one with the courage to turn on your internal headlight and reveal your spirit without shuddering.

Passion without hunger, is like hunger without passion---
Mondeli deli

Substance Abuse—

Collapse into your easy chair and think of nothing—your intuition has been kidnapped by a computer program. This first step should be followed by this next action but preceded by that click and accompanied with that format, which should produce this result. It doesn't sound very intuitive to me, unless you think of your mind as a connection of sequential events, transfused by a slave at a desktop without barred windows. There's a reason why they refer to it as 'Artificial Intelligence'!

Unless your enviro job is specifically database or administrative work, there is no reason to be spending five hours per day every day in front of a video display terminal. Take a look (you've got nothing better to do!):

8am—10am: Sign in, check emails, review documents, return calls.

10am—10:30: Coffee break, restroom, personal phone call.

10:30—12: Concentrate on work priorities.

12—1pm: Lunch

1—2:30pm: Return to your dungeon and shuffle documents.

2:30—3pm: More coffee or energy drink

3—4pm: Try to concentrate, make progress on your 'in-box'.
4—5pm: Work slow-down, get outta' Dodge!

Four hours of productive deskwork per day is the national average, allowing one to maintain sanity, minimize stress and not make much progress in life. You can blame it on the EPA mandatory reporting requirements, or the constant interruptions from Joe Public, or perhaps it's your buddies knocking on your virtual cubicle door, enticing your participation in 'beer-thirty'. By the way, someone should inform Dolly Parton ('9 to 5') and Bachman-Turner Overdrive ('if your train's on time, you can get to work by 9') that for most of us worker bees, the job starts at 8am latest.

You know what makes me happy? Pizza--an authentic, better-than-decent pizza. Good pizza should have sufficient olive oil, oregano, basil and real tomato sauce with a hint of garlic. If it's deficient, I order a side of marinara, and if the waiter charges me for it, I take a buck off their tip. You can call me stingy, but what about the pizza?

Not unlike pizza, environmental leadership must also have substance, character and flavor. Oh-so many environmental programs tout their commitment to diversity and biodiversity and inclusive approaches yet end up skimping on environmental program content. The deep-dish description of the comprehensive public lands protection program on your website is in reality, extra thin crust. Your stakeholders committee appears to be a game of musical chairs, but now you have more chairs than community members. You wonder why you don't have as many customers as you'd like—who is waiting on whom?? And do you get what you paid for, or are you paying for what you get??

Mildew or We'll Do?? --

Josh picked up the office phone from the speaker setting.

"Environmental Health Department, can I help you?"

The party said: *'I must have called the wrong number, but I really have to speak to you"*—

That got my immediate attention from my nearby cubicle. This was going to be an interesting conversation, to say the least. This poor lady needed help to the point where she did not want to hang up the phone, despite the fact that she was in dire need of non- environmental assistance. We all claim to be busy but seem to find enough time to check our personal emails or clip our fingernails. Instead of trying to help this needy person unscramble technical eggs, Josh asked her *"What can I help you with?"*

"Oh mercy, I'm not sure…my son keeps leaving the door unlocked…maybe I need to have you come over…".

We think we have it hard? Josh was able and willing to let down our highly polished departmental armor and our sometimes-snobbish attitude, succumbing to our heartfelt concerns and coming to this woman's rescue. There really are no words for such pure caring.

When asked which comes first, 60% of respondents will say 'lightning before the thunder'. Many first-time visitors to Colorado believe that deer turn into elk at elevations above 8,000 feet. Why? Because that's where they see all the elk! No matter that the larger ungulates prefer the mountain climate, solitude and protection. Kind of like hail turning to snow, what we Enviro Leaders see, and where we see it, goes a long way towards our reasoning and rationale. Rural denizens are thought of as more ignorant about social activities and the arts. City dwellers are oblivious as to which way is due north. Most of it is hearsay.

We are Environmental Argonauts--adventurers engaged in a quest for cobalt mountain lakes and primordial river canyons, traveling slower than the speed of sound. We try to avoid skirmishes and altercation, as they tend to inflict wounds or reopen battle scars. Yet our environmental hankerings are more intense than that blueberry pie on the shelf— further out of reach, if in fact you can even get a glimpse of what it may truly look like! We wish to nurture nature and then go about and cultivate culture with one fell swoop. I for one am so glad to sense your ambition!

'My belly's full, but I'm hungry… a hungry man is an angry man…'

Bob Marley

How to Lose Friends and Negatively Influence People—

Simple answer: Take them for granted.

My next Colorado environmental job felt like I was going to Catholic Church—something I hadn't done for 35 years and have no intent on doing again. During the first two weeks at work, I was showered with heaps of praise and a sense of adoration. Things quickly morphed to feelings of guilt, suppressed thoughts and the omnipresence of a Mother Superior with a stick up her posterior. There were a lot of nuns too—none of this, none of that! Heaven- help me if I tried to inject a dash of humor into a conversation.

I had nothing to confess but my desire to take this holier-than-thou board of directors and spank their behinds. I once recommended that we provide a non-alcoholic beverage at a meeting (thinking to myself that we didn't come here to die from both boredom AND starvation!).

"Ugh", said my supervisor. "These are serious, critical issues."

"Ugh", said my mind-- So serious and critical that we intend to use monotony as our key weapon! I like to appreciate presence by presenting appreciation. Others may associate generosity with some innate weakness--such as the white-collar elite mixing with blue-collar grunts. Our environment is often a public school that is uncomfortable with those professing private or parochial beliefs.

Room & Bored--

Our current day environmental bandwagon has not come to a screeching halt but has certainly downshifted and tapped on the brakes. In a period when we need to expedite our universal efforts to address greenhouse gas emissions and accelerate efforts to enhance community-based programming, we can't afford to slow down or coast for too long—so why have we? Is it that we see the Mohave Desert directly ahead on our roadmap, and that we are feeling prematurely thirsty? Yes indeed, but that's no reason to sputter. At a time when intense programmatic hunger and thirst is valued and praised, many an environmental leader has opted for their climate-controlled offices, reclining chairs and a secure, limited environment. A good number of our environmental forerunners are innately afraid of direction that requires movement, repositioning and alteration. They keep trying to kill two stones with one bird.

If you picked up this guide for self-help, you'll be happy to know that you are 80% of my intended audience. If somebody picked up this guide for you, then you should be forewarned that there will be a scoche of sarcasm, as well as a significant amount of leadership lambasting coming your way. Getting your attention (and keeping it) should be a semi-rude awakening for some, and a stinging ouch for others. You have most likely been partly responsible for the underperformance of your environmental organization. You may be adept at performing your day-to-day duties, but when the rubber hits the road, when the conservation community skillet starts to heat up, are you prepared to be seared like a fresh filet of ahi? Have you been able to consistently stir your potage of possibilities? Or will the anguish of lost environmental opportunities result in blackened responses and deep-fried bailouts?

You set your own alarm—decide when you want to wake up to the environmental challenges that abound us and surround us. In case you're not yet comfortable punishing yourself, I will promise to zing arrows and slingshot unpleasant sensations to your conservation cranium. I'm trying to raise an environmental leadership ruckus, and you're invited to hoist the flag, carry your torch and scale this rugged mountain.

You can admit to this admonishment, pawn it off on other staff or ignore me all together. But I do care. I care enough about our sensitive environment and our all-too-often cavalier attitudes that I will try very hard to detonate a greener grenade within your grasp. I'll continue to pluck environmental chords until I find one that resonates with you. My objectives may occasionally be objectionable to you—better to be out of tune than out of touch.

'The truth is hard to grasp, as the fingers prefer to strum'—
Kekchi

Malfunction Junction-

That's the local name for an awkward intersection in downtown Helena, Montana. Five roads come to a confluence. There are stop lights, stop signs, arrows, pedestrians, bicycles, cars, skateboarders, dogs, you name it. You kind of know which way you want to go, but there is some uncertainty or hesitancy as to who should go first. Some drivers prefer the rolling stop method, creeping forward until you really need to brake. Others err on the side of caution, coming to a complete standstill, signaling their intention, but then seemingly waiting for confirmation from higher beings. Coming to similar environmental crossroads, many of our teams appear lost, frozen or dysfunctional. Somebody needs to take the lead, provide the drive and accelerate efforts.

Democratic discussion amongst teams is worthy of praise, yet staff and followers expect environmental leadership to steer them in a certain direction. Certainty can be a tricky thing, but when supplemented with courage and willingness, will easily supplant indecisiveness. Overcoming obstacles and changing course are normal and expected components of environmental leadership. As an afterthought, when we leaders map out our strategies, it would behoove us to have contingency plans.

While performing public health work for Project Concern International in Belize, Central America, I once accompanied a Mayan health nurse on a jungle trek to a remote village. Receiving over 300 inches of rain per year, the trail was more like a wet sponge, sucking mud from each step like a toilet plunger. After several sloppy hours, one of my running shoes surrendered, as I post-holed into a knee-deep mud hole. The only thing I retrieved was a sock-full of muck. My nurse guide thought it was quite hilarious, and waited for what I would do next. Lacking options, I fished around with my arm at elbow's depth until I retrieved the shoe. Then I put it back on, mud and all, but decided to walk backwards.

'What are you doing?', she asked.

"Well, if I lose my shoe again, at least I'll be looking at it from the front-side".

She laughed so hard, and when we finally made it to the village, made a point of broadcasting the event (in Mayan dialect, so I don't know the specifics) to the entire community. From a leadership perspective, sometimes you need to show your humbleness and allow others to show their strengths and true colors. After all, she wasn't wearing any shoes, yet proved to be a guiding light and trustworthy companion.

No threats are idle, no truths are sincere.
Wind blow pelican 'da way he wanna go--

Belizean proverb

So whaddya' gonna do about it??

But what if you are just a gnat, getting blown away by powerful windbags? Do you accept the verdict that is handed down, and then go into damage control mode to minimize the pain inflicted? Perhaps, but that's entirely (well, not entirely) up to you. Here are a few possibilities that should be examined, along with the myriad of untapped scenarios that are stashed somewhere in your heart and head—

In no particular order:

1. Make a recommendation.

2. Strive for 'confrontation-lite'.

3. Ask some 'what ifs'.

4. State your case.I

5. Take a stance.

6. Brace, and then embrace yourself.

7. Inform others of where you're coming from.

8. Believe in your beliefs.

9. Ask for clarification—Clarity is normally seen as a positive communication process—it reinforces the aspect that you want to know more, even if it's not what you want to hear. Just be careful that if you've been run over by a truck, that you're not asking to kindly back up over you again.

10. "I've done some research, and I'd like to run this by you...".

11. Offer assistance—Complicity, but with other agendas in- mind.

12. Experiment.

13. Make suggestions: "Have you thought about …".

14. Siphon similarities.

15. Request more information—the chopped liver & onions are so good that you're going back for more!

16. Build support.

17. Socialize, and then stir the pot.

18. Before refusing, sample the offerings—you don't have to swallow them! Express your interest (and maybe your intent).

19. Admit mistakes, reveal imperfections—in order to get down & dirty, you start by getting down. White collar, blue collar no collar.

20. Show desire.

21. Build on commonalities & agreement.

There's no rhyme or reason for feeling caught between a rock and a hard place. Conditions might be overrated, and maybe over-stated, but there's always an alternative to the Colonel's original recipe. Hell, you might even be substituting for a substitute, making fake tofu out of chicken. It can be done!

Clip Joints & Hair-raisers·

I am no friend of filthy coal or nasty oil & gas. I do flick on the lights, watch occasional television, use a desktop computer and will continue to cook on our gas range. But I remain determined to aid in turning the mining and fossil fuel industry upside-down. How?

A) Excavate & Energize Leadership Capacity Within Our Conservation Communities. (you've seen this quip before!)

B) Promote Internal Climate Change (organizational, behavioral, economic & political).

C) Develop those 'Liquid Linkages' and Fluid Approaches to Environmental Progressions.

D) Swear to a Team Approach (the WHITEWATER concept).

These are my Fantastic Four.

None of these are easy, especially depending on how much of a tremor you want to trigger. I compare it to the hair that covers most of our body—our surface cilia provide protection from UV rays while also serving as a sensor for cold, heat and foreign matter. Our follicles (or fur) act as a soothing, attached, organized entity. Yet once a hair is cut, trimmed or plucked, it immediately becomes a separate foreign body, a misfit, an irritant. So why does the normal hair on our neck not produce the itchy, scratchy sensation of a cut hair? I think it's due to the fact that our human forest has been 'logged' without permission, and while the roots remain, the felled follicle is sensed as coarse, incomplete, debilitated and out-of-place. One is deep-rooted while the other is an alien body, a stowaway.

Non-renewable fossil fuels and their parent industry make us bristle and feel less-than natural. We (environmental leaders) feel compelled to alleviate the clear-cutting, gas-fracking and coal seam extraction that can produce intrinsic, cosmetic or utilitarian value, but that harvests our planet in a non-sustainable, climate-altering degrading fashion.

Talk about hair-brained ideas, here's a 'How are we doin' concept:

Please fill out this questionnaire independently and confidentially, without asking questions for clarity, and using your individual interpretation. Estimated time for completion = 90 seconds.

$$0 — 1 — 2 — 3 — 4 — 5 — 6 — 7 — 8 — 9 — 10$$

Abysmal   **_Excellent_**

1. *Using the above scale, how well is _____as an organization performing?*

2. *How well is the **Executive Director** performing?*

3. *How well is **your division** performing?*

4. *How well is **your Division Chief** performing?*

5. *How well are **You** performing?*

Results are strictly confidential, no names required. Results will be tabulated and shared with all staff within five working days. Thank you!

If you were to create such a questionnaire, you might be cited as a subversive or a pinko socialist. So, I'll take the revolutionary credit, and all you must do is share this possible approach that this weirdo came up with. Yeah, it's still somewhat threatening, but it could also be invaluable! Don't like it? Rearrange it! After all, the objective is to evaluate and eventually modify your respective plans, practices and environmental processes.

Scrutiny on the Bounty—

To describe a bombastic enviro leader as a 'micro-manager' is usually mincing words. What we really mean to say is that while under the microscope (a location that we never personally chose from the get-go), our crew is being marginalized, segregated and dissected. The microscope is only needed for those that are unable to view things clearly at arm-length or greater distances. Untrained leaders are less interested in finding out what makes us tick and more interested in regulating the ticking. Productivity, policies and procedures are prioritized over human potential—yet if properly assessed and nurtured, both could mutually appreciate in value.

The crew on the whaling ship Pequod was constantly under the obsessive and vengeful eyes of Captain Ahab. His leadership was useful for only one purpose—to seek and destroy Moby Dick. The captain's use of fear and intimidation was not aimed at producing any sort of shared vision of a rosy future.

Many green avengers feast on the submissive loins of their own crew. This chronic, barbaric maltreatment of key team players eventually produces a backlash of discord that power-pushers rarely see coming. Inharmonious and contemptuous behavior starts to brew in the ranks, before the bile builds to revolting levels. Thar she blows!

Charting a clear course is like calling a football play on first down—you either advance, retreat or standstill. Then you immediately re- group and try again. With a true environmental leader at the helm, one can make adjustments and steer clear of titanic obstacles. Yet with a keg of brilliant green bile on-board, an astounding 77% of enviro-linked organizations under-correct, over-correct or underestimate the magnitude of the situation within their flotilla. Yet despite their flailing efforts to 'maneuver and direct' such complex organizations, these quasi-leaders somehow manage to sustain their meager existence. They play chess games, with environmental pawns exposed to friendly fire.

That in itself is quite a talent, often confusing exploration with exploitation, and rational decision-making with token gestures. Talented leaders value their team from bottom to top, while feckless leaders treat staff like expendable casualties of war. Leadership practices are fraught with absurd contradictions, and enviro leaders can't succumb to the 'lose a few to save the many' business and military philosophies. Nor should we submit to a higher power. We must commit to holistic voyages that offer attractive engagements, pool potential synergisms, embolden inclusive sharing and harpoon positively green multiplier effects.

I believe there is a relation or connection to these aforementioned irrational interpretations of reality—explanations that are fraught with contradictions and absurdities. I refer to it as unintentional lie- ability. The disservice produced by not being open, transparent and receptive starts to corrode the very trust mechanisms that keep the organization afloat. Let's take a step back.

<u>4 Things you should be able to ask of your Environmental organization:</u>

#1: What is the salary of the Executive Director?

#2: Right now, as we speak, what is your #1 program priority?

#3: How large is your 'rainy day' / emergency reserve funds?

#4: What have you accomplished over the past 30 days?

There are undoubtedly many other burning questions, but these four should get the juices flowing. In terms of rainy-day funds, I would expect 12 months for most organizations, up to (but not exceeding) 18 months. If your organization, no matter what its cause, has more than a year of reserve operating funds, they need to take 50% of it and do something great, something impactful, something monumental—and then start over again. Otherwise, you're making reservations for programmatic fail- ure, putting a down-payment on the Last Supper, so to speak.

Pretending to be holier than thou, only proves that you have more holes--

Cement Mixer

Mental Floss--

As if I wasn't enough of a glutton for environmental servitude during my first tour of duty, I opted to return to Hawaii to serve as Sanitarian IV. My duties are to inspect retail food establishments throughout upcountry Maui (Haleakala Volcano area). Being a trail runner, this sounds pretty good so far. Then when I get 'seasoned', I can go out to Hana town and crack down on the illegal huli-huli chicken operations. Yeah, right. A skinny, white Haouli guy telling a huge Samoan dude that he needs to get a license, and while he's at it, to rebuild his hut with an approved kitchen, a hand-sink, potable water and septic system. And when I really find the time, go over to the islands of Lanai and Molokai and do more of the same. I guess that if I'm going to feel as alienated as a leper, I'm going to the right place. Too bad Father Damien is no longer around to care about us martyrs.

Luckily, time is not critical in Hawaii. Things will get done, but it might take several people several attempts to get them done. In the meantime, 'talk-story' with the locals, get to know the neighbors, soak in the culture and keep my nose clean. It turned out that the sumo-size guys were very friendly, feeding me quite regularly (a violation in most states, but in Hawaii, it's a gift of Aloha, so enjoy!).

Stand in front of your desk and give it one sharp karate chop down the middle. Now that you've experienced excruciating physical pain, it's time to deal with the mental anguish. My pain came, as I should have expected, not from the community but from the honcho of Consumer Protection. Since I wasn't a local Hawaiian, nor a member of the Asian mafia, I was an easy target for verbal barbs. Instead of succumbing to direct nips from a powerful, vicious feline, or waiting for psychological cavities to form and take permanent residence, I would escape from her bile plaque attacks by creating daily exercises. My first painstaking step was to actually acknowledge that my positive assertions and proclamations were going to go unappreciated by others. It was a horrible first step, but when faced with the alternatives of stagnation or ulcerating decay, it was my preferred choice.

The next step was awesome—it involved being nice to others. Providing assistance would soon follow, but the expression of kindness opened many doors. I wouldn't call it sincere kindness, because I barely knew any of the individuals at the sushi houses and bento lunch places that I would be inspecting. I would reflect on my horrid office environment, trot out onto the field, exhale, and feel liberated. I would come back to the office in the afternoon with a look of confidence on my face—a look that would cause greater suspicion about what I was up to. Pity the poor leader that attempts to control the forces of nature. Personal conviction and persistence can produce results and resolve—perhaps not immediately, but over time.

You can't have any misgivings, if you haven't given--
Lithuanian proverb

Wreck-Creation—

The environmental coast is unclear and littered with leadership landmines, so don't think for a moment that you can bask in the sunlight. Keep your eyes peeled and your ears perched. Sniff out trouble before it arrives on the scene. I keep harping on having true environmental leaders do more, try harder, dream bigger, live larger. This strategy is far from foolproof.

A major challenge is in determining how and when to apply sustained injections of environmental leadership that nurtures and mentors our environmental teams and our programs. High-octane leadership is aimed at increasing the intensity of environmental efforts, signaling stimulation and positive vibrations. When properly applied, this leadership aphrodisiac should create excitement of a different nature—but for how long?

Environmental leaders must make judicious use of this leadership opiate, as staff and communities should (must) become addicted to their own environmental cause and not to your personal calls for action. The big risk is that a certain form of numbness may develop, and that 'follow the leader' becomes dependence rather than an option.

While working as a Water & Sanitation Program Manager in Belize, Central America, I took off my leadership shoulder pads and joined in on a full day boat ride and fishing trip in the Gulf of Honduras. There were fourteen of us, and the boat held eight comfortably. No worries, as calm seas and a first-rate captain kept us cheerful. The snapper and grunt were fighting each other for our baited hooks, hand-held lines (no poles or reels) and spark plug sinkers. Just in case you hook a big one, best not to wrap the line around your wrist or fingers!

When it came time for lunch, there was plenty of chicken to go around. The first drumstick tasted fine & spicy, the second one really funky. I put my leadership hat back on:

"Did you guys cook the chicken well?"

'Ya mon, really well'

"And did you refrigerate it overnight?"

'Ain't got no refrigerator'

"Well, did you keep it on ice?"

'You want cold beer or cold chicken?'

Spoiled chicken—figured it would take about eight hours for Senor Salmonella to unpack his suitcase, after the long voyage to strange lands. The intestinal mariachis didn't start their party until we got home, thank goodness.

We know very little about the intricacies that take place around our environs. Plan for the best, prepare for the worst. The queasiness caused by faulty leadership can be acute or chronic, depending on how many straws of blame are placed on our backs, and whether our backs back up to others. The foul bile is pervasive (programmatic, problematic or both), yet not always obvious. Latency periods can be hours, days or weeks before recognizing your ill fate. But it shouldn't take months or years, unless you're looking in the wrong places or talking to the wrong faces. Would you care for some garden-fresh anguish on that dull pain?

Oddity or Commodity? (being the odd man out)—

The vintage Archie comic books used to advertise the mail order promotion of 'sea monkeys' for your home—pour them into a glass and just add water! What kid could resist? Not me. Of course, the monkeys were just brine shrimp awaiting some moisture, but they did come to life.

Then there was the 'Mexican Jumping Bean'—a seed pod containing moth larvae that spasms or 'jumps' to roll towards a more friendly, humid environment. As far as I know, nobody sued over false advertising, despite not getting what we paid for. Welcome to the world of make-believe.

The crew probably thought, well, it's too late now—I'm so far into this thing, that there's no turning back. Their incarceration within the ranks of a do-good organization is quite confounding. It's amazing how executive arrogance or egocentric behavior can subdue the creativity of sprouting conservationists. They will be cropped before maturation, limited to severely short growth spurts and confined to specific roles that are either mundane or will soon become so. Simply working for a 'good cause' is no excuse for stunted personal leadership growth.

A commodity is something that is subject to ready exchange or exploitation within a market. This got me thinking—our environment is not orange juice. Instead of promising economic goods and services, why don't we focus on good services? Business and military leadership aims to gain an advantage over an opponent. Environmental Leadership, on the other hand, strives to be gauging and engaging, planting and supplanting, finishing and refinishing, hounding, pounding and expounding.

Our training will be questionable, rarely sufficient, solely related to the job at-hand plus an occasional reference to the organization as an entirety. We've grown fat and lazy as a feedlot cow, looking down, not up or out or behind us. You too can become an environmental castaway, a Jughead or jumping bean. You might not have a choice. But if you do (and it's happened to me), ensure that you take the time necessary to go into a recovery mode. Jettison those thoughts and fears of being less-capable or less-desirable—if you have true environmental desires, then there's no doubt that you can improve your capabilities and take your skills to higher levels.

There's no guarantee that your next environmental position will be much better (or worse), but it's your skills, your position and your life that you are leading. We are all 'Significant Others'. We all have a life expectancy, and I expect to be preaching environmental leadership for my entire life, and then from ten feet under—which might be easier, as I'll be less-prone to criticism and in closer proximity to the under-performers.

Preparation & Putrefaction--

From a food safety perspective, potentially hazardous foods (meats, fish, cooked veggies, stews, etc.) can be prepared and safely refrigerated at <41*F for up to 7 days. After one week, the mutiny begins—the foods start to deteriorate (from the growth of competing organisms, or the resurrection of a previously dormant entity), eventually becoming foul and repulsive. The same holds true for teams and Environmental Teams in particular. Minimal preparation takes place, supervision and team direction is given, and then management 'chills out', assuming more of a barometer, fire lookout or emergency response. Tasks that are not completed in a timely fashion will turn stale and sour the enthusiasm of our best-laid plans. Worse yet, such damaged goods and services can be haphazardly pushed and marketed for immediate consumption, with no freshness guaranteed, or your money back.

I managed a watershed monitoring project in the Eastern Sierra that began to show signs of dullness and needing a real boost. Volunteers were getting tired of grabbing the same samples from the same creeks, season after season, and getting the same results. I figured it was time to turn up the juice, and introduced new stream segments, more team integration and pizza! It was that simple, and Abracadabra… conditions vastly improved. Sometimes (often) Environmental Leaders figure that doing the mundane fieldwork, because (according to the water science textbooks) it's the right thing to do for the environment, is sufficient. That's the box of salted crackers that you'll find on aisle eleven—simply one generic element in your shopping cart, but with little substance or uniqueness. You'd be wise to bring a six-pack of sparkling sustenance to this party.

Other efforts and small successes are preserved by practice, repetition and organic doses of humility. While working with Community Health Workers in Equatorial Zaire (present-day Republic of Congo), I conjured up a village-based nutrition song in Lingala dialect that goes to the tune of '100 bottles of beer on the wall'. Better to compose than to decompose.

No Wedgies, Please!-

I previously mentioned the Western Slope Conservation Center in Paonia, Colorado as an organization that I admire from a simplicity standpoint. They simply 'do things' with their members—group hikes, festivals, parties, river floats, Waffle Wednesdays, karaoke, you name it. Granted that the environmental leadership role is way more complex, and involves extreme multitasking, but the staff and WSCC members show exuberance and vitality that is dazzling. They laugh at rancid, tainted programs from years gone by. They stick their necks out, while others bundle up in scarves and earmuffs. They thrive on life, while others try to survive on pints of fear and distrust, then going back for refills. Instead of such organizational dread, this inspirational group is being led, fed and bred.

I was working on creating a collaborative, unified stance against ill-conceived, industry-touted regional oil & gas development in Western

Colorado. Sound science shows us that oil and water (quality) don't mix, yet the oil & gas industry and their political allies continued to harp on 'finding middle ground' and 'playing nice in our sandbox'. Dude, our environmental communities are a bit more complex than sandboxes, and usually there's a bully that tries to wedge sand into our not-so public places. That's not the middle- ground that we anticipated! It goes to show you how the extraction industry views communities. Wise environmental leadership picks and chooses its battles when it can, and recruits and trains more environmental leaders when it can't.

There is a highly touted Montana conservation effort known as the Blackfoot Challenge. It has been given accolades and national recognition for community involvement, stakeholder processes and watershed protection. Yet when I made three inquiries on three separate occasions to three distinct members of the organization, I received zero response. While this initially riled me, I slowly began to understand that the group had little to offer outside of its own organism.

Their internal ideas produced pieces of their environmental puzzle that already existed—but had to be re-examined, re-positioned and reiterated. The Blackfoot Challenge was an internal process to produce environmental cohesion by examining conservation links, neighbor concerns, wildlife priorities and concerted efforts. They couldn't provide me with advice, because they did not have the external know-how or gutsiness to make suggestions for others. Blackfoot Challenge happily and contently chewed their-own cud. They knew fairly well what worked for them, but also realized that they were foreign to the field situations of others. I could not glean information from them, and if I persisted, would have been wasting both our time. Independence prevailed.

CHAPTER IV.
ENVIRONMENTAL CONSERVATION CHALLENGES

'Catch a Whiff'—

600,000 gallons of raw sewage spills out into Waikiki Beach. After a two-day closure, the bathing waters are magically re-opened. Say what? Barely enough time to determine the cause, to mobilize teams, to evaluate human and wildlife impacts. Two days?? Ah grasshopper, there are 'other issues' to consider—namely the life support system of Oahu's tourist-based economy. Politicians can make things happen, if you paste the dollar bills smack-on their lips. I knew more than a couple of these 'polluticians'. Plus, there really wasn't much to do—perform a few water tests, clean up some unsightly areas, reduce fecal transmission and wait for the tide to turn.

The U.S. EPA has been holding Waikiki's bare feet to the fire for over three decades, warning that the municipal sewage treatment plant needs a major overhaul. Thirty-five years of under-treated effluent and still counting. Are there any environmental leaders out there, or is your snorkel clogged with toilet paper and short-term profits? The City of Waikiki is busy investing in light rail transport instead, so tourists can get to the bleached coral and sewage-laden waters as soon as possible. Without a flush of current leadership, the situation appears bleak.

While it's true that small organizations need to find their special niche, it would behoove medium, large and extra-large organizations to 'huddle up' with the little guys, creating symbiotic relationships. We small potatoes must prove that we have the capacity, agility and dexterity to produce ingenious projects and positive outcomes. Bigger guys need to fill gaps, in order to enhance communications, increase diversity, but most importantly, to improve the odds of creating successful, united environmental interventions. The Department of Defense consists of the U.S. Army, Navy, Air Force, Marines, Coast Guard and other special forces. Add to the equation the National Guard, CIA, FBI, state police, county sheriffs, plus the private sector, and you have a force to be reckoned with. Not only do they enforce, but they can also reinforce, if they want to.

Our environmental defenses are much more piecemeal. The U.S. EPA provides financial resources to all 50 states to perform the services that they could not realistically perform themselves. The same process holds true for the Federal Highway Administration channeling resources to State highway departments—and while there are still plenty of inefficiencies and waste, the highway projects are much easier to identify, earmark, monitor and confirm. But when it comes to State Health Departments, the vast majority of them are convinced that county environmental health programs could not plausibly perform much more than restaurant inspections, basic consumer protection duties and septic system permitting.

Thus, the states hoard their dollars, only allowing meager percentages to be doled out, with minimal circulation reaching the extremities. And our states begin to build empires to handle everything from communications and infrastructure to emergency preparedness and ombudsman offices. Each state has its Air Quality Division, Water Quality Protection Bureau, Epidemiology Section, Hazardous Materials & Waste Management office, and so on. What trickles down are technical advisories, programmatic updates, regulatory rulings, perhaps some 'mini-grants' and bureaucratic heavy-handedness. It doesn't help that the Governor's office is within close proximity of the State confines, and that environmental leadership is regularly bestowed by too many politically appointed, eco-centric environmental make-believers and ego-centric career bureaucrats. Admittedly, they can voraciously latch on to valuable resources, but often lack hands-on knowledge, environmental leadership experience and bile-resistant opportunism. From pittance to perches, it's time to wake up and branch out!

Crimson flames tied through my ears, rollin' high and mighty traps
Pounced with fire on flaming roads, using ideas as my maps
"We'll meet on edges, soon," said I, Proud 'neath heated brow Ah,
but I was so much older then...I'm younger than that now---
　　　　　　　　　　　Bob Dylan, My Back Pages

The Double Whammy—Habaneros & Hyenas:

Can you feel it? Not so far away, another Environmental Manager is shaking in his / her boots, sensing the uproar from citizens' concerns about a company's illegal dumping. It will take more than one thorn in the side of the lion in order to get his attention—and it won't be the first time that I've been called a prick by industry. Not that your actions need to be alone, either.

Can environmental leadership be taught to those lacking desire? I fear not and would focus on two other possibilities. Number one would be to go up the food chain, get the attention and support of top brass, and produce inorganic change by executive orders and demands. Select the hottest pepper in the jar, acknowledge its potency, but don't back down. Bring on the heat. Precedent for such a process includes directives by the Governor of California to impose sweeping water conservation efforts, Georgia Attorneys General creating integrated school systems and the New York City Chief of Police mandating actions in response to police shootings. Leadership by command and force has been aggressively performed by humans and wild animals, but since we are addressing inhumane issues that need solving, wilder and wider alternatives should be explored.

The other approach (and there are surely more than these two approaches) is by addressing environmental bile build-up and program stagnation via the HYENA method. If the lion won't get his teeth out of the antelope, let's bite and nip and yelp and cackle at varying angles and hind quarters, creating such havoc and annoyance until 'it' leaves the scene with tail between its legs, in total retreat and embarrassment. Hell yeah, environmental action (HYENA)! It's the incessant attack by a pack of disturbed animals (us) that finally convinces the lion to leave its prey. Antagonize now or agonize later!

Where do you fit into this scenario? (I hope you're not the antelope!). When the lion backs off, will your pack treat the impending vultures in the same vein as the lion? Can you adjust the heat of your inflammatory comments? Can you handle being an instigator, despite its negative connotation? Are you an environmental raven searching high & low, near & far for greener sustenance, or merely accepting the role of the picnic table pigeon, waiting for daily handouts? Feeling morally-obligated to produce environmental progressions will greatly assist Les Miserables at the community level—but only if true sympathy and empathy is ratcheted into your actions, and if your leadership spices are savory to your group's desire!

The black of night only shields the eyes—
Bush Doctor

Trumped, Toppled, Trodden—

In a speech regarding our global warming crisis, President Barack Obama justifiably stated:

"The biggest risk we face… is not acting".

Simply stated and straightforward to all environmentalists, fearful words for industry, and nothing more than mere words to the naysayers, creationists and ignorant folks in general. We environmental leaders possess the combined potency of greenhouse gasses, able to influence our environmental climate via intense actions and incensed reactions. Yet as individuals, we resemble a solitary fart on a windswept mountain.

New Mexicans fondly refer to their weakling leaders as 'Sopapilla Supervisors', referring to the lightweight, hollow and inflated dessert pastry (that goes stale after several hours). Too many of our crusty conservation curmudgeons are nothing more than clueless managers with sizable salaries. With little faith in such bureaucrats and plutocrats (that are much talk with little action), the table is being set for new leaders with true community connections—but only if we encourage integrative processes that are receptive and welcoming and cohesive.

I chuckled after observing a doctored US Forest Service emblem patch of a cow 'servicing' a forest ranger—that's how many environmentalists visualize the fondness one has for the other, with a whole new definition of multiple use. Contrast this impression with an innate desire to do some major environmental good in our world—we green leaders contend with incessant guilt, crazed hysteria and blatant mistrust while others reap the rewards of our misguided actions or passive resistance.

I'll opt for disorderly conduct over orderly misconduct any day. Yet while striving to distinguish ourselves as liberated, independent entities with free choices and open mindsets, we mistakenly and unknowingly extinguish our collaborative EL potential. We could be a forest fire (if we wanted to) but opt instead to smolder around a primitive camp-pit. Believe it or not, we're replacing clout with doubt. Where is the tenacity?

If it does not build character,
it may promote character assassination—
Thomas Teul

Oh Say Can You Tsetse—

I was at the tail end of my 28-month Peace Corps stint in Zaire, suddenly turning weak, jaundiced and urinating the shade of Coca- cola. I was diagnosed with Hepatitis type A. I probably got it several weeks earlier, when eating some juicy undercooked crawdads from a polluted section of the Congo River. Or it could have been that communal pot of elbow-deep fufu. The staff was considering my medical evacuation to the mainland U.S., but I'd come too far, worked too hard, and was about to depart on a 40- day solo journey through Burundi, Rwanda, Tanzania and Kenya. I somehow talked them into staying on this dark, brilliant continent, as my service was ending in two weeks' time. I promised the doctor that I would 'take it easy', consume no alcohol for two months (so any liver impairment is not exacerbated) and 'stay in-touch'.

I didn't tell them that my multi-country trek was going to be via bicycle, but they didn't ask! My Chinese crank-yanker had no gears or speeds, just pedals and crappy handbrakes. Trying to maintain control and rubbery contact on the miles of downhill stretches, I wore out my tennis shoes before making it through Rwanda. By the time I arrived at the Burundi border I was feeling much stronger, getting ready to trade in my French and Lingala dialects for English and Kiswahili-speaking Tanzania.

I packed a bundle of caps and t-shirts in an old U.S. mailbag (probably a federal offense) and strapped it on to the back of the bicycle. It would serve me well while communicating with strangers and bartering for a night's sleep and two handfuls of safou. What I didn't count on was my slow speed on the sandy paths, the grueling half-day distance to the next nearest village and the ability of the tsetse flies to catch up and penetrate their needle-like proboscis right through my blue jeans.

I figured I ungraciously received the equivalent of twenty-two painful injections over three hours on my back and behind and was nearing tears. Blinking for clarity, I thought it might be a mirage, but low and behold, there was a tiny enclave up ahead! I took off my sunglasses for a better view, and whammo, an incoming fly collided with my left eyeball! Now I really was crying, and quite a sight to behold--this teary-eyed white guy on a cheap makeshift bike limping his way towards the first stranger I could find. No English comprehension yet, but international body language pointed to the exact location of my pain. Without hesitating, my newfound friend clammed up a nice big gob of sputum in his lips and launched it at my iris. It felt shockingly good, and I thanked the gentleman profusely for spitting in my eye. He could have his choice of t- shirts, and did he know of a cheap place to crash?

When we ask for help, a splash of specificity can go a long way. Please join us at the public library this Thursday night for a community discussion about non-motorized transit options. Please consider becoming a member of the Jerusalem Cricket Consortium with your $20 annual contribution. Or please help us figure out what the heck we are supposed to be doing, as our leadership message is foggy at-best.

Pretenders or Contenders??

I don't know of an environmental entity that is magnificent. Groups such as The Nature Conservancy, for example, have delineated a tactical plan to accomplish its goals of securing valuable natural resources. Their plans are based on considerable science, and they go to not great, but pretty good lengths to describe current plans to the conservation community. They will contend that critical landscapes require immediate protections, and that they can expedite the securing of such wildlife and watershed-sensitive parcels by entering into contractual agreements to purchase, lease and protect.

I agree with all those assertions, but I have also seen that such land stewardship can get bogged down in its own wetlands. How so? While working on sensitive landscapes and prime habitat, aspects of their environmental science tend to hypnotize and desensitize large segments of our environmental community. The crown jewel properties are touted as superior to most of our homelands, and our cottages can't compare to their castles. Environmental leadership has unwisely prescribed tranquilizers for those seeking tranquility. I think they may want to opt for a greater degree of stimulating, thought-provoking scenarios.

Surely conservation leaders didn't mean to have this sort of result, and it could be rectified rather easily. But alas, the current approach draws in the almighty dollars needed to "sustain our efforts". Changing the way that we do things might make us more community-minded, but could it potentially make us less prosperous? Why mess with success—we'll let the other guys work on environmental education, current & future regulations and holistic environmental / conservation approaches. I give TNC and the Trust for Public Land credit for not pretending to do what they have not done, but there is so much more that can and should be done! From mauka to makai, our inbred love for the land provides perfect opportunities for a collaborative effort! It will take a leader like you to create such change.

Having more than twenty-five years of environmental science and conservation programming under my belt, from ridgetops to reefs, you would think that I would be able to provide sound, professional advice. Yet a close friend asked me what specific skills he would need to land a job with the Nature Conservancy—as he keeps applying for positions but has yet to receive an interview. I suggested that he send direct inquiries to the TNC President and CEO, requesting some divination as to how others with similar skills can enhance their odds of attaining employment at TNC. If their inquiry would have included a potential $1000 donation, I'm sure the response would have been more immediate. Excuse me, but that's a sorry state of leadership affairs for an enviro organization. After a follow-up inquiry, my buddy did get a response to his request for job application insight. While far from ground-breaking, TNC suggested the following environmental leadership guidelines:

a) Ask environmental staff members and teams to dedicate time to learning and development each year. (My reaction: You can ask 'till you're blue in the face—leaders produce the voracious longing and the insatiable passion for our environment!)

b) Follow a four-step (ugh!) process:

    1. Define excellence in leadership

    2. Assess individual performance and behavior

    3. Set learning goals

    4. Offer learning opportunities and coaching to staff and teams. (I personally believe that TNC needs a healthy dose of IPA here and think they should ask the local Montessori School for clarification).

c) Raise money to expand our learning and development programs to create systems and processes that will allow us to better execute the four-step process.

Execution sounds good, but collaborative programming and community participation should be valued as benefits, not envisioned as costs. Do we have the precious time to continue to work as distinct environmental entities?

It is this enormous potential that causes me to be critical of the environmental status quo. I would wager that the term 'environmental leadership' will be passé within the next 6 years. We will need to conjure up new approaches, most certainly. But the ineptitudes and inefficiencies within our current systems can be, dare I say, exploited?

The word 'exploit' is sandwiched in my handy Thesaurus between the words 'explode' and 'exploration'. Perhaps if we psychologically detonate some major sedentary mindsets, we can release environmental program energy into new trajectories--spaces and places that have value, pathways, meaning, merit and real worth! So, try harder, try different, probe into concepts that Edward Abbey profoundly joked about, (including knowing thy enemy) and communicate openly with your allies. Take little avail over no avail, every time.

'And so castles made of sand, slip into the sea,....eventually—'
Jimi Hendrix

Sloths, Slugs & Environmental Retardation--

During my lifelong environmental science and conservation pilgrimage, I've been chronically exposed to shabby and shoddy leadership. Directing under such negative influence (DUI) should be categorized as a criminal activity, in terms of the felonious assault on the good albeit ugly environmental ducklings in the same pond. On the other hand, positive and regenerative environmental influence can be proper, befitting or downright necessary—our eternal swan song.

Take watershed alliances for example—diverse groups can work on erosion control, non-point source pollution, stormwater management, and non-degradation efforts, merging into the collaborative stream from multiple vantage-points (with effective environmental leadership at the helm, stern, or somewhere else on the raft). But it's the 'under' in the DUI that suppresses and distresses qualified leaders, potentially driving them to drink. I've worked 'under' Boards that would run to Executive Sessions faster than a rat up a sewer vent. Their rationale for such top-secret meetings would often be in order to feel secure (amongst other insecure top brass), and to gain direct, uninhibited access to something material. I'm talking about the rat, of course. Yet akin to the rat, circumventing the light of day and securing stashes of coveted secrets can expedite an organizational downward spiral towards environmental plight or plague, where human resources scatter and fend for themselves.

This cheesy process of top-level confidentiality is full of holes and will lure environmental teams into sticky situations and more- catastrophic programmatic traps. Putting a lid on the organizational dumpster will only allow internal efforts to putrefy, and succumb to avoidance, decomposition and dissociation. I argue that executive directors should in-fact be members of its very board and have a voting right as well. Enlightenment is best achieved by those who open their eyes to team possibilities, rather than sticking to a Three Blind Mice scenario of heinous, self-preservation leadership from a gnarly, gnawed-on tower.

Conservation staff should not allow their subservient totem pole status to deter them from latching and grasping onto environmental leadership aspirations. Watershed groups are more primed to flex their environmental leadership muscle than Rudy Giuliani ever could—it's all about experiential learning. Screw the term leadership if it's too intimidating—introduce team building, outreach, in-reach, encouragement, progression and skills development. Continue to promote the casual conversations at the coffee shop, as growing confidence levels will be a coefficient of self-determination. As teams become more actively involved and witness honest effort, the possibilities will start to appear, turning former sloths into environmental sleuths and ambitious, savvy, enlightened leaders.

Our conservation world needs leaders that are not on their heels, not spinning their wheels and not making backdoor deals. We need leaders that strive, drive and thrive at all levels of the playing field. The earth is our turf!

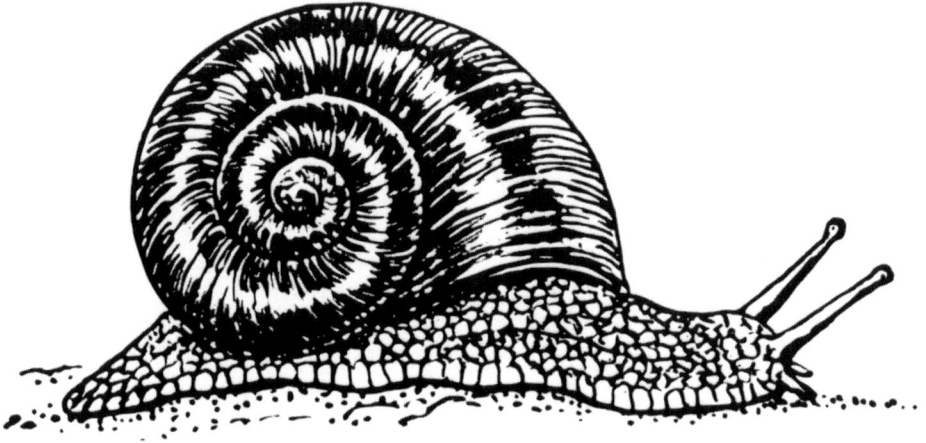

E.S. Cargo Ltd—Leadership on the move..for over 70 years..

Fun fact: Garden snails have a band of >14,000 teeth on their tongue. Now if they can just find a greener garden…(Sound familiar?)

Reign drops keep falling on my head…

I opt to use water terms as my environmental fulcrum because water has dimensions as well as relatives. These 'liquid linkages' can facilitate the channeling of fresh, crisp, fluid approaches. We can immerse ourselves in the shallow or deep end (I would suggest mid-stream), and stumble through our whirlpools of self-doubt. It may take a while before we rename our ocean liner from Leaky Dinghy to Intrepid Voyager, but commit to taking the cruise, and you will experience first-hand journeys and a better understanding or appreciation for the unknown. I dare you!

While inspecting an upcountry Maui restaurant, a Haiku dishwasher looked me straight in the eye and calmly stated that …

"The dishes dry quickly…the dry one's dry even quicker..".

He seemed so stoic and so sure of himself. Was this some sort of epiphanic moment? Some sort of Karate Kid awakening, or Kung Fu proverb for the grasshopper?

I coveted this crumb of intuition, not knowing when again I might use it. Perhaps the dishes he was referring to were members of our society? Or maybe he meant the pain and anguish of human life? Maybe when we inundate ourselves with fresh ideas and spirited cooperation, our souls are temporarily saturated? But dehydration quickly ensues, and we need to immerse our minds into fresh waters of enriched thought. The dryness produces brittle, inflexible approaches that leave one with an intense thirst for preferable alternatives. Or maybe the dishwasher was stoned. Either way, our search for an un-bitter variety of EL starts here and now!

Speaking of thirst, while moonlighting as a water operator at a Durango, Colorado subdivision, I discovered a swollen marmot that was lodged into the drinking water tank overflow. I figured he'd been there at least a couple of days. So, I professionally pried the dead critter out with a screwdriver, took out the bleach and shocked the entire water supply, and then waited for the nasty phone call complaints from homeowners. I solved the problem by screening the 4" pipe—it wouldn't happen again, not on my watch. A lesson in prevention, but I got a feeling that we were drinking mammalian spa water over the past few days. Sure enough, the phones started ringing about the bleach, but nobody reported any illness. Some days are luckier than others.

When faced with corrective actions, environmental leaders must gauge their responses, estimate their doses, temper their responses and prepare for spontaneous reactions. Suffice it to say that indecision is not a viable option.

Science Friction--

Sticking with my flow analogy, the embodiment of many enviro programs is based on the gurgling of sound science. It is an illustration of how an organism or organization thrives within a fine balance of essential elements, finite resources and natural phenomena. Things can get out of whack really quickly, and nobody wants to fall off of the balance beam. Yet as opposed to natural processes and organic forces that provide distinct direction and movement (from an area of greater pressure towards a less-hostile climate), many leaders opt for the reverse osmosis approach.

Using an opposing force that causes a reversal of flow, this process can remove impurities and produce a more potable solution. For example, a program manager could exert pressure on an environmental technician to expedite a soil survey, producing a timely, sterile, shrink-wrapped report. Or perhaps taking an about- face, by injecting cash flow into a resource-poor pollution prevention program—precipitating a forward march in a new direction.

The danger, however, is that the flow of free energy is greatly shifted and fragmented, resulting in an extreme level of filtration (of environmental ideas as well as inputs). The reverse osmosis approach depends upon external pressures that result in a more homogenous product—but it is not a disappearing act. A reverse osmosis unit designed for an individual home that produces 10 gallons of potable water can result in up to 50 gallons of wastewater discharge. To further complicate the situation, the wastewater is more concentrated (sodium, potassium, chlorides) and may be detrimental to the receiving soil and vegetation. The condensed report can present itself as soup without the sandwich, with a side of shortcomings.

This unorthodox process of pressuring groups, filtering discussions or promoting unilateral decisions is far from efficient. While trying to distinguish between resources and waste, unnatural flows can unintentionally extinguish efforts to diversify our environment. Such awkward and misdirected paths of persuasion can lead towards cul de sacs of confusion and coercion.

Taken to extreme levels, the lack of differentiation can result in extinction (with little recourse), while what we're really aiming for is distinction. Yet our environmental organizations attempt to deal with fractions of populations, while minimizing the levels of friction between them and within them.

We talk of coexistence, but it all-too-often boils down to a struggle for survival that is far from healthy or pleasurable—more like a shotgun wedding. If we environmental leaders are to truly engage in inclusive discussions and mutual benefits, we should not stop there, but continue to work endlessly to transcend our distinct differences (social, cultural, economic & philosophic) and shift towards embracing a desired sustainable and healthy environmental outcome. Engagement is good, embracement is better.

The additional strife and discord come in the form of programmatic and internal team fractures. Environmental scientists try to avoid the unknown at all costs. I refer to it leadership-wise as 'a substance without substance'. Water scientists will spend months or longer pouring over data and formulas, murmuring incantations that appease the statistical gods, being productive in terms that they alone fully understand. But as soon as we throw in adaptive strategies or restoration approaches that have no identified quantitative value, our science coequals give us weird and creepy glares. Environmental leadership is ultimately responsible for discerning the appropriate level of fizz in our lemon-lime soda, as without a clear direction, a concerted approach and some well- reasoned rationale, science and environment can fall flat and listless.

'It's the terror of knowing What the world is about Watching some good friends Screaming 'Let me out'---'
David Bowie - Under Pressure

Antics—

Henry's got a bad case of the 'tudes'. Firstly, it's his attitude—poor, bad, somber, negative, maybe indifferent, sometimes trashy. Life is a case of the blahs, and his job sucks.

It produces solitude, as nobody wants to be around Henry, except for the Gothic community. They can read his body language and observe his actions and inactions, all bad vibes.

Henry's solitary confinement produces servitude, as he is now enslaved by being unpopular, unexpressive, uncommunicative and seemingly ignorant. He is hesitantly fed information as needed and confined to his meager workspace. People look away when they see Henry coming.

Henry has very little latitude, as his level of trust is slim, and few want to interact with him. Communication with others is minimal, and he mutters to himself.

There is no gratitude, as he shows disdain for his current position, with no light at the end of the tunnel.

The magnitude of the situation grows and festers, as Henry's bitterness and aloofness starts to volatilize. Trite comments and impersonal organizational platitudes (such as 'think globally, act locally') only add fuel to the fire. Oh Henry!

Henry's not 'going postal' on you, but there are surely some triggers that keen environmental leaders can clue in on. Save him and save your coveted program a lot of grief. Each of us possesses entrance points (intestinal fortitude) that do not create intense confrontation, unless you prefer going that route. The idea is to consider the multitude of entry points that can be attempted, frequented, visited or circumvented. I will not create this list for you, because it is your list. I'm certain that you can come up with 4 good entry points within 60 seconds. Ready? Go!

The clock is ticking. Just do it!

Are you chicken? 'Fraidy cat'!

For those with less esteem, give me 3 push-ups or 3 entry points:

1. _____.

2. _____.

3. _____.

C'mon, just list 3 viable avenues that open doors or create passageways, shedding light on dark situations:

1. _____.

2. _____.

3. _____.

How did you fare? What if you take 15 minutes and discuss your reactions with others? Compare notes, but don't cheat yourself. Here's one example of mine:

Personally extend an invitation to those on the sidelines. With genuine interest, ask spectators to actively participate (and accept 'no thank you' as a small success towards near-future interactions).

Madame Fasaqhe'--

NEPA is the National Environmental Policy Act, and is the number one resource for commenting, questioning and participating in vital environmental reviews. I refer to the NEPA process as a gentleman addressing a French woman named Madame Fasaqhe', or M. Fasaqhe'—Major Federal Actions Significantly Affecting the Quality of the Human Environment. Any time that federal dollars or resources are allocated towards a federal, state or local program, the NEPA process kicks in to take 'a good, hard look' at the proposed action and alternative actions (including 'no action'). The NEPA process can be excruciatingly detailed and arduous, as the affected environment and environmental consequences are formally addressed through draft documents, public notice, community meet-ings, revised drafts and comment periods. Madame and her entourage go on a lengthy tour.

The GMUG management plan previously mentioned will be closely scrutinized from a NEPA perspective. Resource Management Plans that fail to consider significant environmental concerns under NEPA can be rejected by federal officials and the legal system. All of which brings us to the definition of 'significant'.

Leadership, Fellowship, Followship-

The Colorado Air Pollution Control Division (APCD) has hidden behind the term 'significant' for decades. What is significant to the neighbor's lungs is oftentimes insignificant based on a threshold amount inscribed on paper. Granted, we all need to have some essential numerical specifications and identifiers, so that we actually wake up in the morn-ing. But why are we not out in the fore-front and in lockstep, trying to enhance the integrity of our airshed (rather than watch impurities creep closer to a Maximum Contaminant Level)? It's so easy to shrug respon-sibility, blame it on State regulations, revised statutes or federal laws. It's quite ironic that the Colorado Air Quality Control Commission and APCD leadership uses a smokescreen of 'no significant impact' to place a shroud over a blue-sky alternative.

When local Colorado communities have (and continue to) tried to create local environmental reviews of oil and gas development, they are regularly sued by the Colorado Oil & Gas Control Commission, stating that locals lack the regulatory authority. Yet some of those commissioners retaining such iron-clad authority are some of the crappiest types of envi-ronmental leaders that you can find. Sorry, that's wrong. They are not envi-ronmental leaders. Nor did they ever intend to be such an enviro-gelical thing. They are frequently corporate cronies or money mongers, except for a few saints that sit on their Board and try to influence subdued, spiritless events. Woefully, this is often the hand that environmental leaders are dealt. Who's up for changing the mindset of a petrified wood?

So, we know what doesn't work, and we know that we can't give up, but what else can be done? Lawsuits to correct environmental deficiencies play a key role, maybe as much as 8% of the time. The rest of it is up to us environmental leaders. If you happen to be an alcoholic or drug abuser and refuse to get help, you're usually doomed. Likewise, environmental organizations need major help and sizable support. Your reprieve starts with addressing the leadership deficit, but also calls on fellowship and 'followship'. You'll see more on this concept very soon.

Empires and State Building—

We half-jokingly referred to the Montana State Capitol as the 'Vampire State Building'—the bloodthirsty congressmen / women (mostly men) would regularly, unhesitatingly suck the life out of any conservation program that did not prioritize the cattle culture. This was their religion. Their myopic view and short-term memory would ignore our pre-bovine, old-testament culture, insisting that Moses himself was a cattle rancher. What udder madness.

You'd think that bison might interest the free-range cattle coalition, but you'd be thinking with an open mind. Montana environmental leaders would regularly suck the teats of the beef barons, attempting to sway grazing practices towards greener pastures, one nipple at a time. Conservation programs often resorted to this bottom-up approach as a method to prove themselves worthy, willing, integrated and inclusive. That's okay, as long as environmental leaders have a plan to wean themselves—whole milk, then 2%, then 1%, and ultimately fat-free. In the interim, too many so-called leaders sit on fence posts, gazing at the fecal flow from cattle operations entering directly into the Yellowstone River. They see dilution as a gradual, tried-and-true solution to pollution—we green leaders see it as a delusion.

We obviously need to limit our cowboy calcium dependency and bone-up to the truth—that our constituents consist of both raw and 'pasture-ized' populations (cowboys, goat-herders, soy beaners, coconut huskers, almond dreamers and hemp believers). Enviro leaders need to have both maternal and paternal instincts. It's interesting to note that it is normally our maternal side that is defined as 'devoted, caring & nurturing', while both maternal and paternal figures are defined as 'protective'. One is bullish, the other nourishing. Where has Father Nature been hiding?

Too many of our enviro leaders serve as fat globules dispersed uniformly throughout our milky way. The bile may be invisible and elusive, lurking and brooding, gloomy and doomy, congealing and restricting flow. We often forget how to be scavengers, when scavenging may be our best option.

The 'state' that environmental leaders build, brick-by-brick, is a state of mind as well as a state of embodiment. Our greenness is an incarnation of a coveted environmental quality and a manifestation that materializes in greener paths and sustained patterns. Environmental leadership gives concrete form to an abstract idea. We become real-life avatars. We rise above levels of saturated programmatic excesses, and refuse to conform to more predictable, homogenized ideas.

String together wishful thoughts;
fool yourself and fabricate your future--
Chagrinster

Damned if you do,

What in environmental damnation is going on? Why the hell do we slither along environmentally, when we can adopt a fly-like-an- eagle approach? Is it because there's greater risk of being shot down? What in tarnation will it take to be free of our very own imposed shackles of self-righteousness and insecurity? Obviously, we need to cross rivers of change, and we can't afford to stop and scout every little trickle. We need to catapult to the next level and beyond, if we're not capitulating to external pressures or holding ourselves back. Should we practice at joust-ing windmills?

Here's a simple green presentation tool that I call '10-cubed':

Prepare for a 30-minute environmental talk of your own choice. Break it down into three 10-minute segments, with an amusing musical timer, letting folks know when their time is up—

1. What's the subject? (Take 10 minutes to explain who we are, why we are here, and what we're talking about; background, concerns, simple facts, and a sense of presence and vitality).

2. What are we doing about it? (This section could be a little, could be a lot; what has been tried in the past, what we're currently focused on; make it relatable and take your 10-minute time!).

3. Next steps: Allow 10 minutes to wind down, answer a couple of questions, leave some thought-provoking questions and let folks know that they can contact you for more info; but end on-time.

The audience will spread the word like wildfire—they learned a few things, it only took a half-hour, they didn't fall asleep, and dinner didn't get cold! You'll be praised as an innovative thinker, just by not wasting people's precious time. They left with an appetite for greater environmental contemplation and can do some of it on their own! And they might just come back for more! In a complex enviro world, simplicity can hold the key.

The cautious seldom err—

Confucius

Bamboo Leadership—

This is a phrase I coined a good two decades ago, and then I came across an interesting book entitled 'Water the Bamboo'. The author Greg Bell brings up several interesting issues, and my favorites include the following points:

1. Success is about engaging in activities that matter most to you. (I think of it as following a personal non-trivial pursuit).

2. Make your vision become vivid, alive and compelling (see it, feel it, breathe it, sense it)!

3. Become a disciple of yourself, every day. (Adhere to self- discipline, because people believe what we project about ourselves).

We surely need to develop our core strength, maintain our flexibility, become utilitarian, and send out 'runners' that will establish bamboo-like leaders in neighboring areas. We need to be as opportunistic as aspen groves in succession after a pinon pine forest fire. As Jane Goodall, the chimp lady, refers to it, '..*Developing your roots and shoots.*.', and nurturing the personal growth of your inner bamboo.

And talk about succeeding, I would not suggest waiting for a glacier to warm up to your ideas and ambitions. Find receptive avenues, search for hungry minds and incubate your greenness. If your coveted ecological appetizers are as bland as a generic side-salad or if your patience for lethargy is wearing thin, concoct something more palatable. Come up with a special sauce, and have others weigh in on it. Just remember that lots of folks would be happy to eat burgers every day, but there are a zillion different types of burgers. Bamboo leadership bends but doesn't break— no bun intended.

Slap a Good Person Today--

Well, not literally, but do your best to induce, invigorate, foment, provoke, excite, stimulate and rouse. Constantly be on the prowl; explore the outer limits!

Option 1: Discuss

Option 2: Disgust

In southern Belize, a local Punta Gorda fish monger named 'Man-man' produced the most-tasty fresh-cooked snapper and chips, with one problem—he kept his cold beer supply in the iced fish cooler.

Thus, the beer had an obvious aroma and taste. Man-man's response:

'You're eatin' fish with 'yo beer, aint 'cha?'

I couldn't argue with Man-man's rationale—in fact, I accepted it as his reality. He could invest in a second, separate refrigerator, but why? As long as his clientele remained loyal to his cheap, cold beer and fresh snapper, then it ain't broke, everything's cool. But if we hungry fellows start walking down the road to Angelina's place, then we present Man-man with an ultimatum.

Within the minutiae of retail food inspections, it is a minor violation to store utensils with their mouthpieces protruding upward. The supporting science is that wait staff and customers will come along and grab the mouthpiece of the spoon or fork with their bare hands, thus potentially contaminating the eating surface. The solution is to simply store the utensils inverted with the mouthpiece down into the somewhat-sterile utensil holder.

Yet as soon as this non-critical violation is noted and communicated, I observe the kitchen staff grabbing the open-ended mouthpieces (with their bare hands) and inverting them into the utensil container per my instructions—problem solved, easy enough. I failed to get the cross-contamination message across— my stress on the up or down elevation of the handles clouded the actual issue of bare-handling. The beer was still fishy.

Environmental Leaders regularly face similar eco-challenges--such as dealing with hazardous waste sites. We focus on the removal of the dubious 55-gallon drum, while underground migration of pollution should be our priority-concern. Similarly, tribulations continue vis-a-vis managerial direction. We instruct that an emergency response task force be formed, yet we are unsure of what our human utensils will be used for, how they will be applied, how frequently they should be used, and what our finished product might look like. Resources are within one's clutch without having a grasp of the situation. So, we assemble, convene, discuss, question, recommend and think. Environmental leaders will appreciate the dichotomy between thinking and believing, and how we go about handling situations as instructors.

If you cease to resist, then you cease to exist---
Julius Seizure

Larry King's Suspenders—the nature of the beast--

I used to listen to Larry King's radio show before he went on television, and I really enjoyed his inquisitive mind. The guy took a genuine interest in what makes things tick—his interview style (especially when watching him engage on television) gave his complete and undistracted attention to his guest. He looked as curious as an owl, and he communicated openly and naturally, eventually resolving the questions as to 'why' such and such happened, 'what' triggered the response, 'how' the incident was precipitated, 'who' was primarily involved and to what extent, and 'when' the actual events took place. Larry King provided me with much impetus over the years, with his intense curiosity and hunger for answers.

Larry was a genius at getting to the core nature of the human environment, which got me thinking about his trademark suspenders. I'm going to purchase a pair of suspenders for myself, and label one strap 'nature' and the other 'culture'.

Nature and culture, those are the two key elements involved in environmental leadership. Sure, there are economic underpinnings and political ramifications—but focusing on the natural and human environment from a culturally-sensitive ecosystem perspective will pay the greenest dividends. Plus, I can't bear to picture Larry King in his briefs or boxers. It's our results that are endowed with the greatest value, our environmental fruits of the loom.

I define the term environ-mental as using our brains to protect the earth. The environmental impact of creating nature and culture synergisms may be the most potent resource that we possess. Environmental leaders can best address critical issues such as wildlands protection and habitat preservation by considering the nature / culture nexus in great depth. Low impact development takes this very path, by examining social and environmental costs and benefits. As leaders, we don't have to perform the full analysis ourselves—that's where integrative programming and natural resource management may be better equipped to perform the necessary tasks. We just need to ask the Larry King-like questions, and to express our environmental passion and concern for the ecological biodiversity that sustains our existence and offers full suspension.

Total Maximum Daily Loads—

I previously mentioned the terms point and nonpoint source pollution. A point source is the identified sewage discharge pipe, the industrial smokestack emitting a nasty plume, the dastardly villain in that melodrama. The non-point source is a dubious, skeptical character, assuming various shades of green, depending upon his / her benefit, but ultimately contributing a larger percentage of pollution than the point source—stormwater runoff from every parking lot in the watershed, agricultural nutrients draining into nearby streams, dog poop from more than one pooch.

From an environmental leadership perspective, one would assume that your hero, your point source would be lean and green, and that, as within our watershed communities, the majority of our organizational bacteria, erosion and sediment would be derived from non-point sources (throughout the ranks). You really need to verify whether you believe that is the case, and how your leadership efforts can maintain or enhance the integrity of our natural and human environment.

The task of the environmental leader is to determine 'how much is too much', and to set what we refer to from a watershed perspective as the Total Maximum Daily Load, or TMDL. When stream monitoring reveals physical, chemical or biological impairment (excessive bacteria, nutrient-loading, heavy metals, sediment deposition, algal blooms, etcetera), analysis is performed to identify water pollution 'contributions' (too nice a term) from all sources.

Basically, developing a TMDL for an impaired water body is a problem-solving exercise—the problem being pollutant loading that impairs a designated use. It's actually quite simple, until it becomes complicated. Let's compare the TMDL water impairment to an overweight human being. The diagnosis of obesity is a result of excessive caloric-loading and deficient calorie-burning. Both the river and Big Dan need to go on a diet. Developing an action plan is the next big step—less fertilizers, less bacteria, fewer jelly donuts.

Having the resolve to exercise restraint sometimes means doing less. Environmental leadership exercises all available options, but with the realization that ultimate action takes concurrence, coordinated efforts and commitment. All too often we should raise the enigma "how much is too little", in terms of effort, thinking, fixing and prevailing.

We need to ensure that excess pollutant-loading does not impair stream water quality, while at the same time ensuring that feeble leadership doesn't compound our difficulties or impound our efforts. If we expect more from supporters, we should demand more from ourselves.

How much can your body assimilate without becoming debilitated— and how about your mind? What is our 'load capacity'? Need we pile on potential pollutants until they are near a level of concern? And then, when impairment is ultimately confirmed, are we all that confident that reducing loads will bring about adequate and timely recuperation? Are you at work or on vacation?

These are some tough questions, and here are some more—is anti-degradation to be considered an achievement? What about preserving or shoring-up our current EL capacity? The premise is that a specified level or concentration is maintained, and if not, the escalation is listed as 'impaired'. If there was a human continuum, at what point would impairment be reached? When our blood pressure skyrockets? When we are thirty pounds overweight? When we lose faith and wave the white flag?

Environmental Sclerosis--

A lady walked into a New York deli and approached the counter—

"Sam, I'll have a half-pound of potato salad, a half-pound of bologna, and a half-pound of leadership".

The butcher chuckled and said, "You must mean liverwurst".

"Okay", she retorted, "Same thing".

What's this world coming to, when the best that we can do from a pollution prevention perspective, is to quantify how much crap our rivers and creeks can handle over a 24-hr. period? TMDL's try to speak up for the silent streams, by saying (on paper) "...enough already!". Yet when we work on the process of identifying such maximum loading, there will be naysayers—*"Aw heck, the river always looks that way this time of year, get used ta' it…"*. Getting accustomed to being dumped on is not acceptable practice in this leadership guide.

Your workday starts with a cursory check of emails, setting the tone for the next morning hour or two. But you see the phone message light blinking and figure it might take priority over the emails. The gist of the phone message: Please respond immediately, as blah, blah has serious concerns about the wording of the comments you made in this morning's paper… No time for coffee, go get the paper, locate the potentially hazardous materials, try to make sense of these comments, sans caffeine, and assess the inflicted wounds.

The phone rings again, and you instinctively pick it up (because you love your job, and because if it were to leave another worrying message, that would be two strikes without even swinging). You wish it were a wrong number, but no such luck. Sorry, I forgot to tell you, but despite your job description responsibilities, there is an addendum stating *"...and other duties as required to fulfill the needs of the department.."*.

When stuff starts to pile up, the 'woe is me' feelings of self-pity and clouds of despair start to hover overhead. Why are these people such jerks? They've never worked a day in their lives! They should take this job and ....--just then you realize that you do not currently have a Plan B or Plan C. The rent is almost due, the computer has become your prison-mate, the people up top are demanding answers, and you are supposed to be providing leadership?

This is no joke! This sort of scenario is a common occurrence amongst managers and directors everywhere. One day we are standing tall, pointing at a distant mesa, sizing up our strategies for getting there, making plans, delegating duties, employing tactics, taking charge. But what happens the very next day? Cease fire, call for full retreat, with tucked tail between our legs, run for cover. Self-doubt—*I should never have agreed to work out a compromise plan with our stakeholders....* Self-pity—*I always seem to get the brunt of these problems....* Lots of selfs, not many us's.

'Take a load off Fanny, take a load for free, take a load off Fanny,,,, annnnnnd put the load right on meee!..'
-- The Weight, by The Band

tion or be shunned--

It should be common sense and second nature to us—since we work full-time and full-throttle on critical environmental affairs, the issue of our actual daily work environment should be a priority concern as well. Darwin's role in the workplace is not survival of the fittest, but rather to make adaptations that benefit the team, the entity, the whole enchilada. Initiation, Participation and Accentuation all begin with recognition.

I worked with a wildlife conservation organization that did not have a workspace ready for me. I was coming in as the new Conservation Director, and they had three weeks to put in a desk and a chair, maybe vacuum the place (if they could locate the vacuum). Instead, I was faced with detritus from day one, along with a Grateful Dead attitude. Sucking it up, I spent two hours each day for a week, struggling to establish a proper working environment. Whatever became of <u>preparation</u>?

Others would only assist me if I asked them, and even then, somewhat begrudgingly. I knew better than to take it personal. For most of them, my new job paid twice theirs, so why make things even better for me? I switched gears and worked on improving the common area. I became the self-proclaimed tidy bowl man. Several staff expressed some slight <u>appreciation</u> for the availability of two chairs that they could now relax in and read the newspaper during the last 'working hour'.

The Latin suffix 'tion' refers to a state or an action. It is a condition or result, but does not necessarily signify progress—stagnation, or starvation, for example. Here's a corny group exercise that I introduced in my Environmental Leadership training curriculum:

Complete the following sentence by filling in the blanks with a resounding word ending in …tion. Perform the task independently for 1 minute, and then share your responses within teams of 3:

My_____has produced considerable _____that will ultimately result in_____, or at the very least, some degree of _____.

An off-the-cuff response might be:

My <u>intuition</u> has produced considerable <u>consternation</u> that will ultimately result in <u>revolution</u>, or at the very least, some degree of <u>humiliation</u>.

What I enjoy about this menial task is that after feeling relatively confident with your first response, you feel somewhat less secure or ambivalent moving forward, and yet end up with a certain sense of accomplishment. The first response is normally a personal attribute (whatever 'normal' is), while the other responses rely on effort, outreach, <u>assertion</u>, creativity, <u>repetition</u>, <u>ambition</u>, nerve, chutzpah and who knows what else.

Leadership can materialize and leadership can vaporize, despite having similar environmental agendas. One senior staff member was 'working from home' three days per week. Ask the rest of us that are stuck in the office what we think of that! I would surmise that in the backcountry desert environment, some gopher holes are more extravagant than others, but usually their alleyways are interconnected, providing escape routes, rest stops, dance halls and brothels. The very lives of gophers and us environmental groundskeepers evolve around <u>observation</u> and <u>interaction</u>, and their ultimate survival is dependent upon such social processes.

Let's revisit our friendly prairie dog colony. What plagues the pups is, well, the plague. One day you'll see a hundred <u>progression</u> of playful rodent rascals, and several weeks later, a silent <u>regression</u>. What plagues us humans is our inability to work as a society to nurture nature. But like the asymptomatic canine, some of us appear unaffected, despite our leader-of-the-pack role on our environmental team. Who would you rather work for, your mother, your brother, your Uncle Fester? I know, that's a helluva choice! We'll shortly address both <u>evolution</u> and <u>revolution</u>.

The Elephant in the Room--

Do you like quandaries and predicaments? Please say 'yes'! Narrow stream channels are normally deeper, cooler and more diverse, while wider stream channels tend to be shallower, warmer and more prone to erosion, sedimentation and excessive run-off. At the same time, a jungle forest canopy consists not of one towering tree, but of a complex, distinct mélange of trees and vines, old growth and new growth, woody and leafy, furry and spiny. Are streamlined processes missing out on vaster, broader opportunities? Are our trailblazers avoiding or skirting circuitous routes in the name of efficiency? Are we bypassing valuable resources to get to a desired outcome? Is our environmental destiny an actual destination, or is it the pathway towards future objectives that have yet to manifest themselves?

Environmental leaders will concur that we certainly do not have a dominion over the earth, but rather a responsibility to protect and nurture our planet. Environmental leaders need to oppose the close-minded, parochial, regimented approaches that have led to dramatic intoxication of our airsheds, foodsheds and watersheds. We are in dire need of an environmental insurrection that topples the detrimental mindsets that have led us astray. Environmental leadership can revolutionize our vast potential, with an array of enlightened ideas and transformative actions. What can we do to espouse and sustain such efforts?

*Create alternatives to alternatives—you may wish to choose between white, rye, whole wheat or sourdough. You might opt for tortillas, baguettes or bagels. You can mix orange Fanta with Diet Coke, though it sounds pretty nasty! And there is always the 'do nothing' alternative, which suits the bill for those mindsets that have a 20-year shelf-life.

*Take it to the limit— Open the floodgates, if only for a short time, to scour our shorelines and inundate our minds. No stagnant ponds of mundane thinking will suffice. Let 'er rip!

*Get primed—We're going to pump you up! Train, push, build muscle, charge, and then recharge!

*Do the Twist—Take advantage of what is available, squeeze out every drop, then lick your fingers of the remaining goodness.

* Practice 'bumper cars' in a relatively safe environment—do no harm, but try to impact others, through both giving and receiving! You don't have to be an environmental martyr but attempt to play at the margins. Jump up and down. Actually, just jump up—the downers need to take care of themselves.

My cat, it has 3 kittens, 3 kittens has my cat,
and had it not 3 kittens, it would not be my cat---
Mystic Man

Communicide— (alter or falter)

You can grunt, groan and grieve for as long as you'd like—it's better than killing yourself, yet considerably worse than making a concerted effort or honest attempt at altering or amending unsuitable conditions.

As the Associate Peace Corps Director for Water & Sanitation in Mali, W. Africa (not to be confused with Maui, though I did work in both magnetic opposite locales), I was responsible for checking on the overall performance of my 50+ Volunteers throughout the country. Half of them were nearby, some came by to see me (maybe too often), but the adventurous types that were most like me were stationed in the remotest confines of the earth—or at least they should have been.

I made a special effort to plan a trip to the village of Kayes, the hotbox of Mali. Bad enough that the ambient temperature was 114 degrees Fahrenheit, but inside the train it was about to get hotter. The 6-hour rail trip was quickly becoming 9+ hours, with breakdowns and overheating of the locomotive every hour on the hour. When I finally arrived at my destination, I jumped off and waved good riddance to the departing train. Now it shouldn't be too hard to locate the only American in town and treat her to a beer. Say what? You say she went to visit friends on the beaches of Senegal? That's illegal, immoral, unsafe, unimaginable, incomprehensible, but true! Young people take risks, despite consequences.

Well, I'll still go for that cold beer and cool my temper—you only have warm beer you say? Okay then, warm beer it is. And when is the next train coming by? Next week you say? You'd better bring me another beer. I calculated that if I could make it twenty-five miles down the road, that I could catch a bush plane out of Purgatory tomorrow. But it is the rainy season, and the dirt roads are flooded, making it impassable to cars or taxis. Maybe I can rent a bicycle? Oh boy, that got quite a laugh out of the village people. It's time to regain my leadership composure.

I am invited for a cup of tea, and despite the sweat pouring out of me, I graciously accept. The kind gentleman asks me my name—in Mali, all Americans are given Malian 'family names'. The bearded skinflint on my left is Mammadou Coulibaly, with family roots to the bean growers. Sedou Wattera owns the tea shop, another family tradition. My name is Bakary Fofana, from the iron-forging clan. The eyes light up on the guy in front of me, as his name is …. Bakary Fofana! We are un-natural brothers!

Environmental leadership cannot ignore the myriad of displeasures and disappointments that pollinate our communities, ranging the gamut from severe flooding to dry-as-a-bone river bottoms. When given the choice between superfluous, fluffy programs and hard- hitting, concerted efforts, it has been my experience that environmental leaders take a 'wait and see' attitude, opting not to make any choice at all.

But back to Bakary—I pull out my wallet and count its contents in front of him. About twenty bucks, maybe a spare five in the secret compartment for emergencies (it's not an emergency, yet). I waive a ten spot, explaining to him that it's worth about two hundred dollars in his currency. That's a lot of dough! Like maybe four months wages. Plus, he's my brother, so what can we put our heads together and come up with? What are my options?

This again illustrates the unique phenomena of collaborative environmental leadership—other types of leaders would matter-of- factly strive for superiority or influence over competing interests. While there is frequently an 'us versus them' mentality, too many environmental leaders regularly sit on fenceposts and develop calloused behinds. They are never on the summit when lightning strikes because they have never been to the summit. They hike to a safe mesa above raging floodwaters and express their concern from afar. They interpret their own echo as a sign of affirmation. There is a fine line between deception, discernment and deceit.

My brother Bakary has a lightning bolt of an idea—he'll pay the guy that services one of those little diesel-generated rail cars (like in Disneyland) to get me out of Dodge. He'll pay him half and keep half, but who cares! It's dark now, and we're speeding down the tracks, my teeth chattering as the temperature dips. My job is to shine the flashlight, in case there is a cow ahead. And then what-- jump? We actually make it down the tracks, two hours before the bush plane leaves. Thank you, brother!

'I don't want to wake up dead'—
Earth Funeral

My Sediments, exactly---

While hitchhiking through Utah's deserts, I came across a graffiti message under a railroad bridge:

'To gain experience, one must experience the experience'.

Such a heavy statement, and without any spelling errors, I surmised that this was someone's epiphany without the assistance of drugs or alcohol. My takeaway was not immediate in any sense. I just jotted down the words and held onto them forever. From a watershed perspective, stormwater runoff is exacerbated when precipitation flows over impermeable surfaces (pavement, driveways, parking lots) where natural drainage has been significantly altered. Poor or murky organizational sentiment can cloud the water as quickly as a thunderstorm, imposing ill will throughout an environmental team and effectively choking free spirit and communications. I would emphasize the word 'throughout', as office turmoil and turbidity travels downstream rather quickly.

Environmental leadership recognizes that processes are dynamic and change certain. Not all human runoffs can be contained, but impacts can be buffered by making timely use of all available resources, and then making key adaptations in an expeditious fashion.

We hear of people readily reacting to a bizarre episode and then trying to explain the astronomical event—but falling far short of the overall sensation. '*You had to be there...*', they state, in almost an exasperated tone. And they are very correct on two fronts:

<u>You have to be</u> (your self, your best, your future).

And <u>you have to be there</u> (some place, some time, some moment).

'Ya gotta show up, put in the hard work, get down & dirty. Reveal your leadership prowess, and revel in your environmental intensity!

> *'Where there is a flame, someone's bound to get burned But just because it burns, doesn't mean you're gonna die You gotta get up and try, and try, and try*
> *Gotta get up and try, and try, and try...--'*
>   Pink

Engendered Species--

What do you do when you accidentally button your shirt off-kilter? Well, you would un-button, and then re-button, of course. And when you put the t-shirt on backwards? Same thing, it's another easy pres-to-change-o. But when acts and emotions within your enviro team don't seem to fit with your intentions, there is rarely a quick fix for such irregularity. The air starts to slowly bleed out of your inflated environmental ambitions, and you hopefully start to take notice. It's not the end of the road, especially if you are carrying a spare thought, and better yet if you can access the jack and crowbar to make minor mental repairs. And if you're unprepared, who 'ya gonna call? Bilebusters!

Being able to rely on external support is different than being entirely dependent upon others. I had a friend that I used as a personal reference one time too often. He told me via an email "*...I'm sick to death of helping you out like this...*".

I don't think he could have told me that in-person. Worse yet, he served as only a mediocre reference, and our friendship fizzled. When I pondered over it, I felt guilty at first for asking for colleague support three, four, perhaps five times too many. But you know what? Asking for help can be tempered by offering assistance and performing acts of kindness to others, without hesitation and without feeling indebted. One hand washes the other, but it may be the hand of another. Our internal environmental windshield gets chipped and cracked, but rarely does it shatter.

In my recent recount, our boaters Eddy and Helmut were consumed by both fear and confidence—one shrinking, one gaining, both ultimately losing. While there's little beauty in demise, the environment can be unpredictably exotic. There's little doubt that non-leaders will consider many of these anecdotal remarks strange, seeking refuge in their economic and political shelters and bunkers. Environmental leaders cannot risk becoming impregnated by political persuasions and economic vortexes. Our green organizational culture is in-fact the very culture of our organization.

Environmentalism is in our bloodstream, infused with our social and cultural wealth. Selfish, seedy leaders somehow think that engendering environmental actions could potentially endanger their status—and they have reason to worry. Arousing environmental enthusiasm can trigger and provoke a myriad of responses. Sordid leaders are concerned that future team successes may detract from their ultimate power-hold and are equally concerned that any detrimental responses (such as protests or letters of opposition or discovered pollutants) may jeopardize their upstairs position.

The leadership imposters may claim that we are imposing our will on them. Excuse me, but we do in-fact want to implant and transplant our green will and greener ways. The blatant truth is that we want to train the trainer, support the supporter and exploit the exploiter. We wish to promulgate, deftly disseminate and clearly demonstrate enviro issues and actions. We have a proclivity towards intrusion into enigmatic 'no trespass' zones, hoping that the environmental transgression becomes lawful, sinless and addictive. We enviro leaders act with clear conscience, sincere in our beliefs and persistent in our efforts.

True environmental leaders recognize that significant areas of our environmental jurisdiction may be imperiled, and the hazardous waste we confront may emanate from the second-floor office. Provocations are located somewhere within our environmental leadership toolkit, stored next to instigations and liberal agendas.

I aint never goin' back to Tallahassee, Cuz' I aint never been there yet!--

Brown Boots

I'll take 2 jelly donuts, a large coffee, and a medium order of risk—

I often wonder, besides performing at the entertaining twenty- minute Golden Temple snake charming tourist attraction, what does the snake do all day? Sleep? Eat? Hide? Does it prepare for the next day's event or contemplate about the future? And is it the music that charms the snake, or just the wiggling of the flute? All I know is that the Snake Charmer himself appears pretty damn confident. I'm sure he has calculated his risks and has learned from his mistakes (either that or he's a damn fool!).

You're a pathfinder, scout and leader, all packed in one. You've paved the way, made inroads, put in the miles, and all of a sudden come to a major crossroads. You need to make a critical decision as to which way to veer. You have several options, with some routes more secure, others wilder (crazier?). You've trail-blazed, explored the unknown, sought newer horizons and ventured beyond borders. Which way dare you go now? Just don't say 'the way that life takes me...' or I'll surely puke. You might not have total control over your destiny, but I would suggest you shoot for 80%, and never settle for less than 60% of you being directly involved. You are smart enough to realize when environmental intentions are half-baked, and what is most vital to your desires and deeds.

Vitality and zeal should be prerequisites to any plausible environmental project. Become the environmental dynamo that gets the undivided attention of current leadership. If that is not you, then get intimately involved in the creation of this monster. Find out what you want, and then spend the rest of your life trying to achieve it! Sorry for my brutal honesty, but it's profoundly true!

Riddle: What's the difference between 3 cannibals and 2 cannibals? (The answer is forthcoming).

Oregon's municipal bio-versity program intended to emit ideas of environmental sustenance, enrich the lives of inner-city youth and promote more time outdoors. And despite the apprehension and misgivings of some VIP's, the program was very successful. It provided interventions of the third world variety, as it created experiential learning opportunities for curious and adventurous youth. And field staff allowed the environmental outcomes to flourish without creating too many rules, guidelines or impediments—a shining example of unique, green shrewdness.

But sadly, the bile did not dissipate; it awaited the return of the multi-cultural youth team from a one-week affair with Mother Nature. And it came back with a vengeance. Program leaders were scolded for taking risks with adolescent lives. Reports were filed regarding pocket-knives being wielded as weapons. Rumors of sexual promiscuity abounded. And the program was hastily shelved. Was nature more dangerous than the inner city, where you could buy a knife at a 7-Eleven, and sex around the corner? The environmental leaders at the program level felt betrayed, as well they should have. The only solution would be to take these very VIP's themselves on such a journey, so they need not experience the trip vicariously. But there was no such interest, and it was time to go back to the standard, mundane role-playing skits in the safe haven of supervised sessions. What a crying shame!

Answer to the riddle above: One less napkin!

How many of you even attempted to come up with your own answer to this riddle? Or did you simply wait until the answer was exposed? Life in the environmental arena is a gigantic riddle. It riddles our watersheds with waste and riddles our wildlife with such a magnitude of anthropogenic threats, that I'm surprised that I ever see the pueo perform his stealthy maneuvers. We can't afford to wait for someone else to reveal the answers to life's riddles. Plus, there's always more than one answer. Model, inspire, challenge, enable. Bring back the mice.

Sustainability, to me, is the essence of our survival, in a place we call home. That place may be a traditional log-built homestead, or a fully furnished condo, with utilities included. When we discuss holistic resource management at the watershed level, beaver habitat is the first image that pops into my head. Sticks and mud, gnawing and smearing, gathering and constructing, securing and defending— these are all vital elements to building a community. Beavers wholeheart-and-tailedly subscribe to the WATER mantra—We All Take Equal Responsibility. As big-brained humans, you'll recall that We Help Integrate Technology & Education, and We All Take Equal Responsibility (WHITEWATER).

How many of you stopped reading when you saw 'pueo' and tried to figure out what I was referring to? How many of you ignored it and read onward? How many of you want to be better leaders for our environmental future? It will take innovation and creativity, sometimes with new creations, other times with better (different) interpretations. And if it loses something during the interpretive process, it gains something else.

'There are dams, damns and damn dams..'—
Smirkle

All of a Sudden..Never mind..

It comes without warning, or does it? Perhaps you never saw it burrowing down on you, but chances are you could sense that there was a mild disturbance, a peculiar premonition or a bizarre vibration emitted.

At sunrise in my Peace Corps village of Ikela, in the Equatorial Province of Zaire, I made the morning ritual over to the outdoor water closet. My eyes barely open, I saw a slithering black baseball bat ahead of me, heading in the same direction. After pissing my pants, I edged forward with a machete now in hand. Carefully opening the outhouse door, I saw only the large banana leaf that covered the latrine hole (to keep the flies out). Prying it back, I still saw nothing, until returning with my flashlight. The black mamba tried to hide under the leaf, falling into the six-foot-deep pit latrine. I would visit him ('Slippery Pete') several times a day for the next five months—a captivated audience of one. Pete survived on recycled water and an abundance of roaches. Not the life I would choose.

Something's in the air, intimately altering our optimism, creating flurries of sudden insecurity, resulting in flashes of self-examination and survival instincts.

What is a 'sudden' anyway? Is it just another part of the brewing process—knowing what may be missing, what needs attention and how much is too much? That's probably genuine intuition, but what suddenly appears can magically disappear--now you see it, now you don't. Environmental leaders that spend the majority of their time captivated by regulatory policies and procedures better be willing and able to freely regurgitate the information and knowledge they gleaned, lest old acquaintances be readily forgotten. Rigid managerial survival techniques may appear seamless, and while not useless, are virtually senseless.

Maggie recently bought a set of used snow tires from a scam artist. The price was cheap, and the tires looked like they had plenty of tread life left on them. She took advantage of the good deal, but by the next morning, already had one flat. Maggie cautiously limped over to the nearest service station. After a quick examination, the tire experts revealed worn and pitted sidewalls—and the fact that they had discarded these very tires onto their scrap heap just two days ago. Maggie had been taken, and quickly learned that cheap is expensive, and that expensive can be cheap.

When we tirelessly invest considerable time and energy into our primal ways and means, and ensure that we include those with hands-on knowledge, we tend to expect superior performance. This is where the rubber meets the road. Humans have the capacity (and audacity) to glaze over what may be team-beneficial, and convince themselves of the utmost, unconditional necessity for self- preservation and security blanketing. But others in the work environment can plainly see (and feel) just how attentive or retentive you are with your worldly knowledge. You can try to conceal authenticity, but not for long.

Merely striving to transform potential team energy into a collaborative, connective direction, no matter what the subject du jour, will kinetically convey more than substance—in this case, willingness, perhaps even tenaciousness. Perform dutiful rotation to avoid programmatic wear and tear. Make a concerted effort to frequent your internal goodwill store—share, donate and recycle your ideas, making your first-hand thought processes second nature.

'States are not moral agents, people are, and can impose moral standards on powerful institutions'—
Noam Chomsky

Orientation--

I'm running late…. We're all running late…. And what do we do? We take shortcuts! And what are the ramifications? Sometimes we hold our breath, cross our fingers and get lucky, but most times the shortcuts meet up with dead ends, thorns, thickets, poison ivy and rattlesnakes. We're in need for some real 'trailheaducation'.

I often stop and scratch my head when I come to a trailhead sign that displays an obscure, faded map and a minuscule, indiscernible arrow stating, 'you are here'. It's comforting to know where you are, but I find that many of the signs produce other degrees of disorientation—they don't show where north is, they lack a scale of miles, fail to indicate elevation gain and rarely show stream crossings. They are better than nothing, and if you are in dire need of help, such identification sites are a decent place to hunker down and signal for assistance.

Signs are rather objective and can be seen or detected by others. Vomiting comes to mind. Symptoms, on the other hand, are rather subjective. A symptom is a phenomenon experienced by an affected individual, with 'affected' being the operative word. A symptom can also be a perception. Nausea, stomachache and back pain are all symptoms—others only know about it if we inform them, whether they like it or not...

Environmental leaders are on the lookout for signals and indicators. We get a feel for when we need to huddle up and work as a team, and when we should provide for timeouts and recharge. I don't enjoy getting lost, either at work or in the backcountry—but with sufficient experience and poise, we're never too far adrift. Providing environmental challenges and allowing teams to chart their chosen course is both entertaining and enlightening. We need to know not only where we are, but what we are. After sundown there is sunrise, count on it!

Shake things up!--

It's a simple matter to sit down at an environmental strategic planning session and share what works and what needs fixing. We confirm the importance of being important—the community depends on us to protect the Yampa River watershed. We are the 'go-to guys', we are indispensable. We can use our position in the community to expose water polluters, and to engage the public in discussions in favor of smart, responsible growth. We've proven that we can create a groundswell of public support that will enable us to move our pollution prevention programs forward (progressively, of course).

Sounds pretty good, huh? I trust that your 'nature' and 'culture' suspenders are well-aligned and adjusted, and that your personal bamboo leadership has not gone brittle. I feel obligated to stress that community support waxes and wanes. Support needs to be garnered, appreciated, nurtured and never taken for granted. Don't believe, even for a minute, that just because some couple donates $40 and becomes a 'member', that you can therefore speak for them. You represent a cause and are appreciative of the resources given to your organization to pursue the cause—a just and joint cause.

The same holds true for one large $4,000 donation. You don't truly represent the donor—you exert environmental leadership that makes the most efficient and effective use of your combined resources. Is it easier to manage the one-party grant over eighty $50 donations? Is your membership a burden, a blessing, or both? How does it affect your ability to perform nimbly and definitively? And what about your prized and precious financial forecast? What if this large donor selects to go elsewhere next year? How free are we? Can beggars be choosers? (I will argue yes). We all have strings attached (ask my wife) and resist some movements more than others. Your board of marionettes might prefer one style of performance better than another.

But just how does the puppet create synchronicity with the strings? I don't know the answer to this question. I have tried the 'keep your feet on the ground' approach, and yet still managed to trip over them. I've tried jumping and leaping to new limits, only to get tangled in proverbial power lines. I've tried creating my own 501(c)(3) conservation non-profit, but as soon as it becomes a legal corporation, it's no longer yours.

I've tried sitting on boards to get a feel for the front-row seats, and it has taught me a great deal about the power of persuasion. I have a new-found empathy for the 'under my thumb' director—the one that wriggles, finagles, resists and persists in that worm-like fashion, despite being squeezed and scrutinized by a group of pale green higher-uppers. Review boards and oversight committees also need sufficient environmental leadership skills to inquire, recommend, commend, advise, support and act! That's how functional systems operate. Otherwise, the watchdog spends its time watching the watchtower, remaining oblivious to outside interests or internal threats.

I've drifted too far from our conversation about gaining overwhelming public support for eco-smart, sustainable, responsible growth. Somehow, someway, we must emerge before the emergency—that is to say, if we can proactively unveil the multiple layers of secrecy and bureaucracy within our public and private sectors, expose the troublemakers or road-blockers, and shed light on a key concept or pronouncement, we can emerge as environmental leaders.

The term 'to emerge', after all, is derived from medieval Latin 'emergentia'—to bring to light. The alternative is to reactively wait for the actual 'emergency', a need for help or relief, created by some unexpected event. Oftentimes the urgent care unit arrives too late, as the noxious gas weeping from organizational fissures reaches precarious levels of intolerance. At that stage, organizational suffocation has become an 'I told you so' reprimand.

Amory Lovins at the Rocky Mountain Institute said it best when he refers to "...*wondering in the bewilderness..*". I truly believe that time spent wandering and brain cells charged with wondering will add up to something unique and special. I also don't think that you can realistically compare the two—you can wonder what the cannibal is going to do with that napkin, or you can wander over and observe others in action (at a safe distance). Environmental wondering is more guesswork (making an 'educated guess') but perhaps more genius. The environmental wandering is more experiential and perhaps a bit riskier. Together they stimulate creativity—I'll take one of each to go!

Enviro programs that neither wander nor wonder are straight, narrow, bland and flat. They lack the glimmer that is derived from exploration, risk, trial and error. They resemble isolated, protected monocultures with a short growing season--susceptible to fewer external threats, yet aloof from natural reality. On the contrary, diverse environmental programs rely on the cross-pollination of an extensive variety of inputs, resulting in greater opportunities for environmental leadership propagation—the morels of our mind.

The heart murmurs, the brain swells.
                                        Anonymous

Smoltification and the Outer Limits—

There is an internal metabolic process which enables salmonid fish to adapt from fresh to seawater with a minimum of stress. But when their critical habitat is impaired, chronic and sub-lethal effects produce reduced juvenile growth, increased incidence of disease, reduced viability in adults, and increased susceptibility to predation and competition. Substitute the word salmon with human, and there are many parallels to us fleshing-out our environment.

Environmental leadership is well-positioned to assist with averting on-the-job stresses, but I have a real problem with us green avengers developing bend-over-backward tolerance. I'm not saying that we should be intolerant, not at all—but that we should be cautious about being overly tolerant towards leadership deficiencies that need to be addressed rather than dismissed. When your less- competent supervisor claims that you have 'great potential', does that make you feel like a recipe card in the vintage cookbook, or perhaps more like a rusty mortar shell?

Use wisdom wisely and ensure that experience does not become an overdose of doom and direful reality or comprehensive liability. Concentrating on limits reinforces them. Twenty pushups sounded like a lot, as my mental goal was twenty-five. I resolved to double my vision, and with daily practice, I'm currently up to forty-two. If persistence and resolution don't take you beyond your present limitations, daily activities may become a form of servile surrender. Playing 'not to lose' at work, along with a 'don't mess with success' attitude normally results in failure or chronic underperformance. Football fans are well aware of the cautious fourth quarter 'Prevent Defense'—it normally self-destructs and prevents you from winning. You don't give up the big play but are more prone to the dinks and dunks that result in the same losing outcome.

You should always be on life support—support your life and environmental career by being particular, and by promoting your positive qualities and opting for professional incarnation over cremation. You undoubtedly have some strong characteristics that are under-utilized and not regularly exercised. Adapt because you want to adapt, not because you are being hung out to dry. Go on that personal leadership safari, explore your inner beliefs and grow in whatever direction you prefer. You shouldn't have to push yourself to start, but you might have to force yourself to stop. Finally, don't always go with the flow--you might not feel like you're in-charge, but only retired or exhausted fish float downstream. Spawn on!

When the flounder succeeded at graceful swimming, it was just a fluke—

Angle Iron

CHAPTER V.
EMPOWERING OTHERS TO TAKE ENVIRONMENTAL ACTION

Future Shock—From Here to Infirmity--

We are somehow able to envision an image of apocalyptic environmental turmoil yet have greater trouble imagining a utopian society and sustainable world. The fearful image is graphic, gruesome and dramatic, while the hopeful dream remains distant, intermittent and fuzzy. A bumper sticker asks us to *'Visualize World Peas'*—while quite humorous, it's also a stark reminder of how incredibly difficult it can be to picture an extremely doubtful outcome. Some religions are able to vividly contrast heaven from hell. Yet to imagine heaven-on-earth is nearly impossible, especially if we are not the dominant domino.

When we embark upon our environmental aspirations, we seek guidance and valued leadership—yet all too often that environmental capacity is already within us or within our reach. I still do not possess a clear environmental vision, but my rationale is that the pictures of possibilities that flash across my mind are infinite. I'm not comfortable with that, but I do admit seeing a multitude of green flashes (which in my mind, is way better than ghostly apparition and morbid decay).

For those that are not aware, the 'green flash' is an actual-but- somewhat-rare microsecond event that can occur on the ocean's horizon at sundown. At the same moment that the tropical sun disappears (as if drowning at sea), a dazzling green burst of light and energy can take place. I've seen it four times, and it is magical.

During your environmental leadership expedition, it would be easy to say that all the ingredients are included (within yourself) and that all you have to do is just add water (or air, or wildlife). But I admit that it's much harder than that. Amidst all the environmental hysteria and saving the planet hoopla, there will be substantial booby traps and boondoggles that you will inherently step in. Environmental leaders are environmental learners—excavating scientific facts, exposing fallacies, flexing green muscles and deciphering traumatic traces of imposturous green alchemy.

Why Environmental Efforts Regularly Fail:

Unclear Goals   Settling for Less

Non-measurable Objectives   Conflicting Agendas

Hidden Agendas   No Agenda

Backstabbing   Boredom & Under-preparedness

Free Rides, Free Lunches   No Obligations

Fear (our old nemesis)

Perhaps it's time for you to add a few more personal favorites:

1. _____

2. _____

3. _____

There, that wasn't too hard, was it?

'Ya Gotta Hook-em to Cook-em....

I like fish tacos. I like them better without the fishbones, but in Dangriga, Belize they only come one way. I accidentally wolfed down a pointy bone and it lodged in my throat—I was literally hooked. I could breathe okay, but swallowing was quite painful. Since I was still near the taco lady, I pleaded for help. She handed me a whole banana and instructed me to swallow the whole enchilada, er, banana. Bowing to her wisdom, I followed instructions and nearly died from choking and asphyxiation simultaneously. When I was able to gasp for air and swallow, the fishbone was still attached somewhere in my larynx. I scrambled back to my hotel room and drank several glasses of water, but the pain throbbed on. The saving grace was a hot shower, with my head tilted to the sky until the barb shook loose.

Sometimes we leaders don't know what to do but feel compelled to say something worthy of our eminence. Yet we miss out on a grand opportunity to convey leadership to the next level. Simply by stating '*I don't know*', we can convey the need for assistance and acknowledge the importance of others. After all, isn't that why they placed the 'Help Wanted' sign to begin with? But lacking valor and fearing incompetence, we make up responses to the unknown, hoping that the needy swallow our advice, hook, line and sinker.

> *Some folks are born made to wave the flag,*
> *Ooh they're red, white and blue,*
> *and when the band plays 'hail to the chief',*
> *ooh they point the cannon at you, Lord…--*
>
> --Creedance Clearwater Revival

In Stiffness and in Health—

It is the third stage of death; the breakdown of the sarcolemma causes additional calcium to enter the cytosol, activating the formation of myosin-actin cross-bridging, binding the troponin of thin filaments. In other words, rigor mortis has set in. In the case of a cow, if the post-slaughter meat is immediately chilled to 59 degrees Fahrenheit, the muscles shrink by one-third the size. When the meat is then electrically stimulated, the muscles tend to relax. The carcass gets more attention than the being, with tenderized consumption being the ultimate objective.

If environmentally enthused workers are better treated while alive and kicking, and if programs actively reveal their environmental rigor, they will serve as living proof that flexing our managerial muscle can produce core strength, bamboo-style. Instead of ceasing to exist, the strategy is to seize (the moment) and assist.

I won't kid you--our incessant search for the elusive green leprechaun will encounter impoverished conditions, unexpected suck-holes, marital strife and mental anguish. Examining a hornet's nest at close range is not the world's safest occupation. Why should we have to search high and low, near and far, for our environmental niche, when our enviro needs are so glaring and so ominous? Why is it so damn hard to help people and the environment at the same time? I suppose it's because every environmental program is simultaneously operating as an enviro business, with its unique organizational and administrative framework and unequivocal bottom lines. The more we compete, the more we need to strategize and seek advantage, and the more that it detracts from our shared green mission.

We strive to be environmentally omnipotent leaders, implanting claws on our sparrow, when all she truly needs is what she is (those of you in the food court, defend yourselves!). Nurture nature, and you just might gravitate towards enriching the human environment, earning your wings along the way. But if you downplay the human role, you'll be side-stepping more than one pigeon overhead.

> But I know the reason why you keep your silence up,
> No you don't fool me
> The hurt doesn't show, but the pain still grows
> It's no stranger to you and me
> And I can feel it coming in the air tonight, oh Lord
> >   --Phil Collins

Waltzing Matilda--

I enjoyed the musings in the adeptly titled book 'If it Aint Broke, Break it!' by Robert J. Kriegel and Louis Patler. The authors do a fine job of stoking the fire burning in your heart and providing examples of having superiors *'fire hose'* you—effectively dousing your ideas and enthusiasm. They mention the extinguishing of creative ideas with *'Yeah, but...'* responses. Instead of building on your innate potential, bile-full leaders quickly smother any possibility.

'I was thinking that we might consider the local conservation district as a resource, building upon its close rapport with the agricultural community...'.

"Yeah, but they have their own soil and water agenda.... "

'Perhaps we can mutually benefit by working on sustainable food & water initiatives?'

"Yeah, but we've got so many issues already on our plate.,."

On top of that, we often firehose our own ambitions without knowing it, because changes are surely scary. I refer to such opportunities and consequences as 'Germinate or Exterminate'. It's very similar to the fate and transport of groundwater pollutants, with Environmental Leadership taking its own migratory path within our worldly domain.

If I intend to make this book useful to the very people and situations that I write about, then I need to provide more than a modicum of hope and encouragement. My hope is that you take these EL messages seriously (at least some of them!). I encourage you to either step aside or step forward and take the EL leap now, today! Please, none of that 'free beer tomorrow' tomfoolery. If you're not composing, you're decomposing. I urge you to resist taking the path of least resistance and to explore your ultra- personal leadership frontier.

I can relate to the difficulties in changing our current-day playing field and wish to pursue some intentional veering off-course from an environmental perspective. It drives many a director furious, seeing that their well-intended plans are being questioned, tampered with or discounted. We are all custodians of our environment, with differing values and perceptions. You can refer to us as stewards and I'll accept the term yet will always think of the friendly skies. And with Environmental Leadership, the sky is the limit!

The term 'custodians', as I've previously suggested, assumes that we work on cleaning up our environment. We perform the grunt work, are frequently underpaid and under-appreciated, and regularly watch our restoration efforts being trashed before we can empty the garbage cans. I respect the hard work of organizations such as the Surfrider Foundation— recruiting volunteers to work together to clean up our beaches. When we walk around picking Styrofoam containers out of the beach sand and plucking a gazillion cigarette butts from every other stride that we take, surely the observing offenders will feel guilty, right? But what do we find at this same locale several weeks later--maybe some improvement, maybe not? Less butts, more cans, used condoms plus a nasty mattress and a box-spring. This really infuriates me! What's the solution?

I'd like to make a call to arms for our enviro-conservation community. Can we create some definitive program synergies by holding hands, embracing strategies, speaking as one, sharing resources? Probably not, but we should! We can call it our organizational orgy—a way of gorging ourselves with enviro issues that we have such a grand appetite for. Water mongers, air-heads, conservance-seers, trout aficionados, energy savers, bird lovers.

Create that fury! Take gang green to the opposite extreme and promote flow, continuity, capacity, progressions and leadership!

The only difference between range *management and* anger *management, … is where you 'R'—*

Conservation District Wise-guy

Entering the Fray—

All too often I observe governmental agencies that claim to provide services '*for the people*'. At best, the effort is one-third correct. At worst, the provider succeeds in pacifying the greater good.

When performing services '*on behalf of*' the community, these services are usually only partially performed, in a delayed response, and fractionally successful. Not until the community becomes intimately involved, and until the people are fully understanding the processes and implications, and then voluntarily performing some significant activities, are we able to wind up full tricycle with 'for, of and by'.

Environmental Leadership needs to carefully ensure and assure that programs and projects are owned and operated <u>by</u> its citizens, <u>for</u> its communities and <u>of</u> its inhabitants. In essence, programs cannot feasibly be larger or greater than those that they serve. They are a slice of the pizza, a sliver of the pie, a thread in the fabric of the community.

<u>For</u>: Refers to intentions and purpose, as in 'the candy is <u>for</u> the kids, for Halloween'.

<u>Of</u>: Refers to ownership, as in 'Citizens <u>of</u> the United States'.

<u>By</u>: Refers to inclusion and participation, as in 'the concert was enjoyed <u>by</u> all in attendance'.

When we include Abraham Lincoln's full statement,

'*Government of the people, by the people, for the people, shall not perish from the earth*'.

Long before we coined the phrase 'in God we trust', our United States' motto was *E Pluribus Unum*—out of many, one. Thirteen united colonies formed a single nation. There was almost as much diversity back then as there is today. Without a common will and desire throughout our communities, we shouldn't expect many green bequests. But if we entrust our citizens with shared responsibility, legitimate tasks and candid recognition, environmental empowerment may actually prevail.

Go the extra mile. For a trail runner, that's another eight to ten minutes of varying degrees of pain. But as an Environmental Leader, it all depends on how many miles you've already put on, how much energy you've exerted and what mental and physical condition you're in. The difference between real crab and imitation crab is the degree of authentic crabbiness. Don't get hijacked or hoodwinked--be genuinely bona fide and forge ahead!

As entrusted Environmental and Conservation Leaders, give yourself ultimatums, and laugh along with exasperation. When somebody states that you've got a real attitude, thank them profusely. Acknowledge that you'll be engaging with tinted pastures and talented imposters. Realize that there will be abysmal moments, and hopefully not too many environmental exoduses. Feel rich, substantive and not content. Be perceptive and receptive, but comprehend—understand, from an EL perspective, the Full Monty of the natural and human environment. You can't put things into perspective, until you have one.

ICE Capades—

Why do they call it a comic book, when our superheroes are not the least bit funny?

Why do we pardon the guilty and excuse innocence?

Why do we question our abilities before trying them out?

I've observed naïve female Peace Corps Volunteers in Niger, W. Africa, going to the Grande Marche to have their feet and ankles painted black. They say it looks attractive and makes them blend in with the local women. The native ladies though, have no idea that the black smudge is a local melange of warfarin and coumadin, otherwise known as liquid rat poison. Once ingested by rats, it prevents their blood from clotting and the blood rushes into their brain. The rats and the locals don't know any better. I'm not sure what the Volunteers' excuse is.

The Triple Crown of many expectant organizational messages includes detailed elements of Information, Communication & Education (ICE). Pertinent examples include Health Alerts for influenza outbreaks, weather advisories for winter storm warnings, forest wildfire emergencies, changing your clocks for Daylight Savings Time and remembering to start thawing the frozen turkey four days before Thanksgiving. Yes, once again, it's never that simple.

Though we're off to a great start, Environmental Leadership relies upon more than ICE. It's about time to make some <u>cubes</u>:

<u>Collaboration</u>:

Fill the entire trove of people and places. Do things in concert with others and expect some spillover.

<u>Understanding</u>:

Learn what it takes and how long it may take. Turn apprehension into comprehension and appreciate team chemistry.

<u>Betterment</u>:

Seek potable solutions that are refreshing. Add value and further the cause by solidifying your efforts.

<u>Elucidation</u>:

Filter out the murkiness and confusion. Illuminate the room.

Barrages of frustration and consternation can handcuff our green leadership efforts—converting expectant into expectorant, coughing up viscous excuses and ralphing up rehearsed responses. We need to learn how to make best use of people. Isn't that what we are really trying to do? Not abuse them, but utilize people's skills, energy and strength to benefit our cause as well as their own cause. Using ice cubes is one recipe, not for success, but for initiation.

When we get pulled in all directions, our core becomes stretched and silly-putty-like. We must deal with the curmudgeon, the sourpuss, the bellyacher, the malcontent. We respectfully ask for contributions of ideas, suggestions, recommendations, resources and solutions. We can detect the snickers and sense the snipers. Woe is us. We are on thin ice. At this stage, viewer discretion is advised. A log will float, but it's not a canoe. A dog will swim, but it's not a fish. A drum will beat, but it's not a heart.

To the best of our leadership ability, we need to maneuver, conceive, negotiate, plot, scheme and chart a course. We sleepwalk through solitary scenarios, ultimately realizing that we must find not only our way, but our will! Curiosity killed the cat, but it was mediocrity that turned him into a pussy. You might recall our NEPA methodology—don't just take a sip or a nod or a glance or a wink— take a good, hard look, then keep looking!

Forever 'aint bad, compared to tomorrow…--
Catywompus

Have a meltdown—

Current events eventually become mere events, and then just sheer memories, due to frigid environmental execution and poor circulation. On the contrary, the 'current' should electrify environmental leaders, giving them the jolt that can turn tables, increase volume, create presence and develop our precious liquid interdependence throughout watershed communities. I don't care if you call it collaboration, corroboration or building bridges—you need to show up! Literally come to the table, press the flesh, bend the elbow, speak your mind, lend an ear.

There's a running term called 'fartlek' which ironically distances oneself from the stink of stagnation—you decide to pick up the pace over a determined distance of your own choosing. Running faster for five minutes, then returning to your normal pace, and then repeating the fast-then-slower process while you build endurance.

The same holds true for potent environmental leadership—one can't expect to expedite an environmental response to a significant threat if you are not accustomed to going on strenuous, extended expeditions and laborious green escapades. What we green infidels direly need is nothing short of environmental adultery! Your response to a petroleum spill is based on other recent multi-party responses. From start to finish, stop hibernating, melt the ice from your eyebrows, embrace partners and cause your own transition from timid and tepid to warmer, conducive receptions. Engage with others, stimulate green conversations and pick up the pace!

If we're not engaged, we should be enraged—
Perturbed Environmentalist

The $100 Pizza offer:

What appears endemic to the culture of enviro organizations is our inherent desire to cleanse our minds of clutter, and to produce some semblance of a product that is hermetically sealed, insulated and protected from outside influences. Unfortunately, the final product resembles the solitary effort that led to its creation. Let's admit:

a) We are addicted to the dollars.

b) We conceal our addictions in strict confidentiality.

c) We make excuses for not living up to our potential.

d) We don't know what our potential is.

Go ahead, please add a few more:

e)   —————————————————————.

f)   —————————————————————.

And it's probably a result of enviro groups thinking like businessmen. I mean, they do legally refer to the many of us as 'non-profit corporations'. But do we really have to tow the same line as the banks, utility services and auto industry? I find the term 'brand new' to be the ultimate irony, as the brand identifies ownership and existence, while the new signifies creation and uniqueness. We're not marketing cornflakes, nor ketchup! The fabric of our community might very well need conditioners and softeners, but not without site-specific examination that includes (a la NEPA) the affected environment, environmental consequences, environmental alternatives and community-selected preferences. True green leaders prioritize values over value-added.

Can't we have some appearance of professional disarray? Thank God for places like Boulder, Seattle, Santa Fe, Madison and Berkeley, where we can proclaim and profess green slogans and not feel threatened in the least bit. Let's get together and get to know each other. Here's $100 to get us started. If each of your respective enviro orgs also brings $100 to the table, we can create Boise, Idaho's first (maybe annual) $1000 pizza party! Nobody leaves until the last slice is devoured, and the first pledge towards environmental collaboration is set in-stone. Getting started is so easy, so let's get going! Are you with me?? Are there any hungry MICE out there?

Mirage-a-trois--

Leadership can be fatal to an organization and a community, and leadership is largely responsible for the demise of many organic, community-based visions. Leaders toss around the concepts of success, growth and paradigm shifts as if they were available free and at no-cost. Emerging leaders have been convinced that with will and determination, anyone can lead. The leadership gurus understate the critical element of goodwill and the value of environmental values. No, you can't become an environmental leader without an environmental base and environmental balls. Triumph, rewards and prosperity are tertiary in an environmental world concerned about remediation, sustainability, protection and progression. First things come first.

For every ten newly created leaders in this world, we should be concerned that three out of those ten may directly or indirectly harm the environment. Grit without true grit, determination without self and group determination, persistence without a continued, sustained vision of environmental health—just some scary examples of leadership gone awry. We can't allow mythical leaders to penetrate our environmental ranks, but who's going to stop them (or veer their direction), and is it you that is their main competition?

A mental addiction to environmental leadership can take multiple paths:

One way: Increased amounts of leadership are required to reproduce intended results, such as when technical expertise is coveted by one key individual. Environmental followers lull into a sort of doctor-patient relationship and are not given the latitude to prescribe their own future. Cravings and bad habits are reinforced through dependency on others. A dog trainer also comes to mind.

Another way: Shared leadership produces positive dependence, not on any particular substance, but on substantive environmental programming. Environmental staff and environmental communities are sensitized and stimulated by real or potential successes, and in- turn they seek environmental scenarios and amplified responses. Good habits are multiplied, iterated, fortified and sustained.

And don't forget: Foul or domineering leadership has produced a tranquilizer effect on the already tranquil. Doses of low-level pain and anguish produce numbness, servitude or nonchalance. Every day is the same, and a feeling of imprisonment is recognized, affirmed and readily accepted.

If you've ever stepped on a kiawe thorn, you'll recall the experience. The mesquite hybrids were planted in Hawaii to teach the barefoot locals the importance and etiquette of proper footwear, so the story goes. The thorn resembles a devil's trident, and as one thorn points outward, another tip spears upward, and the third downward. The damn things go right through the beach 'slippas' as well. If only our environmental leadership efforts were so pointed, we would have much better odds at impacting and sensitizing communities. With some research and investigation, blends of each leadership elixir can be readily-observed—choose your own Green Goddess ingredients and concoct your personal leadership tonic.

What would Ike have done??

General Dwight D. Eisenhower (not the guy on the dime) will be remembered as a military expert and a proud leader of U.S. Forces. Outside of military superiority, however, he also possessed a keen vision for the world of ours. 'Ike' expressed grave concerns over the dangers of a newly emerging military-industrial complex, the threat of military build-ups and future arms races. Ike was also acknowledged for expanding the Social Security program.

But Eisenhower's leadership acumen did not arrive overnight. He appeared to have learned from his actual experiences, including military interventions in Korea, Iran, Guatemala, Vietnam, WWI (stateside), the Philippines, WWII (Japan & Germany), Tunisia, plus serving as NATO Commander.

A people that values its privileges above its principles, soon loses both..

Gen. Dwight D. Eisenhower

I would argue that it was not Ike's military leadership, but his patriotic sense of social justice and community well-being that cautioned us about the road we are going down. Yet when even the most experienced caution is thrown to the wind, we seem to end up dealing with possibility and probability, pluses and minuses, costs and benefits, authorizations and stipulations.

Then there's Charlie--Charlie Chaplin once won 3rd prize in a Charlie Chaplin lookalike contest! I have a sneaking suspicion that Charlie found this to be quite humorous, but also quite enlightening. Charlie, you see, was more than a star actor / comedian during the age of silent movies. Off screen, he expressed his thoughts and beliefs on issues as controversial as the war effort, social programs and community activism. His support for the common man and the daily struggles against adversity had others label him as a communist or a subversive. His movies were always silent and full of contradiction, but his messages extremely potent, expressing passion in an otherwise hostile environment. Leadership provides assorted avenues, and environmental leadership brings communities to the forefront, prioritizing nature and culture in a place called home.

I am at peace with God.
My conflict is with Man---

Charlie Chaplin

The Land of Disenchantment—

The State of New Mexico is so poor that they can't afford license plates on both front and back of cars. To save resources, they should contemplate the replacement of red lights with tamale wagons, since we all stop anyway. Add in a half-dozen pay toilets down the road and we'll be one step closer to fiscal responsibility.

New Mexico State environmental job recruiters would mistakenly transpose my Lithuanian surname Urbonas as 'Urbanos'—throw in my nickname of 'Wano' or 'Bueno' and you've got a prime Hispanic candidate on your employment roster. Then this pasty Anglo dude (me) walks in the door, and you can imagine the surprised faces.

Yeah, the New Mexico hiring process can be slimy and laced with nepotism. I've worked for directors who couldn't remember my name, and for supervisors who were at best managers of time and money, not people. I wouldn't mind the fumbles, blunders and botched attempts if they were aimed at creating sincere environmental program improvements. But with levels of ineptitude that could drown a roadrunner, it was quite obvious why there was insufficient team spirit or enthusiasm to fill a taco shell.

Over the past fifty-plus years, when somebody believed they had foodborne illness, physicians would normally diagnose them as having 'gastro-enteritis'—basically, inflammation and gas in the stomach. Nowadays, we place 80% of the guilt on Norovirus, a Norwalk-like virus that is easily communicable via dirty hands, vomit, feces, indoor air, door-knobs, shared toys and other 'touchables'. My apology goes out to the formerly accused salmonella and clostridium perfringens—getting more credit than they ever deserved.

The same holds true for the Blue Canyon Coalition, Save the Desert Tortoise and Vision 3000. Whether we are talking about success or failure, there are a host of responsible parties. Some get the ball rolling, others jump on the bandwagon once momentum is achieved, yet others leap off before the train wreck. People are leery to give it, eager to get it, and less gracious to share it. I'm still talking about credit.

Who pays to see us play in this modern age environmental coliseum? Good grief—your Field Program Manager just jumped ship and joined the Bazooka Land Trust—he'll share your secret plans with the opposing team! Good thing you never shared with him your main objectives and ambitions in the first place, huh? At some point before eternity, leaders need to realize that the protection of open space starts between one's ears.

Like a persistent case of Campylobacter, a reality was setting in. Could the old adage *'it's not what you know, it's who you know'* actually be the First

Commandment? I sent an amiable inquiry out to the Green Enchilada Society (name changed to protect confidentiality) and four other 'leading' environmental organizations, sharing this scenario:

Hello Eco-Neighbors.

I am an experienced conservation and environmental professional and have been creating an Environmental Leadership guidebook that can significantly assist our green conservation challenges. Please review my attached two-page 'White Paper' that should help clarify my intent. Can you kindly provide me with any additional insight or any advice that would enhance our shared Environmental Leadership goals and vision? I would be happy to communicate via phone or email, depending on your preference, and can also meet with you in-person, upon your request. Thank you for your time and consideration!

Then I waited, and waited, like waiting for an old episode of Perry Mason to end. I felt like a time traveler—sometimes to the past, often to the future, but obviously never at the right place at the right time. Qualifications are important, but other factors appear to be just as important. While I never received a complete or satisfactory response from any of the five enviro entities, this is what I gleaned:

a) Live in the area.

b) Know people in the community.

c) Experience aspects of the job.

d) Don't know too much.

Yeah, it's a pretty shoddy list. The first three items were old hat and were reinforced by the scanty responses that I received back from two of the five groups. The final item, not knowing too much, now that took me a while to figure out. It's that battle where leadership is at odds with knowledge, realizing that awareness is hiding just around the corner. Somebody with decision-making authority, with resources in their possession, is trying to figure out if they should expend energy on a potentially valuable commodity (you), or perhaps resort to finding a hidden gem at the thrift store—something that can get dusted off, polished, painted and refurbished as a smaller investment. Or maybe just buy that puppy dog and train it to beg from early on, taking it to obedience school along the way.

Remorse Code--

"*Take me to your leader*", said the alien.

Within one quick synapse, the little green woman calculated that you were not the one. I wonder what gave her that idea. Was it your empty stare, or perhaps your aura of subservience?

Before we started taking choking hazards seriously, we kids could get these super neat, keen and awesome secret decoder rings in the bottom of our cereal box. This chintzy piece of plastic from Japan or Taiwan gave us unearthly powers and extraterrestrial imaginations. We could contrive our own messages and convince ourselves that our covert operations were hush-hush, for your eyes only.

In the world of adults, our most common distress signal is SOS—three dots, three dashes and three dots. We cry out in desperation to Save Our Souls and for someone, anyone, to respond to our emergency. With texting nowadays, SOS can translate to Same Old 'Stuff'—the last thing that an E-leader wants on her resume.

Someone once said that '*familiarity is the enemy of awe*'—due to our proximity to often-unsought freedoms, previously daring situations become less and less remarkable. We sing the song of one bird, and unknowingly telegraph our message in advance, both helpful and hurtful. We silently plea and cry out for assistance, displaying anguish and sorrow. Occasionally we let down our caveman defenses and reveal hints of precious joy and outer space elation. Covet that occasion.

We Environmental Leaders try to process new information and decipher coded signals and veiled messages in a matter of minutes or less. On second thought, I think we deal with minutes of minutia and hours of excrutia. Our internal interpretive processes should make some sense, but not a lot. A true process should fold and unfold, grow and outgrow, hash and rehash. But why do we hear all the rigmarole about community-based communications? Are participative processes all that complicated? Will mixed messages result in frenzy, confusion or alienation? Who cares?

We can lament about the one that got away and adamantly state *'boy, I'll never do that again!'* But I regret to inform you that compunction and remorse come with most environmental jobs, so you'd better get used to it.

For what is man, what has he got?
If not himself, then he has naught.
To say the things he truly feels..
and not the words of one who kneels…
the record shows I took the blows,
and did it my way

Frank Sinatra

Trick or Retreat??

It is tough enough fighting formidable enemies (polluters, criminals, careless corporations, etc.). We need not conduct fisticuffs within our ring of allies, unless our environmental drivers are out of alignment—in which case we need to wail away with emerald green uppercuts and wallops to the mid-section, eventually taking a toll on the core or nucleus. The end result need not be winning or losing, but standing up for what you sincerely believe in, displaying environmental stamina and courage, and potentially leveling the playing field.

Environmental leadership should become visceral, deep-rooted and instinctual—I say 'become', because during your first several rounds of bobbing and weaving, you may not be ready for what is coming at you. You'll probably be relying heavily on your hunches, suspicions and professional discretion. It can be trench warfare in the environmental arena, so watch out for the sucker punch!

There's a term for when you sort of throw up a little bit in the back of your mouth and swallow it—it's called 'vurping' and has to do with the simultaneous actions of burping and vomiting. Bottom line, it comes from within, and seeks an exit. Try to compare it to in- reach and out-reach—two vital environmental leadership skills, often coming from opposing directions. Environmental pleasure- seekers can be in for a graphic leadership surprise.

In terms of in-reach, there are dozens of exercises that you can use to take that scrutinizing, microscopic look within your team ideals and belief system. From an environmental vantage point, I would recommend trying a 1:1 session with nope, not a trusted confidant, but a reliable opponent. Consider it a sparring session, with the intent of not knocking out your opponent, but rather taking a hit to your mid-section and seeing how you handle it. Wow, that could be a pretty vulnerable position to put your-self into! But once you've lived and survived in the malaria zone and return to your safe haven, shooing away flies can be accomplished by a mere flinch.

Jab, spar, dance, float and shadow-box—you're on a mission. Swing, duck, sting, clench and perform—no chance of submission. The environmental arena is a public venue with ongoing events to experience. There will rarely ever be a unanimous decision, and you better be able to give it and take it!

Muhammed Ali enjoyed eating lots of beans… They called him 'Gaseous Clay'—
Rest Stop Graffiti

Suck on this--

While visiting the shores of Tasmania, I went for a jog, or what my wife calls, a 'bikini inspection'. Trying not to stumble on the slanted sandy coastline, I ran by a guy tossing a fist-sized piece of meat on a rope out into the surf. Upon my return a half-hour later, my curiosity got the best of me. He was still there throwing meat at the ocean, my only rational thought being that he wanted to see a shark first-hand. There was no hook on the meaty wrap, and no guys in white coats nearby.

'G-day mate'

'G-day to you too; can I ask what you're actually doing?'

'I'm fishin' of course'

'What do you catch?'

'Worms, of course'

He pulled a pair of pliers and a bag from his back pocket. Evidently, the scent of the bloody meat being tossed out and pulled in through the shallow waters causes these eight-inch worms to stretch their necks out in search of a meal. He scampers over, grabs them with the pliers and slowly tugs them from their animal kingdom.

'What do you do with the worms—do you eat them?'

'Nah, mate—I go fishin'!'

Environmental leadership can often be akin to fishing for worms. For starters, you must show up—that's one-quarter of the battle, so you've already put the couch potatoes to shame. Next, you must actually do something. Actions should produce reactions. Then we 'up' our game from action to attraction, determining what efforts are needed to produce a result. Lastly, when results occur, we evaluate if they are intended (worms), unintended (sharks) and significant.

Hopefully you've gone fishing a time or ten. Experiential learning has no equal. You sense, you feel, you act, you react. Of course, folks will feel more comfortable if they are competing on their home turf. As an equalizer for both parties (your worthy opponent and you), take the encounter on the road to a neutral watering hole— not a bar (never a good idea for clear thinking), but the local creek, river or watershed basin. Bad weather moving in, you say? Go there anyway and have lunch in the pickup truck or local café.

It's quite commonplace in Lihue, Kauai to observe Asian businessmen sipping a beer during a luncheon meeting. They will nurse one solitary can of Coors Lite, poured over ice, over a 2-hour meeting. Now I don't speak Japanese, but I can tell you that the activities are quite lively-yet-serious, and that nobody at the table finishes their diluted liquid gold until the meeting adjourns. It's a testament to how matters are dealt with in a respectful, professional, sober and considerate manner. While glancing over with sheer curiosity, I always got the feeling that the actual meetings were more vital than the discussion.

Consider it that fishing trip, but without hooks or lures. Your intent is to use your senses, share some feelings, to agree to disagree on certain issues, break down barriers and see what happens. There may be an initial reaction such as *"...man, I'll never, ever do that again...".* Even that would be a learning process, but I will wager that good or bad, you get something out of the experience. And if not, try it again, and notice that nothing is completely the same. Change takes place with or without you. How you influence the flow will depend on how often you test the water.

The grasshopper is the same color as the fish, but don't be fooled— he swims like the rabbit and sings like the frog--

Desert Wanderer

Evolution & Revolution- - (or revelation??)

As an intrepid Peace Corps Volunteer in the Congo, I thought it would be cool to spend a night in a pygmy (Bat'wa) village deep in the Ituri forest. I was there prior to the HIV / AIDS reckoning, when bush people were considered to be offspring of the chimpanzee (aren't we all?). I was offered one of the few beds in the village, and graciously accepted. After only several hours of restless sleep, my back was in spasms from the splintery bamboo ridges, my feet protruding a foot past the wooden frame. At midnight, while getting up to pee outside, my forehead smacked the low-rise hut frame on the way back in, surely waking up the roaches and geckos. By morning, I counted forty-four welts on my arms and belly from mosquitoes, bedbugs and 'no see-ums'. It was probably a good thing that I couldn't view my back.

Was it worth it? No.

Would I do it again? Nope.

Was it a great experience? You bet!

Life on the equator does not always equate. You formulate your own formulas, adding and multiplying, never subtracting nor dividing. The product is a raw, uncertain product, rarely a finished commodity. Environmental scars can be blanketed or dismissed, or they can be examined and considered. A bad night's sleep can be remedied by a good night's sleep. You might have dismal dreams for two years, but it's what you do in your waking hours that reveal environmental leadership.

There is no time for contentedness, unless you are one of those despicable directors or President Mobutu himself. Be as sensitive as the species that you're trying to protect (including your own species). Hone your environmental leadership skills and develop your senses to the point in which you are keenly aware of your environment. Be aware of poignant situations and actively engage in problem-solving. You won't become an overnight sensation, but perhaps an over-life relation. I must personally thank you for your time and consideration.

Do whatcha oughtta, add acid to water—

I always remember the correct methodology by thinking about A&W root beer, in that order. One normally wouldn't think that adding one element to a proposed solution before the other would make much of a difference. Explosive situations tell us otherwise.

If done incorrectly and water is added to a strong acid, the extremely concentrated solution releases heat via a violent, boiling reaction. On the contrary, when acid is added to water, the solution is very dilute, with small amounts of heat released.

Contributing minuscule amounts of acidic comments in an otherwise united or common cause will produce a minimal reaction. While less intuitive, contributing basic ideas and common sense to an intense, acidic environment can be met with incendiary responses that you would never have imagined—picture a human rights activist at a KKK rally, or a Denver Broncos fan at a Las Vegas Raiders game.

Oil & gas producers want no part of environmental protectors, and vice versa. As environmental leaders, we need to be aware of such caustic situations, and to know what first steps to take. If I'm going to rubberneck over a rocky ledge, I get down on all fours—all six if I had them. Environmental leaders like you need to assure your sidekicks and subordinates that you have their backs, and that we peer into the future together.

I've been relegated to reviewing less-ons for more-ons...--
Desk Jockey

Tribes & Tribulations—

Few Tribal agencies have yet to figure out how to employ non-Tribal environmental professionals within the ranks of leadership positions. Sovereign Nations regularly fill vacancies with many potent non-tribal players, but then assemble them as if they were cumin in a spice rack— towards the back, available if / when needed, used in a pinch.

Teams in-general have many Tribal similarities, especially environmental teams. Starting with a core belief system and holding natural ecosystem values as sacred, environmental teams can function freely and effectively with a sense of connectivity to the land and a spiritual awareness. Obviously, Native American spirituality can be much more profound, given hundreds of years of practice, experience, atrocities and influence. My point is that environmental team spirit goes through the roof when two things happen:

Firstly, the possibility of achieving a significant environmental victory must be within range. Environmental leaders with keen senses and sense perception can actively convey program progressions and regressions, keeping constituents eager, enthused and up to date. When changes rarely occur, and skimpy updates reinforce false hope, faith and spirit goes by the wayside.

Secondly, environmental proclivity must be welcoming and endearing to inclusive, diverse audiences, creating a clan of connected green brethren. When environmental programs are tepid, timid and less-than receptive, they are considered by those 'insignificant others' that were excluded from the process as suspicious, deceptive and conspiring.

Tribal Councils wisely or unwisely reserve final executive decisions to themselves. As elected officials, they regularly misconstrue the mentoring role of their chosen section leaders, and rarely envision (env-vision) internal organizational growth. Environmental leaders within such a team can feel frustrated by the slick promotion of mineral extraction revenues as beneficial to the community, and then being directed to 'minimize environmental impact'. That's a tough row to hoe for any leader, and I'm pretty sure there is a native word for bile. To be ultimately effective, teams (including Tribal teams) must practice daily rituals that include perception of possibilities, receptivity of opinions, tolerance of extraordinary thinking and intense, respectful discussion of options that include sustainable outcomes.

It would also behoove Tribal Environmental Leaders to identify the appropriate channels for promoting environmentally sensitive issues to top-level decision-makers early on in the process. All too often, environmental consequences are brought to the table only after initial and secondary discussions have taken place, and the cement is starting to harden. Timing + Effort = Possibility.

<u>Tributary</u>: A stream flowing into a large river (compare to headwaters, or branches of a tree). We environmental leaders are tributaries to our larger environmental goals. We willingly pay tribute to our nature and culture, as we are committed and devoted to this true cause. 'Trib' is derived from the Latin '*tribuere*'—to pay and bestow. While these terms might appear contradictory, both actually imply giving.

Whether you bestow honor or money, and whether you do it voluntarily or under duress, reveal your leadership liberties. Give yourself a moment to reflect on the depth and breadth of the situation. Our environmental tribulations and ordeals can occasionally be portrayed as distress or suffering, resulting from oppression or persecution—very trying indeed! Paying tribute can be tantamount to paying homage to a ruler; we are peons, performing labor for the monarch. We regularly submit to such states out of fear of retribution—vengeance and intimidation may unfortunately be the motivating factor.

Brilliant, lustrous environmental leadership replaces the vile bile of dependency with intense, ingenuous initiatives—we switch from being submissive go-fers to being confident go-for-its. Like a lion in Zion, our 'tributes' are energized with attributes (knowledge & expertise), distributes (opportunity & diversity) and contributes (skills & resources).

Whether our department chiefs are Anglos or Africans, kings or queens, cowboys or Indians, the welfare of the organization must be given primary consideration. There's a huge difference between filling a vacant position and adding to the ability of the team. Ensuring the beneficial use of all team resources will raise spirits and reveal paths of opportunity, sending not-so-subtle smoke signals to regional partners.

And I keep on fighting for the things I want

Though I know that when you're dead you can't

But I'd rather be a free man in my grave

Than living as a puppet or a slave—

                          The Harder They Come, Jimmy Cliff

Be Topsy-Turvey—

The endless internet updates warn us of over-fishing, over-grazing, over-drilling… all of which can be quite overwhelming. Our greener side nervously responds as if we are playing checkers—their move, our move, their move. We environmental hamsters must eventually conclude (not concede) that the spinning wheel of environmental fear, followed by short-term damage control and repair work, builds environmental brawn, but not brains.

No matter how many times we fix the flat, we keep getting flat tires. We can't produce a puncture-proof environment, and labeling our habitat as fragile has been equally futile. If there is even to be a remote possibility of environmental liberation, we need to un- cage and unleash our intimate leadership capacity.

"Just tell me what to do".

Perhaps I could, but it wouldn't be fair—it wouldn't do you justice.

Devoted enviro leaders go the extra mile, or two, or ten. We give 80% or more effort, day after day after day. Take it from a lifelong professional amateur like me, who takes great pride in performing at a level higher than the majority. I know it's just a saying, but let's be real—nobody gives 100%, ever. We can all do better, and for some under-performers, much, much better! Sustainability is often second place and second rate—we have urgent needs for environmental progressions!

In the wastewater profession, we talk about 'floaters and sinkers' and 'dunkin' donuts', neither in an extremely appetizing way. But what I would emphasize is that wastewater is 90% water and 10% waste. We leaders need to scrutinize and analyze this raw 90% using our on-site insight. And when we tap into our abilities, we can create beneficial uses and a virtual groundswell of leadership attributes—values that will ultimately exceed our expectations. Waiting too long will cause us to be waterlogged and prone to suffering the curse of 'muddle management'. Scum, sludge or success—you choose!

Your period of reckoning has already begun. As environmental leaders, we need to be relentless in our pursuit of environmental game-changers. Anything less plays into the hands of the obstructionists. By the way, middle management certainly faces its fair share of agony—from above (upper mgt.), from below (staff demands) and sideways (peer pressure). Yet while the hodge- podge of issues that have been bestowed upon you are wriggling around, there is ample opportunity to put together a workable leadership game plan that includes prioritization, delegation, action plans, projects and constant communications. You'll end up with a product that synthesizes concepts, creativity and experience, but this product is just the genesis for a new beginning.

Trouble ahead, trouble behind
And you know that notion just crossed my mind…

Casey Jones, by The Grateful Dead

Functionality—

A Swiss Army Knife can serve a slew of purposes, but ultimately does very few things well. For starters, people afraid of breaking their fingernails can't even open the darned blade! The micro- scissors get warped after trying to cut anything hard. The screwdriver attachment folds in and bruises the knuckles. The tweezers are like miniature chopsticks, and the saw can cut through twigs that you can easily snap by-hand. Try opening a can with your knife, and you'd better keep a first-aid kit nearby! But it's red and glossy (the knife, not your fingers)! Airport security confiscates hundreds each day—I wonder where they all end up?

Our society is equipped with a plethora of multi-gizmos touting utilitarian possibilities. Some are gadgets (the pocket fisherman, the singing umbrella) and others are instruments (the shoehorn, the magnifying glass).

Instruments can be tools, and instruments can be pawns. Environmental leadership ensures that natural instruments function as intended, and that humans are 'instrumental' in maintaining or enhancing the integrity of our environment.

In the wrong hands or minds, functionality can easily become convoluted. In Southwest Colorado, I inherited an on-site wastewater program that allowed for the installation of open bodies of raw sewage ponds in people's backyards. The thought process went like this:

a) There are no municipal sewer lines, thus a need for septic tanks.

b) There are not a lot of people (yet), so downwind odor is not a factor.

c) The existing soils are tight, compacted clays that refuse to accept wastewater.

d) We have plenty of sun to evaporate wastewater before the ponds overflow.

e) An excavation 35-ft. across and 5-ft. deep in your backyard will cost less than $5K, while an engineer-designed sub-surface system would cost greater than $16K. (That's enough savings for a down- payment on the pickup truck!).

So as long as you can meet the setback of 100 feet from your drinking water well (and from your neighbor's well), let's install sewage lagoons! I guess I was a sort of visionary—I envisioned stinky, smelly poop ponds, mosquito havens for West Nile Virus, horses wading chest-high in refreshing wastewater and a curious kid named Opie, armed with a fishin' pole, hoping to hook a big brown. I could also imagine rednecks installing overflow pipes that drain downstream and polluters dumping who-knows-what in these ponds. I believed that our homes and property have more value when we respect the functionality of our natural environment.

It took me over a year, but I was finally able to convince our Board of Health to prohibit the installation on new lagoons. I coined the new tri-county program Developing Remedial Sewage Utilization Systems (DrSus). Like most political situations, the existing lagoons were 'grand-fathered in' and allowed to remain. The Grinch must live somewhere!

This enhanced natural value was also transferred to resale value, as homes with more expensive, environmentally-sound, sub-surface waste-water sold at higher prices—the owners were able to not only recoup the expense of the engineered wastewater system, but in- fact double their money. Houses with existing lagoons were reduced in value by $12K or more, knowing that future remediation would be necessary. It's amazing how fast you can get a realtor's attention, when you talk about resource conservation in terms of commission.

To Drench or to Quench—that is the question!

It's not really one or the other, unless you're not trying hard enough! Concentrated efforts will naturally have to adapt and take on new environmental challenges, but also new-found opportunities. Consider the mix & match of hydroelectric stations, power generation, in-stream flows and watershed health—can a region's operations effectively react to periods of drought, flooding, wildfire or dramatic fluxes in energy supply and demand? Are recent fish kills two weeks old by the time the event is reported in the local newspaper? Do you really need more work? No, but the effort is not an illusion. You are creating opportunities, excavating potential and exploring new territory. Do you know why dogs can't dance?

Canines mark their turf, but then go around the block to check things out first-hand or paw. Organic or not, territories need to be shared—we don't need to be omnipotent, even if we are top dog. We seek potable solutions that might mean ensuring your strengths are not overbearing, overwhelming or potentially virulent. (Mild, medium, hot, extra hot; not killer!). If your environmental leaders are tilting at windmills, is anybody taking notice?

(Answer: They have 2 left feet!).

*"When life itself seems lunatic, who knows where madness lies?
Perhaps to be too practical is madness. To surrender dreams — this
may be madness. Too much sanity may be madness — and maddest
of all: to see life as it is, and not as it should be!"*
    — Miguel de Cervantes Saavedra, Don Quixote

Open Wide and Say "ugghh!"--

I get tired of brushing my teeth. Some days I wake up and feel as if I was just there—in front of the mirror, gazing at a life-size sticky note. I perform minimal reflection, as we all look like crap in the morning. Dental health will slowly progress towards mental health and a day planner chock full of stuff to knock out. Whether our 'to- do' list is hearty and vivacious or just merely cosmetic is largely up to us.

Sometimes we just have not worked up an appetite for environmental sushi. Our full plate of side dishes detracts us from the main course of green leadership. When we become detached (and we surely will), we'll end up in dire need of some quick-yet- effective repairs that I refer to as 'deduct tape'. We've already introduced organizational enhancements that include 'erosion control', 'stressor response', 'fate and transport', 'professional precipitation' and 'waste characterization'. Our green deductions are yet another work of art (with sound science, of course).

If it's not the car battery or the starter or the distributor, it's probably the alternator that's on the fritz. Why induce further un- pleasantry or hardship on yourself if you can deduce bile formation several yards away? How does deduction work? Ironically, deduction is pragmatically performed best by conducting augmentation exercises:

Jim, a very good friend of mine, once took me over to Montreal to experience Oktoberfest. We ended up getting pretty looped, and proceeded to crawl over to a Chinese restaurant. Have you ever tried speaking French to an Asian person in lederhosen when inebriated? It's akin to conversing in enviro lingo with a banker at a chamber function—it can be accomplished, if you're up for the challenge!

Deduce is derived from the Latin 'ducere', meaning 'to lead'. This is no coincidence! While we normally think of deductions as lessening or removals of portions (such as payroll deductions), environmental leaders effectively use deduction to lead our minds from lesser to greater certainty, from one idea to the next, from drop to rivulet to watershed moment. My personal roll of deduct tape provides me with stick-to-it-ive-ness and community cohesion—cinching slipknots, ensuring associated supply lines and promoting sustainable, utilitarian approaches.

I believe that if you sample the offerings, your deductions will be solidly based on boldness and first-hand experiences. No more blisters of ignorance, fewer major perturbations and you'll be way far away from wits end. Any cowardice will have vanished, as you and I get down and dirty and engage in mutual enviro discussion.

Environmental leaders need to smile brightly and appear positive—yet when we really, truly shine is when we begin to focus our distracted eyes, close our perpetual mouths and listen intently to a voice or two or two hundred. I think that voices whisper insipid messages—including messages of despair, disenfranchisement, discontent and disbelief. Just as vital are personal, unique discussions about programmatic enhancements, possibilities, and juicy, creative opportunities.

That 'fluid approach' that I mentioned way-back when? It may very well be the panacea that many enviro leaders have been eternally searching for. There's no such thing as automatic transmission—we need to manually engage, then shift our gears of motion and emotion, fueling and refueling along the way.

Flexing your Environmental Bowels:

I have a keen nose for malodorous Environmental Leadership. I came to work at the Maui District Environmental office this morning at 7:35

a.m. as usual—ten minutes prior to starting time, so I can say Aloha to folks when they arrive, and pore over the surf report in the local paper. The boss came in right after me, with two buckets of freshly cut bananas. She proceeded to place bunches of 8-10 bananas on the desks of the person in front of me, the person to the right of me, and the office to the left of me. Me?? What the f… No bananas for this monkey! Big shit, I thought. It's only bunches of bananas.

But then my primal ape urge set in—me want banana! I was being unfairly treated, abused, scorned and starved to death. An hour goes by, and I watch the other cave dwellers gumming the delectable treats. I start to salivate, and when the opportunity arises, I pilfer a banana and stash it in my lunch bag. Now it's time to gather my workload of inspections and hit the road, leaving the banana ordeal behind me (so I thought).

But a few miles down the road, today's saga begins to creep back into my mind. I tell myself that I'm in charge of my own feelings, I have a great self-concept, and I'm not going to feel insecure over a measly, banal banana. Yet it starts to grate inside of me. I'll get even, I say to myself. I'll squeeze my first hour inspection into a half-hour, and then take an extended coffee break. I start to seek revenge.

Feeling exasperated and aloof, I gulp down my lunch, sip my coffee without burning my tongue and stare at the banana. It too would leave a bitter taste in my mouth. I give it to a homeless guy. Pao— done— complete—finished—but tough to forget.

Every time I plant a tree,
he say 'kill it before it grow…'
----B.Marley, I Shot the Sheriff

Conservation Conundrums:

No matter if I'm inspecting Chinese, Mexican, Italian or American eateries, I continually find two major causes of foodborne illness:

#1. <u>Inadequate Hot-Holding</u> (soups, stews, beans, casseroles,) Contrary to your wariness, employees feel more secure when their feet are held closer to the fire—not torched nor inflamed, mind you, but ample, sufficient, constant thermal messaging. The warmth conveys ongoing continuing concern, mentoring, nurturing, monitoring and caring. It maintains the integrity of the human resource (just don't refer to your staff as your pot of refried beings!). On the flip side, a hodgepodge of sporadic, tardy, lukewarm and erratic adjustments provides ample opportunities for an insurgency of competing organisms. Things start to get out of control. You get the point.

#2. <u>Lack of Rapid Cooling</u> (turkey, roasts, chilis, etc.). Responding to heated discussions, environmental leaders fully understand the need to cool things down within several hours—not allowing problems to simmer or smolder overnight at room temperatures, and not incubating individual temperaments. Cooler heads prevail, while tepid or timid responses are awakened to a danger zone of bile-ish insurgents and gaseous equations.

<u>Conservation defined</u>:

A) Taking conservation literally: Conserving actions, deeds, risks; preserving the organism, such as nourishing a tree in times of drought.

B) Using our brains, to protect the earth. How simple can one get? (Environ-Mental).

How can we maximize environmental rewards if we under-utilize our resources? Those leaders and leadership books that pontificate to keep it simple, concentrate on basics, don't launch out, protect your base, do this, this and this… and then add some of this… and Voila! You too are now a leader! Yeah, a spunk-less, naïve, disoriented, virgin leader, serving stale chips and watered-down salsa.

Flailing environmental leadership performance is a testament to stifling, soulless, and segregated resource management. Environmental staff, for example, is leery of stepping on toes, wary of competing interests and frequently unprepared to make cogent decisions. With bile build-up on the soles of their walking shoes, they tiptoe around minefields of mismanagement and unexploded leadership ordnances. Instead of detonating green blasts of creativity and ingenuity, we are crippled by a debilitating leadership deficit. We possess a lot of emptiness, and it somehow obscures our acumen.

Leaders all too frequently become enamored with statistics, budgets and forecasts, becoming so engrossed in quantitative predications and assertions that they deprive themselves of quality time with people. We had a Consumer Protection manager implode in front of us, when his planned PowerPoint went haywire. He just couldn't adapt to the situation at-hand and appeared to be having a mental breakdown! We incorporate uncertainty into our computer models, taking into account variability and influences, basing decisions on what appears economically prudent and programmatically viable.

But we are not models! Attempts to calibrate, simulate or extrapolate human dimensions are a lost cause. It's more strenuous of a challenge for an environmental leader to understand and account for human uncertainty, program probabilities, personal possibilities and worst-case team-based scenarios. Strenuous, but gratifying!

Are you currently performing self-reflection or self-microscopy? What takes precedence---reports, analysis, data, permits, protocols, strategies, discussions? I would vote for the latter, making sure that program continuity evolve around open team dialogue. Your leadership will determine how actual on-the-ground environmental efforts are advanced or retarded. Nobody likes to be dissected. We unanimously vote to be 'membered' and remembered, not dismembered.

I used to be uncertain, but now I'm not so sure…--
Anonymous

Urine Nation--

It's usually not a good sign to read about pain, frequency and liquid evacuation in one sentence. Certainty and predictability can have similar connotations, like Big Ben chiming and Old Faithful surging. Someone once said that:

'The best way to predict the future, …is to create it!'

So, let's start with creation. Throughout the Hawaiian island chain, mating and reproduction of the box jellyfish occurs under certain lunar and tidal conditions. Surfers can predict with a high level of confidence that nine days after the full moon, peanut butter will find its partner. The Waikiki Aquarium even shares a box jellyfish calendar—but you can bet bottom dollar that it's not placed in the Chamber of Commerce's promotional gift basket.

Supervisory tentacles can also be stinging—but we leaders won't know until we ford out and experience 'see-life' with others. Most of us can handle pain and anguish on a monthly basis, especially when we develop that keenness, that shrewdness, that programmatic sagacity that transfers into greener knowledge and community pride.

When bathers are stung by the box jellies, lifeguards recommend putting meat tenderizer on the sting to deactivate the toxin. But if you are courageous enough to ask the locals if they have any meat tenderizer in their board-shorts, expect a grinning response. Once they stop laughing, they'll tell you:

'Nah, bruddah, just pee on it'. --

I can vouch for its effectiveness. Environmental Leadership utilizes the resources that are available, affordable and acceptable. How you go about applying your first and second and third and fourth leadership aid will significantly affect your program wellness. From a self-preservation standpoint, veer about twenty degrees from direct confrontation when seeking relief. Unzip your collection of EL collateral and expose yourself to all possibilities— but surely don't turn your back on the mainstream and keep a vigil eye on your ever-moving target.

Our battles intensify when the very agencies that we publicly hold accountable (state & county government, USFS, BLM, EPA, etc.) chronically underperform. We expect a heavyweight performance but instead are presented with lightweight tap-dancing. Overestimation, under-appreciation, misdiagnosis, lack of ambitious goals, soft-serve presentations and nauseating responses all funnel down to weak and sporadic leadership. It ultimately results in profound contempt for our public process and can either produce complacency or fervent opposition. We can surrender or fight harder. Bring in the MICE—model, inspire, challenge, enable. Additionally, there's an urgent need to PEEE:

Presence / Emergence / Engagement / Exposure--

Presence: By design, creation and existence; nourish our communities by serving as an enviro-protection incubator; spawning new schemes and assimilating flexible, fluid forms of our ideas into other receptive communities. Please come in and sit down. Let your thoughts precipitate! When I mentioned that absence of evidence does not equate to evidence of absence, our conclusion should be that we need more evidence—making things more evident takes place by turning absence into presence. That can be quite an epiphany for some folks.

Emergence: defined as a 2-edged sword:

1. The process of coming into being, becoming important or prominent. Ex: emerging opportunities / positive.

2. The process of coming into view or becoming divulged and disclosed after being concealed. Ex: emerging threats / negative.

Environmental leaders can make beneficial use of both edges. For example, clearly affirming the following:

We are Citizens for a Holistic Environment;

We are here to protect our air, land, water & wildlife;

We will scrutinize, monitor, analyze, verify, question, sample, demand, inquire, document, unveil and reveal any elements that pose a threat to our environmental health;

We are not going away; we will persist in pestering and perturbing your anti-environmental activities, and you may have little choice but to recognize us and reckon with us. Only then can we work towards agreeable solutions. (You must decide where and when to emerge as a leader; I wouldn't wait too long).

Engagement:

You can't engage on the internet, even if you're surfing Singlefarmer. com or some dreamsicle version of reality. Engagement requires bodies and minds in the same room, muscle and blood at the same table. It starts with presence and progresses towards mutual relationships. It can't be accomplished at quarterly public meetings, though many enviro leaders opt for just that. Engagement occurs all the time, except when you are presently absent and have the personality of a test-tube. But when your brain is firing on all cylinders and your heart senses that community issues are community-owned, you should be out there listening, interacting, pondering, learning, questioning, thinking and acting. But how do you leap out of your petri dish and become that cooperative, cohesive force? Come up with a plan and try it out, then work on making it better. There's no other way.

Exposure:

In the environmental arena, the only indecent exposure is underexposure. With the degree of dynamic impacts occurring from industrial emissions, resource extraction and catastrophic climate disturbance, there is no excuse for not divulging environmental impairments. Exposure is a double cheeseburger of both disclosure and awareness. Many an environmental organization sits on its laurels and awaits successful preliminary interventions prior to notifying the public—they call it assurance, while I call it despicable.

What we need to practice is a greater degree of our favorite kid's game, 'show and tell'. Dumb down the conservation science, integrate appropriate technologies with environmental education and take ultimate (or at least equal) responsibility for your actions or inactions. Sure, make full use of all media outlets, but don't expect an 'e-blast', webinar or Zoom session to be as effective as meeting over coffee, lunch, or at the local library (neutral locations surely increase comfort levels). You'll reach more people electronically, but you won't touch them in the same way (except for their 'delete' or 'mute' buttons). They won't sense your passion and concern, and you'll have become less-human in the process.

Definitely document and augment your public meetings with electronic broadcasts, making your message as accessible as possible. Take advantage of e-surveys, social media, program updates and organizational 'contact us' information. But do it as an environmental addendum, not in lieu of real-life interaction.

I personally know of an environmental 'leader' who resembles a Venus fly trap—at first, there are sweet secretions and rosy ideals that lure in those that are attracted to environmental justice and forest green promises in subtle and suggestive humane terms. There are daily doses of being Mr.& Mrs. Nice Guy, but the vice- grips are always in-hand. Please quickly share that the kids are fine, our pets are cute, the house remodel looks great, All right then, now stop dawdling, and get your butt back to work! You've been ambushed, cornered, captured—trapped like a rat.

Upon closer examination, there is no genie in the lamp, no matter how hard you wish there was. You've employed your time, resources and most-valuable desire to create enhanced ecosystems within this greenhouse, only to discover that the plant is carnivorous, confining its environmental staff in pods to be sacrificed or preyed upon. Such environmental virtue is dubious and personal integrity is continually questioned. What is utterly disgusting is the ability of such enviro directors to make a profit, usually at your expense. Yes, business as usual occurs within the environmental ranks.

Listen carefully and attentively, be respectful, ask questions, raise doubt and agree to disagree. It's easier to dole out sedatives to the stimulated than to produce stimulants for the sedentary. Both exacerbate environmental situations, one for better, one for worse. Show a genuine interest in individuals and their opinions, and always provide the opportunity to meet again—preferably before you forget what you were discussing.

> *The ocean is a desert with its life underground and a perfect*
> *disguise above; Under the cities lies a heart made of ground but the*
> *humans will give no love—*
> America

Strange Brews & Secret Sauces--

Is there anything sadder in life than watching a wild dog at the zoo, running back and forth within cramped confines and against rigid barricades? His lust for wandering has been denied. Her quest for a maiden voyage has been squelched.

I suppose it is due time to tell you some of my secrets.

I referred to my unique approach towards a combined environmental / conservation leadership training endeavor as my 'Special Sauce', relying on 2 main ingredients:

1. I committed to a <u>watershed-based approach</u> that makes environmental issues 'feel-able and relate-able'. I was trying to attract conservation fellows who have community-based connections to a specific and personal river, creek, watercourse or drainage basin. I wanted to enlist those who can help create the requisite 'liquid linkages' and conservation dialogue, mixing ingredients that create conducive, conservation conduits and palatable, palpable results.

2. I opted to combine sound, simplified and demonstrative watershed science with environmental education messages, attempting to exponentially improve community-based attempts and success rates. I concocted the aforementioned acronym WHITEWATER—We Help Integrate Technology & Education, and We All Take Equal Responsibility. Whatever is your environmental appetite, every food for thought needs sauce for love.

I worked doggedly to share my recipe, methodologies and innovations within the conservation community. I wanted folks to have a certain 'buy-in' to my approach, but as an environmentalist or pragmatic humanist, not an economist or traditionalist. I wanted to affirm our responsibility to lead a life of environmental ethics, using EL as an instrument to aspire to a greater, greener good.

But sometimes the echo is not what you expect to hear. You cringe and try to decipher the mumbled response. Then it dawns on you. It can't be true, but it is—your ideas are not as worthy as others, and regardless of all the hard work and anguish, despite all the opportunities and possibilities, you're being given the Dear John letter. Something to this effect:

Dear Wano:

Thank you for sharing your program concepts with our Evaluation Team. While we very much appreciated reading your (do you really have to read any further??) *proposal, we have received over 400 requests for funding, and unfortunately, your proposal was not chosen for consideration...* (This is where you hope there are a couple of cold brews in the fridge...).

We sincerely appreciate your thoughts and ideas, and while you are in a state of utter despair and depression, we will be sending you mega solicitations to remind you that you lost, and that maybe you are still interested in financially supporting our conventional, mainstream, unremarkable, humdrum undertakings of despondency and doldrums. Please keep in touch.

Sincerely,
St. Joseph and the rest of the Conservation Apostles

You think this made me go berserk? You're bloody well right! Despite the extreme disappointment, I had to find out what sort of scores this Evaluation Team gave me. Yet even before reading the evaluation scores, it hit me harder than a brick on a birdhouse. The Evaluation Team, being diverse of course, consisted of environmentalists and volunteers that knew little to nothing about environmental leadership themselves! (I would see this hypocrisy play out time and time again, like an Environmental Leadership version of Groundhog Day).

Does our age-old experience hold any water with newer generations? Or was I peddling some sort of, I don't know, environmental tincture or elixir--something that might become the effective bile expectorant but might be hard to organizationally swallow (and did not guarantee immediate results). Once again, grant reviewers preferred cuteness over cutting edge, opting for community cleanups and the annual painting of picnic tables, with pictures of pretty little girls in dungarees posted on the webpage.

Then it happened again. I was coming home from visiting my father in Ft. Meyers, Florida. I was never the mechanic that he was, but he gave me one of six ratchet sets that he had stashed away. Going through security, the alarm was triggered, and I had to open the ratchet case. The TSA gal who did the inquisition tells me that no metal items over 14" are allowed on the plane. No sense arguing, but the largest ratchet was 15"—couldn't she give me an inch? She told me it measured 16" and took the liberty to show me on her trusty tape measure. Nope, it measured 15" see, I tell her. No, it measures 16" she insists. I rub my eyes in disbelief—she started measuring at the 1" line. Nobody in her life ever taught her how to use a ruler!

"Start at zero, and have fun with your new ratchet set", I said, walking away with a major headache. It was time to take a guzzle of aspiration.

Moral: There's something to be said about environmental processes, focus groups and engaging folks of all shapes and sizes. We can't expect our common knowledge to be taken for granted— as it was their lack of knowledge that took the grant(ed) from me!

I'm certainly not qualified to provide a detailed, comprehensive ranking of environmental agencies and entities, nor would I ever attempt to do so. Yet at times it's hard to avoid the malodorous rank within our green ranks. There's absolutely no sustained benefit from continuing to fund and perform stagnant programs. I find it hard to comprehend how some organizations appear very content with their Bud-lite and corndog-style programming. Perhaps their impoundment is a self-fulfilled prophecy.

But just to show that I don't have a vengeance towards enviro organizations as an entirety, I'm very impressed with what I see and hear from the Environmental Defense Fund—their message is clear, their audience broad, and their objectives challenging. They face formidable foes within the ranks—municipalities, counties, states and the feds. Yet EDF has a strong belief in its abilities, almost as if it were the abominable snowman itself. The environmental playing field is littered with treachery, tomfoolery and fraudulent, unconscionable comrades. Being replete of environmental integrity surely helps them live up to their promises. As a ten-year old growing up on Long Island, New York, I recall EDF's initial battle against the use of DDT. Fifty years later, their critical environmental work continues, with wise and experienced environmental leadership.

I mean, come on, how much faith did I truly place in my personal Letters of Inquiry to Oprah? I thought that perhaps she could fund an Environmental Leadership training program that would be as cheap as sushi and more effective than her upcountry Maui organic farm. Oprah, in case you misplaced my proposal, just give me a shout-out and I'll send you another copy. It's not too late, not yet, not ever!

Defeating the Purpose—

Bluebird: "Why don't we try to fly upside down?"

Redbird: "Because that would defeat the purpose."

Bluebird: "Why don't we try to defeat the purpose?"

Redbird: "It's hard to defeat what we can't understand."

Bluebird: "Then maybe we can try harder to understand?"

Redbird: "What do you think we are, humans?"

Bluebird: "Do humans try harder to understand?"

Redbird: (hesitation…) …"Yes,…yes they do."

Bluebird: "For what purpose?"

(Followed by sighing of an exasperated bird…)

A defeatist attitude can come into play when teams are confounded over their mission, priorities and direction. We fly by night. We attempt to fly under the radar. We fly by the seat of our pants. I can hear Ho Chi Minh in the distant shadows whispering mis- directives and false alarms.

Environmental leaders must not be dismissive or suppressive and must work within a team framework to minimize chaos and subversive activities.

We in managerial and decision-making positions tend to think of the community-based process as a sort of prerequisite (rather than a lifetime commitment)—a step to inform folk, share ideas and then maybe work towards reaching some form of consensus. And I truly believe we chronically fall short in two areas:

#1: We expect too little from locals.

#2: We expect too little from ourselves.

To right this injustice, I believe that a strategy with great potential is to include decision-making individuals in Environmental Leadership Discovery. I call it Discovery because we humans naturally have trouble recognizing our need for EL training and exercising. I harp on recognition and respect of others, but it takes energetic, curious, risk-taking individuals to recognize that they too can gain greater discernment and greener appreciation.

I tend to envision a community college comparison as opposed to a 'uni-versity'. Creative approaches and opportunistic vantage points can resurrect teams from deliberation to liberation, with newer possibilities on the horizon. Instead of fleeing or being fleeced, teams are provided for, commended for and rewarded for their joint aspirations, ambition and enviro actions. We enhance our EL intentions along with our self-worth.

Cursers and Precursors--

A human is an animal with many desires, few needs, some ideas, rare solutions, long lives, curved tales, short sights and little feats. I spent ten seconds of my life facing a male silverback gorilla in the Congo. I froze for six seconds acknowledging a grizzly sow in the Montana wilderness. I stared into the eyes of a lone black wolf for a micro-second, and I spent twenty-six years suffocating under suppressive, submissive, frail and flailing leadership. It sure puts life as an entirety into a better perspective. I'm positive that some of these environmental leadership concepts and scenarios will ultimately prevent you from succumbing to cages and captivity.

We want our Environmental Leadership congregation to flourish. You can't preach to a choir until you have formed a choir. Then, we preach to the choir, because we need more preachers, and to have others assume their vacated choir seats. That's the transitional flow of environmental leadership. It's not just your time that you're wasting—others rely on you! And if what plagues us is mediocrity, we shouldn't be avoiding the plague, but taking it on as a challenge—becoming contagious, infectious, communicable and impactful!

As environmental ambassadors, we'd better be conservation practitioners, catch-and-release environmental educators, sustainable environmental scientists and compassionate citizens. Create that nexus between your personal life and professional ambitions. Demonstrate leadership via leadership. Writers write, runners run, teachers teach, killers kill, leaders lead. E-Leadership seeks unity. Our arduous tasks include:

*The assembly of mutual organisms and organizations.

*The clarification of concepts and misconceptions.

*The production of something substantial.

*The delivery of an improved product or creative process.

*The nurturing of people and places.

Our laborious efforts can give birth to sustainable evolvement, tangible solutions, transformative actions, positive results and newborn possibility. Environmental progression is unquestionably a critical element of environmental leadership. Don't you think it's finally your turn and your time?

Address and size up your challenges, and don't dismiss potential opportunities too quickly—

'This didn't work, so we tried that, and it didn't work either, so we tried this…'

It's through our creative freedoms, huddling and hurdling that we can expect significant environmental progressions, petite a petite. Sometimes you'll opt for the juggler (a rotating assortment of healthy inhabitants with growing abilities), and other times go straight to the jugular (prioritizing stricter wastewater effluent requirements). With the outreach of an octopus, go explore your outer E.L. limits.

This is what my career ladder looks like:

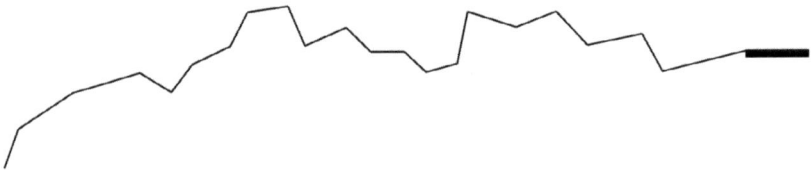

Birth   **Sayonara**

It looks like a set of Leggos. It's not pretty, but if nothing else, it's a solid foundation based on my many experiences—some would say too many. I'm still learning, but I'm also sharing, contributing and trying to develop substantive EL ideas, concepts and approaches together.

There's no dearth of environmental leadership possibilities, only a paucity of creativity and energy. You're low on energy? Call in the reinforcements! When was the last time that you provided staff with a challenge?

"While I'm on my one-week vacation, I want you gals / guys to come up with a way to involve our business community in protecting our watershed—sort of a 'Chamber for the Environment'. I look forward to seeing what you come up with. While I'm gone, you're in charge!"

Sure, when the cat's away, the mice will play—but perhaps their creative play-work will induce unimagined possibilities. And if not, then what's next? I'd give it another shot—what's there to lose? But I bet you'll find some resemblance of progress. You'll never know what took place on

Monday or Tuesday, but Friday seemed to produce something (which is better than nothing!).

It's not a finger in the dike---it's a dike-full of fingers!!
Hollandaise Sauce

Annoy-elation—Where Credit is Due--

Way back in time, before humans started adding question-mark voice inflections to non-questions, there was this City Market grocery cashier who really, really enjoyed verbalizing with customers. He was far from loud or obnoxious, more calming-yet- loquacious. I'll refer to him as Gus Sackett.

'How's it going? Nice fresh apples 'ya picked out…, orange juice for the young-uns…, good-lookin' bacon…—hope 'ya have enough eggs…. Those coffee beans sure smell good…, here's some er, personal products, and by golly you saved yourself $3.22 today! Insert your card whenever you're ready…'

Some customers would opt to avoid Gus altogether, willing to wait in a longer, more-predictable line. Personally, I relished the moment to exchange niceties.

All of us environmental leaders have a personality or two, and personalities come into play, even when it's not all fun and games. The choice is yours—you can punt, pass, hand the football off, or call your own number. Opt for paper, plastic or bring your own bag. Gee whiz, you've had adequate time to process your EL thoughts, so some of this should register with you. Or have you already checked out?

'All your life you had to stand in line, still you're standing on your feet. All your choices made you change your mind, now your calendar's complete…..

Don't wait for answers, just take your chances, don't ask me why…'
----Billy Joel

Bed, Bath and Beyond--

A London hospital commenced operations in the year 1247 under the name 'St. Mary of Bethlehem' and served its constituents well for over 150 years. Change was on the way, however, and royalty commandeered the hospital's use as an insane asylum. The name slurred from Bethlehem to Bethlem, to eventually be known as 'Bedlam'. Into the future, other madhouses came to be called bedlam—places full of confused people. Bedlam even became a Boris Karloff horror film.

We often joke about the inmates running the prison or surrendering power over to those being led. The impression is that sharing decision-making ability would 'lead' to chaos and overthrow, and that once the floodgates were opened, there's no turning back. Run for the hills!

Somehow, we E-leaders need to adjust the flow. There is an environmental adage that 'the solution to pollution is dilution'— reduce the nastiness into tolerable levels of public consumption, and everyone will be happy. Nowadays, we've finally been able to admit that watered down policies and extraneous directives are really just a pu-pu platter of delusions. Instead of severely editing our enthusiasm and energy, or even typecasting our philosophy and psychology, we need to refute dour predictions and formulate fresh solutions.

Fast forward to today, where the Bethlam Royal Hospital serves as a psychiatric research facility--the inmates have become teammates.

"The housing situation is intolerable— it's enough to give one an inferiority duplex.."---
Jimmy Durante

CHAPTER VI.
BUILDING SMART, GREEN MUSCLE

He who felt it, dealt it! (Duty-bombs)--

If only that were true! Decision-makers rarely feel the full brunt of their decisions. They are all-too-often buffered by compromised reports, skewed results, redacted comments and full-fledged excuses. They make a critical decision, take two steps to the side, and await the winds of change. We, the working stiffs, are confronted with the verdict. We collect mental notes but take minuscule action. Then, when the air clears, it's time to emit another stink-bomb of an idea. And the first one is not usually the worst one!

We are taught to serve our superiors and to think with our head, not our hearts. And yet the gut-wrenching feelings we reap lead us towards escapades including time alone, Netflix galore, wild parties, calling in sick, going fishing, or worst of all, returning to that dreaded office, knowing the sort of edicts that we are in-store for.

How do we tame this vicious cycle of offensive ineptitude, environmental irresponsibility and the resulting heartburn from ingesting cruddy directives? Candidly, we do it by not succumbing or putting up with it. Sure, let current events scorch your innards for a couple of days or a week while you gain composure. But don't fool yourself—you are destined for something much better, if you are willing to work much harder.

Some will say that life is a series of compromises, and that the path we choose (as Environmental Leaders) requires compromise in order to progressively advance causes. Organizations and leaders that draw a line in the sand are compromising (whether they realize it or not), some more than others.

A narrow focus and adamant attitudes could very well be holding an entire community hostage. Peering out of our home-made bomb shelters, we cringe while watching raptors zooming towards 'state of the art' wind turbines. We grimace over the blockade of elk migration routes by 'upgraded' power transmission lines. True environmental leaders have both an ability and an obligation to participate in discussions and activities within their (our) respective communities—and to adapt and deal with ever-changing conditions and consequences. We bear witness, but we must continuously testify. Yet as in Mad Max's Bartertown, you bust a deal, face the wheel.

I just dropped in, to see what condition my condition was in—

Kenny Rogers & the First Edition

What's on your green palate?—

If you're not repulsed by the encompassing fear, loathing and lethargy, a non-ambitious make-believe leader might actually relish at the thought of fewer interactions and more computer time. What is appetizing to such leaders is a smorgasbord of status quo.

We all too often accept the premise that iceberg lettuce is the starting point for our community palates. We chew on programs chock-full of inertia and seem very content in effortlessly doing so. No citizen complaints for a week, so we must be doing a bang-up job. I think I'll splurge for croutons today. No wonder why our enviro programs come across as bland, mundane, unsubstantial and malnourished.

Oil and vinegar will ultimately mix. You just have to work at it and shake things up! Instigation is an artful science that nudges apathy and avoidance with subtle-yet-sensitive tendencies and tenderizers, resulting in nothing or something, depending on the particular fossil family you are spoon-feeding.

The French word 'formation' means training. We need to mold, form, build, invent and serve knowledge to the less informed and misinformed (and that includes ourselves). Environmental leaders will be confronting a substantial challenge from the clan of conformity. Bring out the ranch dressing, darlin'.

What's your green leadership druther-- Spinach? Kale? Seaweed? Collards? Mustard greens? Dark leafy green, that's what we need— and you get to choose! We have options, we have choices! Select a leadership action with nutrition, antioxidants and flavor. Get repulsed by that pale, flimsy, impotent, mundane, paltry, pathetic leadership style, come up with something homegrown and hearty, and savor the moment—your moment, endive right in!

> *When we bite off more than we can chew, then we need more teeth!!--*
> Downtrodden

Water & Mystery Meet--

Oh, if I could only be the Spam of the environmental community! I could win over the hearts and minds of every type of Hawaiian, creating an intense hunger for environmental programming, aka 'Leafy Greens' or 'Lettuce Save the Planet'.

For those of you who could benefit from a quick history lesson, the U.S. military brought to Hawaii ship-loads of k-rations of Spam during WWII. And while the troops yearned for fresh fish and bananas, the locals quickly developed a taste for the salty, fatty, meat-like product. It offered a perfect bartering exchange for cigarettes and booze, as the cans were non-perishable and a dime a dozen. Today, the Spam addiction has branched out to smoke- flavored, ranch-style, pizza toppings, and the good 'ole fashion variety. It's very cheap, readily available, and stockpiled by the case in every single Hawaiian home throughout the islands. Even for those that don't eat it, it's good for dog food and for caching for hurricane and tsunami season. There is no group or organization that can be effectively compared to glorious, victorious Spam, but there's a natural, organic, holistic comparison—water.

Water is what people battle over worldwide, whether it is during a California drought or a Colorado canyon diversion project. And the term 'water community' normally refers to those agricultural users, irrigators, conservation districts and water rights protectors—that's splitting the molecule and promoting provocation.

When the U.S. sponsored the military overthrow of the Kingdom of Hawaii, it did so while cognizant that the abundance of clean water would produce bumper crops of sugar cane and pineapples. Fast-forward to current-day Hawaii, where Hawaiians are fighting to regain their traditional water supplies, in an effort to return to more sustainable agricultural fields of taro, fishponds and splendiferous tropical fruit trees. By the time this book is published, we can assuredly add hemp and marijuana (recreational as well as medicinal) to the list. Hawaiians use the term 'ahapuaa' to define a sustained, low-impact, healthy environment where nature and culture thrive in harmony. Water nourishes the soul.

While I was already developing my Environmental Leadership concepts based on Rocky Mountain watersheds and professional experiences in Equatorial and Sub-Saharan Africa, I soon realized that water was soft and hard, acidic and alkaline, hot and cold, simple and complex—but no matter what the dramatic differences were, the water component was easily identifiable—even more than Spam!

> You see I've been through the desert on a horse with no name
> It felt good to be out of the rain
> In the desert you can remember your name
> 'Cause there ain't no one for to give you no pain—
> America

A Mouse's Tale—

I was performing a highly scientific procedure of inspecting the internal hot-holding temperature of a rubbery wiener at a local convenience store. After wiping my bayonet thermometer with an alcohol swab, I noticed the black rice pellets around the trash bin. Peering inside the cabinet, I could tell that it was the making of a cozy mouse condo unit. I sorted through the adjacent condiment drawer looking for gnaw marks or contaminated single-serve packets. The ketchup looked fine, and so did the mayonnaise as well as the mustard. But the relish packets were completely devoured by the varmints, as if they were pouches of intravenous fluids performing rodent rehydration therapy.

I doubt if mice can read or distinguish between the different-colored packets. But their sniffers must be so intense that they can determine what's inside each one, opting for the relish whenever available. I wonder what is their second-favorite choice, maybe 3 Mouseketeers bars?

We humans have our own unique preferences, tastes and lifestyles, and Environmental Leaders should be able to relate to our animal instincts. Frankly speaking, we muster up what energy we have, to perform in a professional and collaborative fashion, day-in and day- out. We seem to always be playing ketch-up, as the incessant phone calls and emails distract from our priority tasks all too frequently. We relish the thought of having some free time to evaluate our programs and to plan for enhanced environmental efforts and strategies. And alas, all of this trouble, turbulence and turmoil lead us crawling into the front doors of the Mayo Clinic.

Underdogs—that's what we are--

Do we have any input or leverage?? Have we been making real-life strides, or have we been assigned to designated treadmills? Did we wake up one morning and realize that we will always be working for Cleopatra or King Tut?

Get used to it. We will always be underdogs. Deemed as rascals, scallywags or worse, we are thought of as subversives—too smart for our own pants. Superiors keep an eyeful watch on us, or rely on the coconut wireless of rumors, innuendos and fictitious, disparaging remarks. The Authoritative have a decent hunch that lava flow can alter direction on a whim, so they clamor upwards and observe human metabolism from higher ground. Yet while some big shots personally tout temporary impunity, those of us with environmental leadership intuition can, little by little, start to infect others. We are weak and obscure viruses, but we spring up here and there, and if we really persist, we start to develop resistance to the sterility of the top-down directives and the incoherent mutterings of power-players and their sidekicks. We become Morpheus—the one that shapes and forms our dreams and ambitions.

Speaking of turbo-dogs, environmental leaders do not need Lassie to come running over and tugging your pant-leg, letting you know that little Tommy has fallen into the well. It's obvious that you need to take action, and it's up to you to establish what steps to take. I've mentioned WHITEWATER, MICE, IPA, PEE and others-- I'm willing to toss out as many ideas as necessary, and then some— how about you?

I have hopefully shed some smattering of light on Environmental Leadership—by now you should be fully aware that increased turbidity (within our watersheds and our working environment) causes the following:

*An increase in total dissolved solids—more clutter, more chaos, more ambiguity.

*Increased suspension—suspense, settling, then more suspense.

*Reduced photosynthesis—we can't see clearly now; the reign is far from gone.

*Erosion & abrasion—we are pulled, torn, unstable, detached.

In totality, turbid situations cause havoc and turmoil to our working environments. Those in need of clarity depend upon Environmental Leaders for guidance. Your team may not act or react like fish out of water, but they may lack a clear vision, appearing lost or disoriented. Environmental Leaders convert dependence into reliance, and then reliance into support, drip by drip.

'When you show the moon to a child, it sees only your finger'--
Zambian guide

Pu-Pu Platters—

Environmental leadership requires innovation, and it can be approached from many incongruous vantage points. I helped promote the idea of a natural gas-fired 'hot-box' that would prevent the coal-fired fireboxes in the locomotives of the Durango-Silverton Narrow Gauge Railroad from the perils of iron expansion and contraction (and resultant cracking). This cleaner fuel technology would eliminate the need to have three or more coal-fired locomotives idling 24/7 just upwind of little Jimmy's bedroom window and Aunt Martha's oxygen tank. With nighttime soot emissions equivalent to nineteenth century London, no wonder there are so many complaints of respiratory illness!

I set up air particulate monitoring stations in order to document potential air emission violations. The bleached white filters would turn jet black within 12 hours, but when weighed in accordance with EPA protocol, did not produce enough mass to exceed ambient air quality regulations. Thus, there was a need to work on our natural gas retrofit alternative from a 'good neighbor', non-regulatory perspective.

But alas, the Railroad considered the new technology as an abomination, a slap in the face of historical coal-burning, American freedom and personal liberties. Community health was not a priority, and my leadership effort was unsuccessful. So, you try again, with more adaptations, trying to get the attention of other fearless leaders, examining the 'maybe this' and 'perhaps that' approaches. Or you can take a nap on the tracks and hope something special rolls your way.

The island of Kauai has its problems with feral goats that were introduced long before statehood. The bearded ungulates cause hillside erosion and vegetative habitat destruction yet haven't found their way onto the State's top twenty list of 'things to do' for natural resource protection. Dealing with the bigger picture of rising sea levels, algae blooms and coral bleaching should indeed take precedence. Maybe we need to train the feral goats to munch on algae, and then maybe we can teach them to swim, and then to dive! But if they possess a dislike for algae or perhaps develop a craving for sushi, then we're really screwed!

You would think that the environmental leaders would appreciate such outlandish brainstorming of the 'maybes', as it helps build a case for the more-sane solutions. Nature compensates for weakness, danger or impairments to the environmental immune system by developing adaptations and varying forms of resilience. If our purpose as an environmental leader is to be an enabler (enabling communities to take progressive actions), then we need to encourage, engage, entice and envision. Green envy, for sure!

Fellow the Leader—

A simple twist on our childhood game reveals how to abstain and refrain from the despondency of adulticide. The last words that the bush pilot said after dropping us four paddlers at the headwaters of Desolation Canyon was:

"Don't encourage erosion down this hillside; spread out."

We were only four in number, and we were not going to create a stampede to water's edge. We were not trying to consciously ignore the pilot's instructions either. It simply didn't sink in. After taking ten strides, the pilot hollered back at us:

"What did I just tell you guys?"

Our brains were honed-in on the river below, and we were less-able to focus on the task at-hand. We must've looked like sheep to the pilot herder.

Focusing in on guidance and direction entails more than following instructions. If we, as Environmental Leaders, listen to the message, the next task is to acknowledge it. Any one of us could have said:

"You go there, and I'll go here.".

The acknowledgement is communicated, and usually deserves a concurred response—

"Okay, Roger, ten-four."

When the plane departed from New Orleans to Belize City, I would be leaving the U.S. for a two-year public health stint with Project Concern International. It would actually take two flights, as our pilot some-how forgot which country he was going to and landed the first time in Tegucigalpa, Honduras. He was close, at least, as Belize used to be part of British Honduras before independence. The British military still protects Belize from neighboring Guatemala and Honduras, flying Harrier jets overhead that occasionally break the sound barrier—that's probably suffi-cient to scare the crap out of a ragtag group of riflemen with few bullets and no instructions.

But just to impress upon any potential revolutionaries that they didn't stand a chance, the Brits would conduct military exercises with real tanks and paratroopers. Nobody parties harder than paratroopers—I guess they figure that if they survive the float through the air without being shot down, that they are invincible. To celebrate their continued existence and vitality, the paratroopers would literally take over the local bars, getting drunk, crazy, naked or all three.

While the Brits nursed their hangovers, somebody was always on-guard. The other regiment within the British Army was the Gurkha—these were ultra serious-minded troops from Nepal, who carried a trademark 18-inch curved knife on their hip. Despite their relatively short stature, nobody messed with the Gurkha.

During their military invasion of Nepal in 1814, the British East India Company suffered heavy casualties at the hand of the Gurkha. Instead of admitting defeat, the Company ingeniously signed a 'peace treaty', and then recruited the former enemy to work for them! What pitiful persuasion!

While it is rare indeed for environmental organizations to hire their corporate adversaries, we regularly observe federal and state government recruiting industry insiders (mining, oil & gas, nuclear, stock market) to fill leadership and fellowship voids. Evidently there will always be economic underpinnings:

* risks & rewards
* costs & benefits
* employment & deployment
* affordability & acceptability
* assistance & resistance
* return on investment
* equity & equality

These are just a few, of course, of the multitude of economic factors that can significantly influence our nature and our culture. Yet they remain as factors, not end products. Economic factors are a subset of sustainability that can drive or forestall program functions but are not in themselves intended outcomes. How a community defines sustainability and profitability is critical, colossal, and perhaps ultimate. Here's my kindergarten equation:

Sustainability (S) = Benefits (B) − Costs (C)

Subtracting Short-term & Long-term Costs from Short-term & Long-term benefits.

The end product = Either a drain or a gain.

I would hope that you would hold some EL discourse around this crucial topic, discussing cumulative value and worth!

The Bogeyman cometh—

So much for me poking fun at that misinformed pilot--I thought that surely, I had finally landed (the second time) in the capitol city. As it turns out, soon after Hurricane Hattie, the Belizean government decided to protect the public from future tropical storm disasters, and moved the capitol from Belize City to Belmopan, a good forty-six miles inland. This is where 'followship' comes into play. The capitol moved, but the people didn't. Why did Belizeans stay put? Better to take one's chances by the seaside than to become an interior landlubber. Who can get fresh conch soup if they don't live by the ocean? And where would we bathe and swim? Despite pleas by the government (if we build it, they will come), Belmopan remains as an aloof administrative center and a fabricated community.

As the primary American representing my organization, I was quite successful in building a collaborative leadership spirit with the Brits as well as the Belizeans. One of my first discoveries was that discrimination in Belize was similar to that in the U.S., with native Mayan communities being on the bottom of this Caribbean totem pole, topped by African-descent Garifuna, followed by mixed Creole populations, East Indians and even some American descendants of our Civil War. As an advisor to the Belize Ministry of Health, my role was more of an environmental health fellow, offering lateral support via public health education, safe drinking water, sanitation and Primary Health Care training.

Environmental Fellows are a crucial component of organizational approaches. In fact, I would say that Fellows are invaluable and indispensable. Fellows can commence by discussing random directions, deliberating 'what if' scenarios, creating group connectivity (and conviviality), refining concepts, experimenting, learning and eventually leading. Leadership is that thirsty end product, but also serves as the beginning for the next green venture.

Using the F-word—

I might be giving you the impression that many of our enviro leaders are a bunch of pussies, incessantly talking about pie-in-the- sky 'sustainability' yet practicing measly, piecemeal programming. I'm sorry that it took so long to reach such an obvious conclusion. Many leaders stress holistic approaches, yet rarely go to the nth degree to ensure inclusiveness and momentum. They compromise from a position of weakness, kowtowing to political pressures. They preach stewardship, yet bizarrely resort to dictatorship. They covet knowledge like a squid gripping an abalone. Their legacy will be that they 'gave it their best shot', while in reality, they were aiming way too low. You might be one of them.

There's hope—but only for those that desire it!

My first recollection of a history lesson was learning in first grade about Christopher Columbus and his ships--the Nina, the Pinta and the Santa Maria. I've got 3 leader ships of my own:

Fellowship: I sometimes wonder if the same folks that enjoy hearing themselves talk get similar satisfaction out of watching themselves listen. I kind of doubt it, but anything's possible in the sphere of environmental pedantic. We wholeheartedly agree that, to the greatest extent, learning should be experiential—yet those that have actually experienced the experience often dominate the conversation (with unwarranted claims of expertise). Sharing entails a generous dose of collaboration and is complemented by more than a polite response. Sharing is greater than giving, and often results in unexpected thoughts and freer emotions. Normal tendencies abruptly halt, while unknown and unforeseen information illuminates and materializes. Collegial efforts form tight bonds, and possibilities proliferate. That's the magic—the green, eclectic, effervescent magic that needs to burst into board rooms and work situations.

Followship: We look over our shoulder or through our rearview mirror to determine who is behind us and how close are they to us. Are they breathing down our necks, and if so, might it possibly feel good? Are you capable of such feeling, or are you an insensitive son-of-a-gun? If you are following a direction, are you thinking about what's up ahead (to the detriment of what you've just been through)? Will you be able to make informed decisions, or are you destined to play the role of mule team supporter? What else will ensue from your leadership lessons?

Failureship: We've talked sufficiently about failing, trying and learning, so there's no sense repeating it—just don't knuckle under to wax museum leadership, regardless of the price of admission.

Speaking of legacy, throughout all corners of Africa, no matter what city or village, hotel or hut that you are in, the names of a Holy Trinity ring clear and true:

Bob Marley, the father

Michael Jackson, the son

Muhammad Ali, the holy spirit

From every marketplace to every mosque, it's utterly amazing how these three supernatural humans have influenced an entire culture, an entire continent, an entire civilization. Environmental leaders such as John Muir, Rachel Carson and Aldo Leopold have also retained a sense of immortality. Whether we fill shoes or follow footsteps is a moot point—but I think we should definitely lay more green eggs, to enhance the flavor of our canned ham status quo. You might just have some fame to claim.

Elementary, my dear Watson—

In order to receive the benefits of in-state tuition at Colorado State University, I spent my first summer in Colorado working at the Easter Seals Handicamp in Idaho Springs, CO. Hands down, it was the biggest personal challenge and most fulfilling job that I ever had—working ten straight days with mentally disadvantaged youth, then the next ten days with developmentally disabled and physically handicapped campers, then back again. I would cry tears of joy on a daily basis and learned more over this summer than in any college course ever. Some of us overcome obstacles, while others deal with them as part of daily life.

During my learning curve, there was an evening comedy event that included corny jokes and costumes. There were a handful of physically and mentally-challenged campers interested in being the Master of Ceremonies, but I had a clear favorite—the kid who could speak clearly and remember his lines. So, when we put four names in the hat to pick the winner, I ensured that my choice was the one selected. In my mind, it was best for the group--the most-qualified, the funniest, and the person I could rely on to perform admirably.

I had no clue as to how much one of the campers wanted this ringleader task, until he pulled a knife on me. It wasn't a big knife, but I was sure glad that I saw it coming. Despite his mental deficiencies, he was certain that I rigged the vote, and now it was time for me to pay for my sin. I changed the subject, challenged him to a game of basketball, let him beat me, and the situation was over. But I learned something about discrimination and honesty; this haunted me for many years.

Based on my Peace Corps volunteerism in Niger, Zaire and Mali, Americans (especially white Americans) are treated special, sometimes like a superior race. I detested this, and went to great lengths to eat local food, drink local palm wine, learn local dialect and 'be one of them'. Yet I would never be one of them. One tribe would refer to us foreigners as 'Anasara', another as 'Tubabu', another as 'Mzungu', yet another as 'Mondele'—strangers, not in a bad sense, but as outside of the norm. In Belize, Central America, 95% of my Community Health Workers were Mayan men—not necessarily because they were interested in water & sanitation, but because they didn't feel comfortable with foreigners working with their women. In Hawaii, I got used to the term 'Haouli', as I would never be a native Hawaiian braddah. Even in New Mexico, Anglos ('Gringos') are different from Hispanics—that's just the way it is, very elementary. Sort of like playing 'cowboys and Indians' as a kid—it became a battlefield for preservation of status, utilizing cultural norms and community pride to fend off outside influence and foreign ideals.

In the job market, I'm sure that African and Hispanic Americans experience this rudimentary, embryonic discrimination on a regular basis. As Environmental Leaders, we would spend days going over diversity issues, not so much to benefit the privileged, but to allow the discriminated an opportunity to vent and to personally share. I learned quite a bit about sexual discrimination as well. What I was probably least prepared for was age discrimination—it still boggles me as to how all those years of wisdom and experience can be dismissed as 'old school' or 'behind the time'. If we are to tout leadership construction over environmental constriction, we will need both proven tools and yet-to-be-proven ideals, to mutually contrive or whip up our green layer cake.

Environmental leaders regularly deal with a senior populace in the field and at community meetings—seniors can also get the ear of County Commissioners and their relatives with greater ease than most of the younger green generation. There's a hefty price on aged cheese and vintage wine, but a clearance sale on getting old. We certainly don't help ourselves by going into early retirement— it's as if we surrender because it's no longer worth the effort. Some of us have little choice but to work until we 'get it right', and 'share the wealth'—it's this group that I admire most.

Lullaby or Alibi??

Jack & Jill went up the hill, to fetch a pail of water?

Does anyone really believe that's why they went up the hill? Oh, they were thirsty all right! And seeking uphill water was a splendid alibi. Excuses abound, and we often get lulled into a sort of funk or environmental stupor. I call it our mental blender.

By the year 2029, ten percent of our nation's energy can be derived via legume combustion. A U.S. company known as Aspara-gas has created a process by which mature asparagus plants are harvested, compressed and volatilized until they produce clean, sustainable energy. The crop can be grown in a variety of soils, is disease- resistant and drought-tolerant. This sounds great, except that no such thing exists. With all our news sound-bites and fun facts, some things get our undivided attention, and we have little time to seek out 'the rest of the story'. We hope it's true, as it would improve our lives. Buying an 'information smoothie' is very refreshing and easier to make than slaving in your own kitchen or workplace.

The vintage television show 'The Wide World of Sports' had a tagline about

"..the thrill of victory, and the agony of defeat".

Environmental leaders need to experience first-hand that agony, because ultimate success depends upon it. Nothing hard comes easy. Hiking a watershed boundary along the East Fork of the Dolores River, I must have picked over twenty ticks from my legs in the course of two hours. Someone had to be there to walk the lay of the land, look for invasive plants, monitor riparian areas and try to sneak a peek at some stealthy trout. You can't just refer to a ten-year old technical report about a demonstration plot and expect it to hold water. Vision statements should be referred to as toilet paper testaments, as they need to be used daily, flushed out and replaced when needed. Ply onward!

Consistency—

The Food & Drug Administration's Code of Federal Regulations (Sec.135.110) for Ice Cream and Frozen Custard standards state:

Except that when one or more bulky flavors are used, the weights of milkfat and total milk solids are not less than 10% and 20% respectively, of the remainder obtained by subtracting the weight of the bulky flavors from the weight of the finished food; but in no

case is the weight of milkfat or total milk solids less than 8% and 16% respectively, of the weight of the finished food. Except in the case of frozen custard, ice cream contains less than 1.4% egg yolk solids by weight of the food, exclusive of the weight of any bulky flavor ingredients used. Frozen custard shall contain 1.4% egg yolk solids by weight of the finished food: Provided, however, that when bulky flavors are added, the egg yolk solids content of frozen custard may be reduced in proportion to the amount by weight of the bulky flavors added, but in no case is the content of egg yolk solids in the finished food less than 1.12%.

Can the ice cream cops please explain to us what this means? Clear as butter pecan, I suspect we are not the intended audience of this techno-slurry. Let us sincerely hope that this is not a harbinger of our substantive efforts to provide green leadership. Discipline is one thing, but there's a reason why they sell 31 flavors. It's interesting that while vanilla and chocolate remain the top two sellers, mint chocolate chip and cookies & cream also make the top four. Unique, unconventionality can be quite tasty!

My buddy Joseph eventually opened his own corner coffee shop, insisting that after decades of 'hands-on experience', he knew what people wanted. Joseph undoubtedly knew the product well, and I give him lots of credit for that. His coffee would never be weak, fruity or bitter. The eight-ounce cup would be 8.1 ounces, not the cheating 7.9 ounces of others. The cream would be true cream, and you wouldn't have to ask for it.

But what Joseph undervalued and underappreciated, was the service—the total coffee experience, the essence! He catered to coffee—good—consume—go, then come back. He underestimated welcome—help—serve—look around—relax--appreciate. Joseph made decent money at his venture, claiming it was *consistency, not rocket science*. I woefully think that this may be how many other professions view their daily tasks. They downplay their abilities and disabilities and concentrate on a trance-like 'do a job, do it well, then do it again' mentality. When one tries to water- down water quality, they've reduced habitat to merely humdrum habits.

'All in all, you're just another brick in the wall..'
Pink Floyd

Unequivocally Speaking..-

During my last few days of trekking the beaches around Mombasa, Kenya, I teamed up with a British guy in order to do a half-day snorkeling trip in the emerald Indian Ocean. With my Peace Corps readjustment allowance almost depleted, I needed to bargain for a cheap-yet-fair price. I had been bartering for everything from pineapples to monkey meat over the past two years in the Congo and was pretty good at it. But sometimes in life, it's not the price you pay but the value of the experience.

The wooden dugout didn't leak but didn't have a motor either. The sailor raised his mast to reveal the name of the flour company that the sack-sail was sewn from. We weren't going very deep, but we didn't know the waters either. After fifteen minutes, the Kenyan 'captain' hands us a mask and snorkel (no fins) and instructs us to jump on in. That was the last I saw of my Brit buddy, as he was a better swimmer, and I, a real good floater. I was amazed at all the multi-colored fish and coral, but they were flying by way too fast— wait a minute, they weren't moving! I was caught in a cross- current! Luckily it didn't take me out to sea with the large-toothed predators, but it pushed me over two miles down the coast to some unworldly spot. When I crawled to shore, the local Kenyans looked at me like I came up from the ocean floor, with sea urchin welts to prove it. I got what I paid for.

When an enviro organization commences with a phrase such as 'I can assure you that…. without a doubt…', you can be assured that there is an unequivocal amount of short-sightedness and close- mindedness. It's not that the wildlife guardians or blue lake coalitions don't know what they are doing—au contraire, they may be very justified in their own minds in taking their stance. They boldly state their cause, pledge and promise, such as 'no new gas drilling...no fracking over my dead body...' or 'no chlorine in my water...it's poisoning us..'.

Such adamant statements are undeniably candid. Yet to be reassuring and also convincing, bold statements and affirmations must leave little doubt. Otherwise, organizational objectives appear wishy-washy or even contradictory. When opportunities for discussion and potential compromise surface, what may be compromised is organizational trust and credibility. The best way to predict the future is to create it, not steadfastly minimize your options or show your lockjaw-like inflexibility.

Many enviro groups see alternative routes as veering off course—do you recall that lady who drove her car mega-miles while wearing diapers, so she could cause physical harm to her ex-boyfriend as soon as possible? The problem (and there always is one with one- way streets) is that despite the internal declaration that it's going to be 'my way or the highway', you will not have a clue as to what others are doing and what direction they are taking. The mad dash and your tunnel vision will get you blind-sided or legally entangled. While your roadmap may take a straight arrow beeline toward your destination, the constant uphill battle will inevitably produce sluggish performance, curbed enthusiasm and potential collapse.

By the time your 'check engine' light comes on, your internal combustion may be extra-crispy. Long distance runners refer to it as 'hitting the wall' and 'bonking'—usually due to inadequate training or not sticking to a reasonable pace. Furthermore, sheer commitment and determination also needs fortified aid stations. A partly cloudy sky may not induce rain but may prevent heat-stroke and exhaustion. (Now that I think about it, a beeline is never a direct route, is it?).

As Yogi Berra was cited as saying,

'If you come to a fork in the road... take it!'.

Choose the scenic leadership route, the one with attractions, amusement parks, interesting (different) people and rest stops. And bring the kids (staff) along! When deciding between the death-grip- approach versus miles of smiles, drive your personal engine at your own risk and pleasure-level. In the same vein, one's individual antics provide a vantage point—whether that proves to be an advantage or disadvantage is unclear. Environmental shots fired may hit their target or ricochet in unpredictable directions. Uncertainty, while not reassuring, may be environmentally enlightening.

> *A cloud is a ghostly spirit—moaning, weeping and searching for a reason to exist.*
>
> *Fulani Nomad*

Environmental polygamy···

Environmental leaders covet their natural and human environment, and that's a good thing! Land and water are rhythm and blues— they play off each other, creating opportunities for harmony, zeal and devotion to join in. They survive through the tough times by practicing natural and cultural adaptations—breathing, weeping, searching and trying not to surrender to silence.

Caress the forest, cherish the canyon and adore the mountain while then emoting feelings of green exhilaration. Go ahead, reveal your leadership fervor and revel in your environmental desires. The wholehearted passion that we harbor for habitat, both natural and human, is our cornerstone. It conveys raw justice and transforms a kaleidoscope of vivid memories into mechanisms to perform our collective enviro responsibilities.

As mentioned, leadership, fellowship and 'followship' need to be in the same league and on the same team, working and playing together. Followers are often misunderstood, misrepresented and under-appreciated. Followers can be public servants—leaders must be. Consider the words from Trustee Leadership Development (1991):

> '*Leaders who see themselves as "trustees" have the ability to see that individual and community interests are interconnected and interdependent. They continually strive to integrate the personal with the professional, the*

individual with the institutional, private with public, and the subjective with the objective…'

When dealing with self, the organizations we are involved with, and the larger community in which we live,

'Trusteeship involves a significant shift in perspective from management (doing things right) to leadership (doing the right thing) …'

Environmental leadership can galvanize all of this—we can indeed convert those fragments of community conservation into a united and potent watershed confederacy. Environmental leaders will not or should not perform the essential environmental tasks of others— we are not competing for environmental superiority, and we can all have a good time! Leaders will do 'the other work', by fortifying environmental capabilities at the earthy, place-based watershed level—making dilemmas personal, touchable and tell-able.

I suppose that you will agree with about 60% of what I have to offer. The other 40% is the formidable foe, the potential for weighing in on concepts that are just that—more concepts, not even theories. The objective is to read, think, conceive, attempt and perform, enabling environmental leadership surges and breakthroughs.

To reach your final destination, prepare for the journey—not with fear or over-anxiety, but with energy, audacity and awareness. Your environmental leadership travels well in that handy companion pack they call the brain—or is it the heart? I always get the two mixed up.

Purple haze, all in my brain;
Lately things, they don't seem the same.
Actin' funny, but I don't know why, '
Scuse me, while I kiss the sky…--

Jimi Hendrix

Bar-ometer—

I haven't had a good, hard laugh in several weeks. Normally for me, a belly laugh of decent proportions occurs several times each day. Perhaps the humor drought was due to the kind of statements that have been puking out of my director's mouth as of late:

"You seem to have an environmental agenda on your mind." "We surely don't need another activist amongst our ranks."

"Why check with your cohorts—they'll only say good things about you."

"You'll have to put your personal bias aside; we work for the Commissioners."

Is there a sane asylum nearby that serves refreshing thoughts over a 'happy hour', and shouldn't we insist upon at least one goodwill hour during each workday?

Nothing is worse than inspecting a Confined Animal Feeding Operation (CAFO). I think pigs smell a tad better than cattle, but I'd have to ask the flies for their valued opinion. A lot of what transpires at environmental agencies each day is slightly better than pig sty slop. The big difference between routine enviro work and hogwash is how we stand or withstand the heat. Pigs do not sweat and must regulate their own body temperature with water or mud. There are times when I think we'd be better off not sweating (especially the small stuff) and go rolling around in our watersheds instead. We might find that when we playfully rumble around with others, when our blue trends are mixed with red values, the result can be green ventures.

Wide mouths can be filled and re-filled; Narrow minds, well, ... they can't.'---

Bishop, CA barber

Amputational Opportunities--

Based on a sizeable war chest of experiences, anecdotes and ordeals to recall and reflect upon, I would consider most environmental programs to be slightly underweight. There are those that are obviously obese and others nearing starvation, but all-in-all, most entities could use additional caloric intake—fuel to perform and produce energetic programs. Environmental leadership deals with how that precious fuel is allocated, and in what forms.

We have a real problem on our hands—the Total Maximum Daily Load quantitative process (that we recently discussed) does not willingly bring watershed communities to the table. We are in the habit of practicing community awareness as if we were posting a hologram menu on a store window—and not always the front window. You can stop and peek at our organizational innards as you are casually walking by, if you just happen to be in the neighborhood. The door is slightly cracked open, the lights are dim, and nobody is greeting you or offering you a seat. There is a huge difference between 'the public is welcome to attend' and 'we are anxious to speak with you about our shared river protection strategies'.

With a full carafe of environmental leadership brewing on the back-burner and wafting through our surroundings, we should be actively inviting constituents to our potluck, asking everybody to contribute to the cause, collaborating on the actual presentation, conducting interesting dinner conversations (food for thought), evaluating our finished product, sharing leftover comments and giving credit where credit is due. On the other hand, if you are accustomed to serving micro-waved pre-packaged empanada-like offerings, you will scoff at this slow-food approach as being time- consuming, unwieldy and non-scientific. No wonder why you might be a lousy leader! Stew on that!

A stream pollution diet must cut back on its 'fats, sugars and empty calories'—reducing stormwater runoff, decreasing agricultural fertilizers, weighing the performance of wastewater treatment plants and measuring the waste instead of the waist. But it does not and cannot force feed or prohibit intake.

When given the chance to function, natural phenomena can accomplish miracles. But it takes time, alignment and conditions of environmental synchronicity. Our stream ecosystem makes best use of its ambient environment to develop symbiotic synergisms with its fish, native vegetation, macro-invertebrates, soils, temperature, oxygen and nutrients--it works towards stability and sustainability. Nature seeks pulses and surges, not arrhythmias nor surgeries. How environmental leaders allocate resources and exercise discretion will reduce organizational impairment, and set the requisite green tone for its potency, capacity and willingness to take on environmental challenges. Whether it is a recipe or a strategy, your modus operandi is an environmental leadership approach—a sincere, heroic attempt, not a hasty retreat, bailout or bile-out.

"Sho, I wanna vote . . . where do ye vote? . . . 'n' whut fer?"

'What, me worry??'—

Alfred E. Newman

Differential Equations:

Stereotypes—our world is chock full of them, even though their sheer existence is based on our vaporous and vacuous mental caverns. What we perceive during our leadership spelunking expeditions can materialize as fast as they can dissipate. Ralph Kramden is our stereotypical, mopey bus driver. Ed Norton is our generic, dopey sewer worker. I forget what Archie Bunker did for a living, but I know that his type just loves Twinkies. Oh, and by the way, our Environmental Leadership honeymoon is officially over.

At a recent broad-spectrum, community envisioning workshop, Rosemary concluded that our conversations were proceeding in too much of an environmental / sustainability direction. She had two points to make, neither one of them well-thought out, but this was her opportunity to contribute to our regional quality of life conversation.

'*I believe it's vital that we have the participation of more working ranchers in these discussions*', she started out saying.

That was sufficient to raise the hair on the unshaven armpits of many of us enviros in the room. 'Working ranchers'—the connotation was that this absentee group was always working hard, and that we in the room were, well, if not hardly-working, surely working less-hard.

'*It's difficult for the agricultural community to attend these important meetings*', Rosemary went on to say.

Her words and gist continued to pierce our environmental armor. Who, with ample advance notice, could not attend a two-hour meeting?

<u>Answer</u>: all of us, if we have other priorities and other excuses. Yet why would the valued time of a farmer be any more precious than the morning of a single parent, or a restaurant worker, or a homeless person for that matter? We all have dilemmas, we make decisions, and while we might not be able to make the time, we can most definitely take the time. If you cannot attend the meeting, well, shoot out an email paragraph that expresses your interests, questions or concerns. Place a phone call. Send me a postcard. Turn off the television for fifteen freaking minutes and contribute to the process! This is how human beings should deal with important matters.

When I hear the term 'delinquent', the first word that leaps into my mind is 'juvenile', as in juvenile delinquent. As a kid, my parents scared the hell out of me with the threat that young troublemakers will get whisked away to reform school. It wasn't a pretty picture they were painting—rodents, barbed wire, bloody noses and shabby clothes to go along with the cold porridge. I've since discovered that delinquency is correlated to a significantly larger degree with parents and parent companies than with our youth or youthful enthusiasm. When opportunities for environmental leadership are squandered, it could plausibly be that they care less or care not.

Do you know how hard it is to pass the Colorado Certified Wastewater Operator exam? It was plenty hard for me, equipped with my honorable Masters Degree in Public Health. Imagine the degree of difficulty for the grease monkey with an elementary education and minimal math skills. Yet the guy with the wrench in his hand and stuff on his feet is certainly better qualified to deal with daily liquid waste problems that involve gaskets, seals, motors, wires and general troubleshooting. The field guy has the hands-on experience, literally. Waste makes haste, so he puts in the time.

We E-leaders are functions of multiple variables of both lower and higher dimensions. We are human derivatives representing divergent disciplines, unbalanced relationships, atypical expressions and (hopefully) favorable solutions. Can we formulate sustainable outcomes that result in desirable actions and reactions?

My point is this—environmental leaders must recognize the potential contributions of a wide array of community resources. Yet while doing this at community events, we must keep the playing field as level as possible. Once things start to slant ever so slightly in the direction of one group (agricultural, economic, environmental, etc.), then we will be accused of 'having an agenda'.

Yet wait a second—I thought that our agenda was quite clear, and that our environment was considered to be a priority? Yes, but when you flush the toilet, things will not magically disappear. The conservative movement came up with the terms 'wise use' and 'takings' to portray images of being stripped of individual rights, while in reality, it was their 'wrongs' that were being usurped— over-grazing, blocked public access, endangered species, climatic catastrophe, and erosion of responsible stewardship. The so-called Sagebrush Rebellion didn't last but was able to create roadblocks and detours that stalled or stopped critical environmental progressions.

How do environmental leaders inch forward without placating to special interests?

1. Require specifics—what is it, specifically, that you are concerned about?

2. Expect assistance—how are you going to help out?

3. Make recommendations—you might consider this…

4. Perform necessary adjustments—based on what we're seeing…

5. Act, then react, then act—adhering to your personal beliefs.

And once again, <u>your turn</u> to come up with 2 doozy ideas:

1) ————————————————————————.

2) ————————————————————————.

I'm so glad that you're finally able to complete these tiny tasks without any trepidation or apprehension! You're now considered to be a major contributor to our team!

<u>Daredevils</u>:

By definition: Audacious, bold, adventurers.

Our environmental impudence can come across as brashness or even arrogance, while our goal, ironically, is to facilitate the serene sensations of untrammeled nature. We wish to convey familiarity of shared watersheds, mutuality of crisp air, conviviality of shared communities and recognition of natural splendor. Our confidence can come across to others as over-confidence and for the easily threatened, insolence. Few of us have nerves of steel, but the battle scars of past environmental victories and sounding defeats have tattooed us as environmental ego and eco maniacs. Yet when we stand tall and perform our enviro-conservation chores, there's a certain confident, comfort level that can be a calming effect, especially for the team players around us.

The other tendency is to camouflage ourselves within a system that is programmed to seek out those that stand out. Once we are selectively exposed, we cannot be allowed to influence the core organizational body. We are cancer at worst and a scab at best. Infection must be cauterized, isolated, zapped and removed. What we are taught is that environmental affection is a nice thing, but don't let it get in the way of progress. We expect some prejudice in our diverse communities, often discover it in our extended families, but to come face-to-face with environmental ignorance at a workplace designed to promote environmental protections? None of us should tolerate this injustice.

But how does the system change if we walk away and seek the greener grass over yonder? And how essential is it that that ineffective environmental managers are made aware of their weakness, laziness or ineptitude? Answer: very important, but not as important as you making and taking the requisite strides towards the environmental progress that you cherish. Don't expect to pick up every cigarette butt that you see but make it obvious to those around you that you are passionate about our natural and human environment. If you're branded as the Evel Knievel of your section or division, seek out other courageous individuals that have dared to look over that ledge, and share your intriguing, personal war stories.

Some of my best friends and environmental bedfellows wonder why I left the decent-paying enviro-related jobs that I worked so hard to get. The explanation would take a lifetime, because I have yet to discover the answer myself. But I know that it is related to folks like John Muir, and it moves on to involve enviro leaders such as Al Gore, Bill McKibbon,

Vandana Shiva, Tom Freidman and everybody that performs the daunting EL tasks, including you and your budding EL aptitude!

There's much more that is still inside, searching for opportunities to launch an environmental leadership crusade. Through my thirties and forties, I always searched to live and work in mountain communities where the elevation was greater than the population. It used to be a lot easier, with fewer folks on our planet. Big cities would eat me up and spit me out, and it was hard for me to function in a large municipality for more than a few days. Many of you may be more urban-inclined, and quite honestly, you're positioned to influence a greater number of people in more diverse situations. Yet whether we crave the local diner or the mega- cinema, we remain daredevils!

> *Tax the rich, feed the poor, '*
> *till there are no rich no more..*
> *I'd love to change the world, but I don't know what to do,*
> *So I'll leave it up to you—*
>
> Alvin Lee & 10 Years After,
Woodstock 1973

Pipe Dreams—-(Fusion or Confusion?)

About every other year, Environmental Health inspectors attend a two-hour session about backflow prevention. In a nutshell, if wastewater 'backs up' in our plumbing, we need to ensure that it does not contaminate our drinking water. The easiest solution is to create an air gap—a physical disconnection that separates potable and non-potable water. This task takes three minutes to explain.

During the next 117 minutes, we are lectured at by professional plumbers about vacuum breakers and backflow prevention devices such as the RPZ double check valve, the reduced-pressure anti- siphon backflow preventer, and the dual assembly Apollo preventer. Yep, it's rocket science to most of us. Every two years there are newfangled devices, and every two years we feel dumber than a mop bucket and extremely overwhelmed.

That's just plumb wrong! Environmental Leadership should never be so convoluted. We should introduce concepts that maintain a steady, sustainable flow of sanity—not a trickle nor a surge. We all jump out of our skin when an air bubble unexpectedly gushes out of our faucets. We frantically leap when surprised by anything that backfires—cars, trucks, generators, managers, spouses. E-leaders strive to be liquid plumbers—we try to sip from the public water fountain without getting soaked. We refuse to allow byzantine leaders to baffle us with bullshit. Uncomplicated, unambiguous leaders are easily recognized and highly sought after. The last thing that we need is more clogs in our societal systems, or more drains in our community pipelines.

At the forefront, we need to avoid the congealing and marrow- mindedness that clogs and blocks our eco-flow. Our skulls are numbed by brainless repetitive activities that don't amount to squat... or maybe they do amount to squat, which is pretty obtuse in this day and age. Our E-programs have gotten diluted and convoluted simultaneously. We refer to 'partnerships' and allude to 'cooperation', but they left the building with Elvis. Much of our wasted effort gelatinizes and then ossifies us into petrified malcontents.

Plumbing solder must first be melted, in order to attach to and then connect adjoining pipe pieces after cooling. The Latin term 'solidaire' means 'to make solid'. The process requires that the solder has a lower melting point than the pieces being joined. We E-leaders must recognize the need to melt ice, mold minds and solidify causes. Our community flux is observed and displayed during coherent conversations regarding water quality and water quantity, generic food and genetic food, visible air and invisible air, inspirations, aspirations and expirations. We don't need to become rock solid—we just need to fuse, combine, blend, integrate, meld, merge and intermingle.

Aye, it's a bizarre world of ours, when instead of being engrossed in positive eco-pursuits we are challenged with obstructing clots and thwarting bile in its formative stage. Our communities most definitely have calcium deposits and programmatic aneurysms needing urgent attention. An affirmative Environmental Leadership prognostic will assuredly be anti-sclerotic, promoting strokes of the positive variety. We E-leaders must be well-versed in heartening of the arteries.

If my clothes were my mind, I would never change them—
Obstinate

Water Activity & Healthy Competition—

Water activity is defined as the level of moisture existing within a vegetative commodity that determines whether organisms can thrive, survive or die. Bread, for example, has a low water activity, and thus does not promote the rapid growth of bacterial organisms. In the same vein, a 'white bread approach' to environmental leadership does very little in terms of promoting organizational growth.

Some of our most prestigious enviro groups have a low water activity—ignoring the requisite irrigation of the roots and shoots of their very programs. It is ironic that even water quality entities can unintentionally be on the dry side—putting a new twist to the term 'conservation'. Even the bile is dehydrated.

Interestingly, molds can act as opportunistic agents, gaining a stronghold in an environment that is absent of competing organisms. Some of our smaller, more nimble enviro groups can (and do) fill this niche—by enacting quicker response times, having lower overheads (and usually less-competitive wages) and setting anchor in shallower waters with the potential to proliferate. For a good read, Malcolm Gladwell's book David & Goliath is very thought-provoking in terms of examining strengths, weaknesses, challenges and opportunities. As your leadership plot thickens, just make sure that your environmental lifeline doesn't start to congeal.

Restaurant Sign: **<u>Today's Special:</u>**

Prime Leadership, seasoned with diverse viewpoints, infused with organic thought, glazed with social overtones, served over a bed of reluctance… All u can eat!

<u>Customer:</u> *'Sounds delicious—where's the buffet'?*

<u>Waiter:</u> *'Over there, at the esteem table…'*

<u>Food 4 thought--</u>

Some introspective leaders have gone so far as to differentiate between a pollutant and pollution—a 'Pollutant', they claim, is merely an ingredient or element, such as Total Nitrogen, Total Phosphorous, or E. Coli. These substances don't result in pollution until environmental concentrations are changed. An altered flow in stream cubic feet per second, going from say 40 cfs to 10 cfs could dramatically result in greater concentrations of pollution. This lack of an adequate dilution factor can result in algae blooms, causing eutrophic conditions to the detriment of the undeserving watershed. On the other hand, a thunderstorm might take a creek from 40 cfs to 200 cfs, inundating it with run-off from its urban interface and hammering the creek with sediment and dissolved solids.

Before change pays you a personal visit, or before rust builds up on your shining armor, practice being forthright and tenacious— galvanize environmental support by taking things personally and sharing personal beliefs. So put a hop in your step, pass on the mundane, and take on what ails you—Initiate, Partake & Accentuate!

Nothing artificial--just real, raw emotion topped with some seared humbleness. Ideas and solutions are finest when organically grown. Just add water!! Make them soluble and soul-able at the same time. Yet they can be just as easily altered, as ideas cannot be eternally mummified. They will erode. Thoughts will decay, confidence will dwindle, and paths will get overgrown.

How do enviro programs go about losing that funk? How do we progress from raw, green talent towards medium-rare efforts, en- route to well-done environmental leadership, without resultant burnout? For starters, let's chop the head off of mediocrity! We need a field of leaders, serving as leaders in the environmental field, not a factory farm of cruddy GMO'd cucumbers. Step up to the counter, raise the bar, order that IPA. Why settle for a lackluster environmental leadership lager when you're capable of more, so much more!

> *I'm a man without conviction I'm a man who doesn't know?*
> *How to sell a contradiction*
> *You come and go, you come and go…*
> *Culture Club*

A Return Visit to the Dilution Factory:

It is a sure fact that once-potent environmental programs eventually get deactivated-- naturally, mistakenly or coincidently. You started with a quality product that is both appetizing and hearty, but felt compelled to reduce costs, hasten implementation and maintain market share. So, you've decided to add fats, fillers and preservatives. Salts and sugars are cheap flavor enhancers, but have zero or negative nutritional value, and have detracted from your healthy environmental message.

"*But we've already got a full plate … no way we can add activities at this time…*"

How many times have I heard this 'but-crack' explanation! The 'full menu' excuse needs to be scrutinized at more than the entrée level. Examine the beverages, appetizers, salads, desserts. Then there's the prep cooks, chefs, wait staff, dish divers, delivery persons and cleaning crew. Full environmental service? At what cost?

The risks of watered-down programming can be countered by environmental leadership efforts that 'concentrate' on powerful conservation actions. Credibility should remain a key ingredient to program success.

Branching out does not necessitate expansion— sharing skills, ideas, questions, challenges and opportunities can embolden and entice environmental programs and ultimately produce program multipliers. Shockingly, environmental leadership may not always be necessary, not every minute of the day. But it must be readily available, accessible and acceptable to others. Having the prowess to engage in common conservation causes can produce fertile ground for our next emerging leader(s).

Leadership-wise, some bigwigs are partially diluted, others significantly deluded. Potency is normally not in their front hip pocket. But when a true green bile-free leader rolls around, the environment lights up with excitement—words turn into actions, having profound positive impacts on team health and community engagement. It leads to phenomenal events--growth is stimulated by a synthesis of nutrient concentrations and the addition of light, shedding opportunity throughout our culture. We can turn pitiful efforts into pivotal moments, no longer relying solely on responses to upset conditions. Proactive, inclusive, watershed-based approaches are environmental leadership in the making--ambition, anyone?

> *"Politicians are like weathervanes. Our job is to make the wind blow..."*—
>
> Let the Mountains Talk, Let the Rivers Run

Be the Equator—

You yearned for some leadership latitude, but what you got back was longitude—they extended your list of tasks and responsibilities, but not the kind that flex your leadership ligaments. Welcome to the 'Oh-no' zone! It's a territory of programmatic desolation without any realm of dynamic influence.

Every beast has a belly, including the environmental universe. You are working within one of the most exhilarating and most perplexing professions that exist, and it is up to you to profess your enviro leadership attributes and desires. There's a jungle of environmental opportunities and challenges, and wading through swamps of bile will take more than a pair of galoshes. You'll need to act now and take advantage of our special offer that won't last long—unless you wish to prolong your own agony.

Internal environmental protection work (within the organization and within you) should always be exciting and enticing—always! It shouldn't be like pulling teeth or working at the morgue (fewer repercussions). Bonus offer—act today, and we'll include an additional bile trimmer at no extra charge!

When we are trying to stay afloat and crest the incoming waves, threats and challenges will naturally produce a significant amount of angst. But there's no time to hunker down and batten the hatches. Become less pragmatic, more idealistic and yes, even impetuous. Don't delay--waiting for the tide to turn is opting for rust instead of lust. Convert your thoughts into environmental action, brush aside the caustic and critical comments of naysayers and yodel out your leadership message over the hills! (Offer does not include processing and delivery costs. If you're not completely satisfied, return your leadership life for a complete refund—you'll be back in your organizational penitentiary in no time flat!).

If you dread the future, the future will be dreadful—
Locks of Babylon

Getting Our Marching Orders—

At our tiny rental cottage in South Kihei, Hawaii, I encountered an afternoon brigade of sugar ants parading across the kitchen counter. I literally wiped out the first battalion with one spray of Windex and paper towels. Only four minutes later, the second infantry was streaming in, and I couldn't detect exactly where they were coming from—just some corner nook, and they were headed for the sink.

Ahaa! They must smell food in the disposal. I'll get out my mighty bleach spray, sanitize the area while blinding the bastards, and have them beat a hasty retreat. But much to my surprise, the sugar ants just kept coming! More bleach, then hot water—I'll scald their skeletons while they send out a warning pheromone that should immediately reverse their direction.

Holy crap, they just keep heading into the sink! What do they smell down there? Is the queen commanding them to bring back bounty, despite the risk of life and limb? Go back where you came from, you can't win!

There would be no defeatist attitude on this trail. Likewise, us two-legged ants can march to the beat of a different drummer, or better yet, drum up our own beat. With some sense of direction, we summon up a green parade, proceed at a comfortable pace, and set our sights on the horizon, peering under rocks along the way. Hazards will abound, debacles will occur, and we will surely suffer some casualties.

I went to the hardware store to get some ant bait. They'll bring the dessert back home and poison the queen bitch. I might have to put up with them for another three maybe four days, but eventually I shall be victorious! Another guy was at the checkout counter with an armful of mouse traps and rat poison, cussing about the musk of dead rodents behind the drywall—it put my minor problem into another perspective. The cashier chimes in:

'Yeah, it was that wet Spring we had, and now followed by the dry Summer heat, they're comin' inside for water'.

Then it dawned on me—thirst. Mice, ants, humans, horses, trees, ... we must drink! It's our liquid lineage, our common thread. The sugar ants weren't kissing up to the queen, they were fending for themselves, doing whatever formidable task it takes to get half-a- drop of water. Here I was, pulverizing them, when all I really needed to do was to hose the trees outside!

How does this relate to us humans? If we 'get thirsty', we seek a solution—a new boyfriend / girlfriend, different job, change in location, or maybe just seek a cold beer. And most of us take the easy way out—we thirst, then we quench, only to get thirsty again. But we do have a choice.

Life is full of ant traps, sticky situations, leg-holds, droughts, floods, riptides and nightmares. This is life. I propose that we remain thirsty for our entire lives. Our thirst for EL is not quenched by ounces of refreshment, but rather by oceans of thoughts, deeds, efforts and dreams.

Remote Control—

We environmental leaders are the batteries that are required (but not included) in most environmental operations. We can be energized as well as depleted. We are bi-polar at times, and proud of it. We bring the crucial topics of 'environmental impact' and EL 'significance' to light—daring green leaders to turn up the volume, change channels and surge forward.

Personally, I don't want my mind to be considered a controlled substance. We inherently know what compounds gel and which opposites attract—yet it's often the prescribed, sequential steps, mandated order and standard operating procedures that keep innovation in a secure and predictable lock-down mode.

Q: *"Would you like to place an order?"*:

A: "Yes, I would like to free my mind, and not be restricted to convenient thoughts".

Q: *"I'm sorry; we don't pre-approve free thought, due to the risks involved"*.

A: "Who do I need to speak to, so I can unleash my potential?"

Q: *"Such a request would have to be made in-writing to our 'Head'- quarters office"*.

A: "I suppose I have to fill out a form?".

Q: *"No form is necessary—just make a convincing argument, justifying why you need to utilize more aptitude than what was allocated to your account"*.

A: "I have an account?"

Q: *"How else would we keep track of your inefficient use of intelligence?"*

A: "Why do you need to keep track of anybody's thought processes?"

Q: *"Without order, chaos would rule".*

A: "Can I get a large order of chaos?"

Q: *"It comes with a side-salad or fries".*

A: "What do you suggest?"

Q: *"I'm not authorized to make personal recommendations, but if I was, I'd go with the salad, as my brain is already fried".*

> *It's mind control, mind control,*
> *Corruption of your thoughts, yeah*
> *Destruction of your soul*
>
> Stephen Marley

Dormant Volcanoes--

Don't get me wrong—Maui is a tropical paradise, if you believe in paradise. Personally, I consider Maui to be a beautiful culture and climate with an abundance of man-made atrocities. For example, in this day and age, the Department of Health still allows the installation of cesspools! You heard it right, not septic tanks and absorption fields, but poop-holes in the ground that eventually migrate to the Pacific Ocean. Bad enough that thousands of Mauians have such 'outta sight, outta mind' excavations in their backyards, but municipalities have been injecting the wastewater of its population centers into the volcanic rock, evidently believing that time and distance are appropriate safety factors (didn't we just talk about distance?). Why the antiquated approach? Lack of environmental leadership is most definitely a strong possibility.

Then every Christmas season, Mauians are expected to thank Monsanto Claus for keeping them employed, even if it means potential ill health from herbicidal spraying of genetically modified organism (GMO) crops and fields. And if you can stray far enough away, then you'll likely be downstream of the Hawaii Commercial & Sugar plantation fields—aromatic, right? The blackest sugar you'll ever see, as cane-fields are burnt in order to minimize harvesting costs, and windswept neighborhoods are blanketed in sickening sweet soot. Why the raw deal? Lack of environmental leadership lends a clue.

These less-than-stellar performances are based upon what people can get away with, by taking the easy way out, finding loopholes and making excuses. We fall prey to the Chambers of Commerce, the Alexander & Baldwins, the Smith & Wessons.

It's what I refer to as <u>Purposeful Defeat</u>:

Q: *Why are you doing it that way??*

A: It defeats the purpose …

Q: *What purpose would that be?*

A: The purpose of doing things differently…

It's not the hope that somehow repeating the same activity will produce different results—even polluters know better than that. It's the desire to continue to repeat harmful activities as long as they can get away with it—habitat homicide, that is.

Sometimes we have great intentions, but they can result in inevitable losses. For example: You intend to stir things up, create some new dynamics, a horse of a different color. But things somehow go by the wayside, and you end up creating a messy situation. Whoops! What to do now? Repent? Succumb? Apologize? Avoid?

For starters, I would recommend a <u>straight-forward game</u> <u>summary</u>:

1. What we did right / what succeeded

2. What we failed to accomplish

3. Lessons Learned

4. Huddle up and call the next play. You can strategize and coordinate from the playbook and observe from the sidelines, but you'll need to convince those engaged in the game that:

   a) You know what you're doing.

   b) You have faith in them.

   c) You practice positive reinforcement.

   d) You're not afraid.

Remember the saying about losing the battle, but winning the war? You win some, you lose some? Showing your environmental tenacity in a losing effort can still impress others—getting them to assist will be easier if they see possibility and optimism, maybe some faith thrown in alongside.

Somewhere, somehow, somebody must have knocked you
around some;
Tell me why you want to lay there and revel in your abandon...
                                              -Tom Petty

Ostrich Alert—

The Paonia, Colorado region, also known as the North Fork Valley, has the highest concentration of organic farms in the State of Colorado. How could this not be taken as a major environmental accomplishment? When methodically scrutinizing how the organic farms operate and bringing old-fashioned and new-fangled conservation into the environmental equation, our suppositions might morph significantly. For example, farms and orchards require water, lots of it. The North Fork of the Gunnison River and its tributaries provide it. But take a good, hard look at river levels, especially from July to September, and figure out how a native trout can survive in a warm, slow, oxygen-depleted trickle.

Most of the organic farms are no better than the conventional pastures in terms of wasting acre-feet of water. Little effort is being put into ensuring adequate stream flows (adequate, not minimum), as agriculture rules the valley. Simple water conservation measures can result in a 20% increase in streamflow. The Western Slope Conservation Center and their innovative, community-based leadership are making headway, albeit gallon-by-gallon. Other local environmental organizations prefer the head-in-the-sand approach, thinking that total and complete opposition to oil & gas development will protect the watershed. It ain't gonna happen.

Environmental leadership cannot pick and choose to attack oil & gas while ignoring coal mining (due to jobs and family connections) or detrimental farming and irrigation practices. In fact, prioritizing watershed health will ultimately be more effective in restraining oil & gas development, as it takes a more holistic, altruistic, sustainable community-based approach to environmental protection and conservation, with the involvement of many cubic feet and feats per minute. I'm not saying that the other groups have no integrity, but they just simply have less of it!

With Environmental Leadership lacking, there is no taste for watershed health, only a dis-taste for new ideas and creative, collaborative approaches. Poorly led organizations quickly dive into survival mode without realizing the shallow depths of their plunge. Their drought of ideas is directly responsible for minimal stream flows, as they have become their own organic sinkhole. The dirty secret of stream-flow waste will hit home within the next three or four years—why wait?

Stubbornness and adamant environmental opposition can only be effective if your leadership message is infective—if you can transmit your green bugs to a receptive audience and watch them start to proliferate, you might have a fighting chance. The Western Slope Conservation Center that I recently mentioned recognizes this environmental germ theory. Alex Johnson, the group's former innovative and open-minded environmental leader, has added the requisite fizz and pizzazz to the generic environmentally-flat soda. My observations and interactions have led me to conclude that Alex's secret sauce for success is based on being receptive, creative, friendly, tired-less, humorous and engaging. He's a smart guy too, but the human nature side is what has opened pathways for his inviting program concepts.

Environmental reality reveals that our levels of community support or resistance vary daily, and that we 'deal with' common colds and feverish pitches, trying to minimize or maximize impacts to sensitive or sensitized populations without a collaborative strategy. We are all susceptible and never immune to our external environment and remain prone to certain activities more than others. Whether you are the Greater Sage Grouse or the Lesser Sage Grouse, don't brood over it, just deal with it!

Run for your lives!

What can possibly happen when you take my advice and become an environmental pyrotechnician? When you turn up the heat on that silent-but-violent volcano boss of yours—the one that has thwarted your innovative potential and ignored your servile requests to do bigger, better, greener things—what might you expect?

To be on the safe side, expect an eruption of Vesuvius magnitude—this way, you at least know the worst-case scenario. Surely provide yourself with an escape route to hurdle the lava flow, but better yet, seek higher ground! Call on your inner belief system to be proud of your granitic greenness. Defend your actions by taking a professional and honorable stance—it won't be comfortable, believe me. But it's a helluva better plan than scurrying down the rat-hole, not knowing which direction to turn, or which entrail to exit.

Some will refer to you as 'an instigator'—take it as a compliment, as you will have demonstrated to others that environmental courage, commitment and conviction are an innate part of you.

Frankly, it gives me the creeps when I get pinned down for some banal task or trite action that any run-of-the-mill voodoo doll can perform.

Be that ignition source! Reach out for an outlandish approach that might not evoke an environmental apocalypse but can at least forestall the hypnotic trances culminating from our mundane daily 'activities'. If we can prevent the environmental coagulation now, we can deal with what may be more conducive and more contributory soon after. We are the proud, the few, the Environmental Leaders.

> *"Throughout history, it has been the inaction of those who could have acted; the indifference of those who should have known better. The silence of the voice of justice when it mattered most, has made it possible for evil to triumph."* --
> Haile Selassie I

No See-ums-

During my first month in my Peace Corps village of Tabelot, in the remote Sahara Desert region of Niger, W. Africa, I witnessed the death of nine infants from a measles virus outbreak. Escalated fever and dehydration took its toll on the prone, immuno- compromised newborns. A regional nutritional analysis revealed that there were also (obviously) protein deficiencies, due to drought, poverty, lack of education and all the other convenient contributors to a destitute society.

The primary local sources of protein around Tabelot were identified as dried goat cheese and a millet / sorghum mix that we Westerners commonly refer to as 'bird feed'. But after living there for six months, I discovered another protein source—insects. Some bugs (crickets, grasshoppers, caterpillars) were intentionally gathered and cooked, yet other creepy crawlers were regularly ingested raw without great inspection or reflection. The insects seemed to be inside most of the dates, whether they were fresh or dried. Don't ask me how they get in there, I'm no entomologist. And after confirming that the petite buggers existed, I decided to cease opening them up and just wolf the whole date into my mouth. They tasted excellent--out of sight, out of mind!

Environmental leaders don't always have to be highly visible. We can be teachers and contribute conservation knowledge that is ingested and further divvied out by learners. We can be farmers and practice sustainability without uttering a word. We can be environmental fellows that support community efforts from the east and west. We can also be followers in close proximity to our trailblazers from the north and south. Leadership can come and go, flourish, then fade back in time. But I vehemently and enthusiastically believe that whatever version of a leadership song is being sung, that it be conveyed with healthy environmental intentions and conviction, and widely broadcast through community messages. Once you crack open that nearly impenetrable shell of bureaucratic stagnation, you may discover creatures with promising features.

Fiber Optics--

In my host community of Punta Gorda in Southern Belize, there were only a handful of places to go to eat lunch. My favorite noon spot, by far, was Goyo's. You could always count on Goyo (owner, cook and waiter) to produce a fine jerk chicken, but what I really salivated over was the beans and rice. Tourists would occasionally come in to cast off their overloaded backpacks and sit down for a ginger beer and hot lunch. They too would order similar lunch items, but it wasn't quite the same—you see, there's a big difference between rice and beans on one hand, and beans and rice in the other.

I would always order the beans and rice, which consists of freshly cooked and nicely spiced beans, poured over a volcano of freshly-steamed rice, topped with an inferno of mango / habanero pepper sauce. Gastronomically, the ethnic food-fare was highly rewarding indeed! Diversely, the tourist menu revealed rice & beans as yesterday's leftover rice, mish-mashed with yesterday's leftover beans, infused with coconut oil and reheated. Oftentimes in life, it's important to let others know just what it is that you're asking for. There's a redeeming value in providing a service to others, especially when you meet their true needs.

Another true tale—on a boat trip in Rwanda, I sat next to a stranger with zero French-speaking ability. I ordered café et croissant, he went for the super-sized omelette. I was hungrier than I thought, and after quickly devouring the croissant, asked the server to 'donnez-moi un autre'—bring me another. The stranger liked the looks of my croissant, so he repeated my verbal request— 'Donnez moi un autre'. He was very surprised when the server returned with another humungous omelette! He got what he asked for.

While we don't always get what we want, the chances of getting what we really, truly need depend on sound communications— including asking pertinent questions. Someone once said that 'there's no such thing as a stupid question'—I beg to disagree. Environmental leaders must develop sound techniques at asking candid questions that promote both their sincerity and curiosity at the same time. Some questions are not only absurd, but they prove that someone was not doing their homework, not listening or only partially processing the information at-hand. Confusing river-right with river-left (always looking downstream) can capsize an expedition. And to build support for our understanding, leaders need to clarify, acknowledge and affirm their desire for more of the same. 'Great beans & rice, Goyo! See you tomorrow!'.

> There is no foreign land—
> It is the traveler that is foreign—
>
> R.L. Stevenson

CHAPTER VII.
THE LAST HURRAH / GREENAGE MUTANT LEADER HURDLES

Waiting in the Wings—

Opportunity may present itself, but it's a rather quick cameo appearance. Environmental leaders need to be not just prepared, but vigilant and on high-alert, ready to lunge forward as a first responder. I distinctly recall house-sitting in Birmingham, Alabama while going to graduate school. The house-confined Siamese cat slid through my legs and out the door, bee-lining a path to the trash dumpster. I shepherded her back into the house within two minutes, earning only minor feline bites, no severe punctures. The wrath I truly suffered was from the nasty, ankle-biting hitchhiker fleas. It was no circus.

Opportunistic organisms and individuals must be anxious, eager, equipped, primed and responsive. Fleas, ticks and hungry environmental leaders can latch onto passing opportunities. Get a good grasp of the situation and then dig deeper into the meat of the organization. Others will try to relieve themselves of you (or on you)—you'll be considered a pest, and their response is merely human nature. But if you want to ascend in rank and put your leadership skills to the test, you'll need to ensure that others recognize your talents, your intensity, your tenacity, your staunchness, your moxie, your potential and your ambitiousness.

Take your best shot, and if you miss the mark, take aim again until you hit your target. Your effort and persistence will reveal your environmental courage, exuding self-confidence and worthiness. You won't feel parched for greater environmental leadership without first exercising your current talents and personal traits. Develop that thirst!

I earlier introduced myself as a failure—not a complete and utter failure, mind you, but a driven, contorted malcontent. I'm a self- described unsuccessful individual and professional instigator, an accomplished loser and a never-give-upper. I hope I have taught you a thing or two about spunk and relentless trying. It might just be my life's calling—getting you to read over this guidebook while simultaneously performing serious self-reflection and self- evaluation, causing you to consider, wander and wonder. I should have recommended pouring a stout cup of coffee, finding a cozy chair and pondering over the EL possibilities (without letting things bile-up)! We're not done yet—I just paused for a moment to talk with you. Some of my best friends are strangers.

We all have propensities and natural tendencies to perform in some habitual way or to function within our comfort zone. Sorry to say, such proclivity normally results in underperformance, as the alternative means more work and more energy expended. Environmental leaders consider the added workload as a fuel supply of renewable energy—we expend because the effort builds confidence, competence and environmental muscle. The human penchant to be mellow and non-confrontational is an easy defense- response mechanism—a knee-jerk reaction geared toward conserving energy and reducing uncertainty--but for what beneficial use? Self-preservation, I suppose. Laziness leads towards laxness, with unpreparedness and neglect as your roommates.

Astute or a Stooge?--

Try to recall the very first 2016 U.S. Presidential debate—not the first one against Hillary, nor the first one against his Republican henchmen (whoops, there goes another 3% of my readership!). I'm referring to the 2011 Comedy Central roasting of Donald Trump. It was one jam-packed hour of humiliating barrages about his hair, his rhetoric, his unstable / irrational behavior and of course, his greed. Mr. Trump sat there with a smug look on his face—tight lipped, clasped hands, minimal signs of emotion, few smiles. The guest comic roasters tossed him f-bombs, with crude sexual innuendos and jokes on the ends of bayonets. And Mr. Trump sat there and took it as if it were a required dose of chemotherapy. Bring it on--give me your best shot! And when it was his turn, he got the last laugh—on the show, and in the world of showmanship.

What a primer for the next ten months of attacks. Sincere or not, credibility was not a critical issue. The man had proven to himself that his mortal enemies (the liberal democrats and overly social conservatives) could be minimized and marginalized, as if he were a super-human wind-shield wiper equipped with razor blades. Only one thing mattered—the fact that he could convince others that he could lead them, not into temptation, but deliver them from the evil of politics as-usual, with Chinese trade wars, Mexican immigrants and Isis terrorists as icing on the cake, Amen.

This version of worldly leadership must be countered and overcome by your version of leadership, with environmental leadership playing center stage. Rachel Carson's Silent Spring sent out shock waves about environmental carcinogens and pointed fingers at human irresponsibility. It was a call-to-arms without the arms. While it has taken decades to reduce the levels of DDT in our environment, this was a clear victory for habitat over hypocrisy. We are more convinced that prevention is better and cheaper than cures or remediation, but convincing requires conviction as well as commitment. Whether we are deterring nuclear battles or harnessing global warming, we will need to garner public support and retain deep-seeded belief that our nature and culture will prevail over profit for some and loss for others.

I truly believe that without Moe's acidic leadership, Larry would not be a Stooge. The guy had real potential yet fell into the wrong ranks and ended up as a submissive. Larry's role is pivotal in almost every Three Stooges episode, yet he gets no credit and is at the brunt of aggressive responses. He relies on Curly for support and little consolation, the same way that enviro staff may end up relying on other blue / green collars, following directives and scurrying around helter-skelter. If Larry can lead, so can you!

Stench Supporters:

Prior to accepting a recent environmental health job at Chaffee County, Colorado, three other companies were after my services— the gas company, electric company and the cable company. Bills to pay, sure enough, but it got me thinking—ignite, electrify and connect. Don't run out of gas, provide an ignition source and drive forward with some direction in mind. Be a conductor and amp things up! Be utilitarian! Environmental Leadership takes energy, and more than just potential energy. Environmental leaders need to kinetically convey energy and enthusiasm.

I never really cared much for the rock band AC /DC, as I always had trouble hearing the lyrics. But I must admit that they did have energy! Energy & connectivity as well, which takes us back to environmental leadership. From a supervisor vantage-point, I believe that the best kind of directors are alternators—leaders who are able to divert energy, convert electricity, recharge systems, ensure backup power and be able to switch flows of current on short notice. Environmental Leaders alternate responsibilities and share the stage, juicing up team efforts (by encouraging contributions from diverse arrays of sources). We need to be staunch advocates for our environmental and conservation progressions, not stench supporters of bygone approaches and regressive fixations. We enviro leaders are charged with converting static ability into engaging, ecstatic performances. Anything less remains nothing more than an annoying buzz.

Coagulation—

While tending to your personal environmental leadership ambitions, you may consider this factoid—ambient noise levels decrease by approximately 6 decibels on the A-scale, for each doubling of distance. It would take over a football field in distance to decrease noise from 70 (irritating) to 50 (acceptable) decibels. Environmental leaders have several options at their disposal—they can create 'buffer zones' to minimize impairment, they can attempt to dampen the impairment with technological fixes, they can require reductions of nuisance decibel-emitting levels prior to permitting, or they can do nothing.

Environmental leaders consider all options, farming out ideas to those with enhanced knowledge of the specifications and detailed operations. Eventually, some concepts will be weeded out and a path will be chosen. Nobody wants to be mired down in eternal deliberations and indecisiveness, but sticky situations happen for a reason. Blood coagulates to avoid hemorrhage, but the presence of blood clots can also impair circulatory system function. Sometimes the plot must thicken before the blood thinners are introduced.

If limited by two choices, I would rather hire a pitcher as a batting coach, instead of a batter as a pitching coach—for the simple reason that batters react while pitchers deliver. Yet as we've seen, deliverance can come from contrasting opinions, from alternative horizons, from dueling banjos. Determine what levels of programmatic consistency you can tolerate, be wary of being spoon-fed environmental policies and seek out natural flavors and community tenderizers.

Premises, premises—

A premise is something assumed or taken for granted--a presupposition. On the premise that people are generally honest, you leave your car door unlocked. A premise is a proposition upon which an argument is based, from which a conclusion is drawn. Environmental leaders carefully scrutinize basic assertions—mine coal to boost our economy; nuclear power is clean energy; dams keep our farms green, beef, it's what's for dinner--you get the idea.

With our awareness honed via environmental leadership exercises and actions, we need to openly criticize zany theories by demonstrating their false pretenses, charades and dubious premises. No, birth control is most definitely not a ploy of world government to manage planned percentages of our various races.

The flip side, of course, is that environmental leaders need to stand tall on the solid ground (for the time being) of climate change and the overwhelming consensus within our scientific community. Environmental leaders must have a combined personal and professional belief system. For example, you can't detest immigrants and work full-time at the Social Services Department. When we are confronted with boastful, baffling and bogus ideas, we need to question the almighty source. Despite being beleaguered by leadership slips and slides, we'll need to roll up our green-sleeves and latch on to firm terrain. And like the kid's game of King of the Hill, when you get shoved, tripped and trampled, you get up and push back.

As the environmental anchorman, you must be a central and dependable contributor to your organization. You must be primed and pumped to run the last leg of your relay team, yet also eager to sprint to the front of the pack. You must be able to set a realistic-yet-aggressive pace, and you must be able to provide aid stations. You must be able—a bonafide, genuine, authentic leader that is true to the cause. You have environmental currency that can be distributed in good faith—the exact opposite of phony, counterfeit leadership built on reproductions, charades, facades and short-term profiteering.

> *There's always gonna be another mountain I'm always gonna*
> *wanna make it move Always gonna be an uphill battle Sometimes*
> *I'm gonna have to lose,*
> *Ain't about how fast I get there*
> *Ain't about what's waiting on the other side It's the climb, yeah!*
>
> Written by Jon Mabe, Jessi Alexander

Calm-frontation—

Poise and composure can really tick off some type-A folks, to the point where they won't cease until they rile you! They want more than words from your mouth—they want to see perspiration, anxiety, tears or turmoil. They want to see living proof of your blood and sweat equity. Your calm demeanor irks and occasionally humiliates them. I often refer to my 'P-soup' of environmental leadership traits—poise, professionalism, persistence. I used to add patience but have come to understand that patience is a tool, not a virtue. Sometimes environmental impatience can result in knee-jerk reactions, but sometimes that's exactly what we need to get the juices flowing. Someone's gotta show up to confront the bile.

Environmental Leaders serve as the glue—we need to be cohesive and receptive, with open arms, sharp eyes, a clear mind and a keen sense of magnetism or attraction. Our stick-to-itiveness pertains and adheres to our community-based values. We work to overcome our conservation deficit disorders by learning from both the abilities and disabilities of others, in essence becoming bile-lingual.

> *'Get up, stand-up, stand up for your rights,*
> *Get up, stand-up, don't give up the fight!'*—
> Bob Marley

Play with fire—

That is leadership—a tool, resource, provision and weapon all in one. Calls for enhanced environmental leadership do not usually directly translate to stoking the fire to provide desired comfort and warmth. It might entail gathering mature wood, ensuring adequate ventilation, furnishing layers of warmth or providing timely tending. 'Beating around the bush' also has its moment and purpose—why try to walk up and pet a rattlesnake? And 'finders-keepers' is rarely a coveted EL trait or desire. On the flip side, leadership can be a compelling opioid--producing strong cravings for demonstrative exercises that diminish pain and anguish while escalating environmental elation at the same time. I refer to such potent strides as 'duces wild' and the finesses offered during Environmental Leadership induction:

*   In<u>duce</u> meandering—Suggest routes and invite exploration.

*   Pro<u>duce</u> changes—Spearhead efforts without impaling environmental allies.

*   Re<u>duce</u> waste—Refuse to accept unworthiness, create worth and gain value.

*   Intro<u>duce</u> possibilities—Challenge conservation communities to be receptive and responsive.

Understand the power of leadership. A dependency on valued leadership can escalate both wanted and unwanted reactions from within the rank and file. By the time it becomes apparent to you, your team may have been lassoed and hog-tied into submissive positions, addicted to the leadership message of another. Surely, it's not your intent to lure in others, but this just may be the inconspicuous, stealthy approach of defective leaders and sordid bile producers. Don't say I didn't warn you!

Sometimes such ill-fated conditions can be ignored or avoided, but in the long run it can become insidious; smoldering in a gradual, subtle way, like the sun's rays on fair skin. Be leery of power brokers making absurd profit and loss statements, along with incoherent claims of forecasted prosperous communities. The tiny mountain town of Kremmling, Colorado was sold this bill of goods by Louisiana Pacific Co. and its incendiary waferboard plant. Cut down the aspen, pollute the sky and we'll all get rich. Impoverished communities get desperate, and without community leadership, can be coaxed into making deals with the devil. Such deplorable bonding between big money and politics needs to be recognized (not respected) and closely scrutinized. We surely don't want to follow Pinnochio's lead and be swallowed by Monstro, so be very wary!

Oooh, see the fire is sweepin', our very street today; Burns like a red-coal carpet, mad bull lost its way..—
                                        Keith Richards / Mick Jagger

Getting Slaughtered or Steering Clear—

If you've never visited a rendering facility, you're really missing out. This multimedia tour is not for the squeamish and will leave you with vivid images and olfactory memories that shall never be forgot. Be sure to wear non-slip shoes. The meat rendering process attempts to convert waste products into a value-added material— recycling, so to speak.

What goes into the vault can include animal carcasses, from cows and pigs to cats and dogs. One rendering operation cooks the entire batch into a gravy-like stew, which can then be sold to the pet food industry as kitty and puppy chow, or to the farm industry as animal feed. Economics seriously comes into play, with the rendering process being less expensive than hauling the animal waste to the landfill. 'Bone meal' sounds a lot better than 'rancid horse entrails'.

Unfortunately, the feeding of carnivorous by-products to a normally vegetarian animal community (cows, sheep, pigs) created a pathway for the spread of bovine spongiform encephalopathy, aka 'mad cow disease'. As they like to stipulate, *side effects may vary*. Carrion my wayward son…

Another 'benefit' of the rendering process is to produce a fatty-content product (such as soaps, greases and candles) that is not susceptible to spoilage. This is performed via cooking followed by liquid extraction and drying. Sometimes I feel as if our watersheds have experienced such rendering first-hand.

Now I'm not saying that our workplace resembles a slaughterhouse, but I have noticed a pile of human carcasses stacking up on the leadership scale. I view death and decay in the EL realm as despicable contempt. Our fats and proteins have the potential to be utilized as an energy source— especially if funneled into a creative environmental mechanism. Yes, it is literally a visceral vittles process that can render our EL efforts useful or useless. The door that that takes us towards the meat grinder should never lock behind us—examine, evolve and escape.

It would behoove us to closely scrutinize all the trace elements that end up in our rendering plants—poisonous plastic waste, flea collars, pesticides, euthanasia drugs, Styrofoam trays and items we don't normally consider to be food-grade. The maggots don't seem to mind this over-coating, and the enhanced food product will be neatly mixed and packaged for your pooch. And how pure is the downstream milk that our dairy cows are now producing?

Are we environmental leaders destined to be livestock or laughing-stock? We need to sniff out tainted politics and decomposing programs. We need to create unusual, noteworthy, environmentally-sound opportunities. We will pay a hefty price if we don't take the lead. If we don't continuously forage for greener pastures, the alternative is to grow fatter with fake fodder, becoming the chowhound chief or bloodhound boss that we cynically mock.

Shallow the Leader--

It's hard to sustain an environmental leadership locus when you're the only fireman or woman. Brushfires will take advantage of drought conditions, and you'll need to prescribe proven anti- inflammatories, practicing prevention via team approaches and hands-on exercises. But when the top tier states that 'You're in charge', the prevention is often kicked aside while you jump into full damage control mode.

It's a similar situation with eroded riparian areas within watersheds. Historic overgrazing has denuded streambanks to the point where river sections have become shallow and braided, warmer and sediment loaded. Erosion prevention is replaced with sediment control as a stop-gap measure, and mitigation efforts are subsequently launched.

Avoiding staff run-off is another difficult task for environmental leaders. I would suggest that a certain amount of flight be accepted as normal, but that concerted fortification of your environmental program will ultimately shore-up the team and minimize the erosion of future conservation projects. How can we leaders be expected to perform similar life-saving measures within our watersheds without addressing the integrity of the mighty bodies and minds within our very organization?

Unfortunately, we do it all the time. For example, we perform water quality control as a blended variety of pollution prevention and site remediation. But we rarely examine the leadership abilities (and liabilities) of our project coordinators and program managers, leaving ultimate authority in the hands of supervisors that seldom get their feet wet. That's a large reason why our expectations are not very great, and also why community-based approaches to watershed health remain far from mainstream—more akin to tourniquet therapy.

Okay, I admit that I too can be a dummy at times—how often have I gone back to the dictionary to figure out the difference between metaphors, similes and analogies? But non-brainiacs can lead. It's just a matter of knowing when to soak it up and when to suck it up--pairing up halfwits, fooling our forecasters, tempting our intolerant, perplexing our politicians, and conjuring up creative, newfangled approaches.

As far as I'm aware, there's no dummies guide to environmental leadership. Adhering to our core environmental principles and belief system will keep us afloat, treading water and staying on top of the situation until help arrives. Then we naturally ask for honest, candid assistance. You might find that you have hidden talents that simply needed exposure and opportunity to present their selves outright. You might not have known how to swim, but had few options but to surface or submerge, flail or prevail.

I found my mind—
Shipwrecked Survivor

Slime—

Underground septic systems often rely on infiltration galleries to collect wastewater flows emanating from the outlet of the septic tank. Within these dark cavities, aerobic and facultative bacteria feast on sewage flows, digesting nutrients and forming the foundation for a layer of bioaccumulation that functions fairly predictably under normal conditions. Flushing sulfuric acid or hydraulic fluids down the drain, however, is not considered normal, nor is flooding from uncontrolled or illicit outputs.

Environmental grunts are the green slime of our gritty operation—the welcome bio-mat and the reception committee. We work in the trenches, day-in and day-out. We can process small quantities of impropriety and neglect but are not equipped to handle significant slugs of bile from noxious leaders. Accidents happen, but chronic virulent outputs will malignantly take their toll by sealing our pores and suffocating our voices.

What constitutes an environmental leader? I would surely mention his or her demeanor, disposition, temperament and character—all difficult to quantify. Within true environmental leadership, there is a green state of mind and a greener-based prevailing attitude towards teamwork and collective conservation efforts. The continuity and connectivity make perfect sense.

A second definition of disposition is '*the act of disposing*'. The judge, whomever that may be, makes a ruling and transfers you to the care or possession of another. I am inclined to believe that being dispossessed would lead towards team abandonment and solitary confinement, turning us into doubters, scoffers and heathens. The bile continues to baffle us with indigestible sludge, odiferous responses and clogged arteries. Somehow, some way, we need to alter our collective mindsets from consumption / disposal into a framework of treatment / beneficial use. To avoid systems failure, environmental leadership is crucial.

"It is not variety that is the spice of life. Variety is the meat and potatoes. Risk is the spice of life..."---David Brower

Platypuses and Impetuses—

Oftentimes, the obvious needs to be clearly stated and not shadowed over. Life is about adaptation. Nature and culture are like Siamese Twins—equal, dependent, interdependent, yet unique. Take the bizarre-looking platypus for example. Female platypuses lay eggs, yet nurse their young like mammals. Stranger yet, the females lack nipples, and exude milk through mammary glands on their belly.

Male platypuses didn't get away that easy either—the males produce venom similar to reptiles, but from its hind legs, as they lack real teeth. Both sexes resort to sucking upriver gravel to break down tough foods. Platypuses do, however, have an extraordinary, redeeming feature—a sixth sense in a phenomenal bill that can detect electric fields derived from all forms of life.

If only we enviro leaders used our sixth sense and our strong suits to their fullest potential. If we only had the stomach to deal with irregularities, and if we could somehow develop the propensity to use spunk and vigor to our mutual benefit—if we were only inclined to be conservation catalysts and develop a craving for innovative, sustained community involvement…. That's just my gut feeling.

No Deposit, No Return--

Sometimes there is a sense of ultimate conservation direction, but you are facing substantial barricades en-route. You are eager to get going, pronto, chop-chop! But the blockage is as evident as an X or your tic-tack-toe O path. Your leadership remedies are too weak, and the bottleneck is hard to comprehend, like a deuce in a urinal (health inspectors see the strangest things)!

Where do you find that commercial-strength decongestant that will provide essential breathing room? Where would I start?

<u>Firstly</u>: Think. Think before acting. If you flush the handle without considering the facts, you may be in for an overflow situation.

Therefore, think!

<u>Nextly</u>: Breathe. Some refer to it as deeper reflection, mindfulness or contemplation. Sometimes we think too hard! Oxygen is our friend.

<u>Then</u>: Put things into perspective, ala NEPA—The Purpose, The Problem, The Affected Environment, The Alternatives, The Consequences, The Proposed Action—slice and dice the situation.

I would surmise that these three steps will potentially solve 30% of your problems. That's not bad for such easy sequences! You've reduced the problem by almost one-third!

<u>Finally</u>: Seek additional resources, ranging from a toilet plunger to an expert plumber.

I'm sure that you'll agree that some things are better sight-unseen, air pollution, for example. Granted, there are industrial emissions that are invisible to the human eye, but let's keep dealing with that 30% visible particulate for this exercise.

We are not defenseless, but most definitely prone or susceptible to respiratory distress, asthma, emphysema and other nasty lung impairments. We are vulnerable—the Latin word 'vulnerare' meaning 'to wound'.

As Environmental Leaders, we conduct Vulnerability Assessments to examine presence / absence, dose / response, frequency / severity, black / white, affordable / astronomical, possible / impossible. Is any of this coming back to you? We are often confronted with double-exposure, aka 'the double-whammy'. At the same time that we resemble wounded warriors trying to breathe fresh air, we are also sensing a considerable level of community distress.

'Why doesn't somebody do something about that guy's burning of his garbage?'

'Why is she able to smoke right outside of my bedroom window?'

'I wish someone would tell that truck driver to turn the damn thing off!'

Environmental Leadership does not always have to deal with all the mounting frustration, but we certainly need to acknowledge it—think, breathe, put things into perspective, seek out resources. EL does more than put a band-aid on the wound, especially if you're fresh-out of band-aids. I didn't solve your problem, but I observed it, recognized it, and gave it some deeper thought—I didn't say 'it's not my problem'. That is brass tacks Environmental Leadership. Make the deposit.

Bitten or Smitten?—

Cats and dogs can be exposed to rabies (Rabies lyssavirus) by snatching up rabid bats with their mouths or encountering virally- infected skunks or raccoons (which are probably lured closer by our precious humming-bird feeders, puppy chow basins and birdbaths). Bats don't bite people, unless you're raising Dracula's vampire cousin as a house-pet. If a human is bitten (usually via an infected cat or dog), the scenario switches to potential exposure, confinement and observation.

Rabies symptoms commence with an early onset of fever, and are subsequently presented with violent movements, uncontrolled excitement, fearing of water, confusion and loss of consciousness--- traits observed in a fair share of our paralytic leaders. The virus starts by infecting muscle cells close to the site of infection, where they can replicate without being noticed by our immune system team. Once of considerable virulence, the disease migrates to the central nervous system, ultimately migrating to the salivary glands—ready to transmit a fearful message to the next host.

Environmental leaders are confronted with a leviathan of socio-economic issues that will most assuredly impact our natural and human environment. Astute enviro leaders see the waxing moon in its early stage, while citizen support is still waning. Not until neighborhoods and neighbors are stricken by noxious plumes, windblown trash and industrial odors do they start to gripe to their elected officials. At this stage, we've already been exposed to environmental harms, and can rarely resort to preventive measures.

Communities can easily become infatuated by the new cinema complex or impending Target store—offering value and choices, and most of all, convenience. We are moonstruck by both the brilliance and the simplicity. Our scowls turn to howls and short-term satiation. We don't bat an eye over concrete parking lots encroaching on historic wetlands—not when we can buy discounted peanut butter in a jiffy. We experience the pluses, the positive experiences, while ignoring or undervaluing sustainable initiatives and low-impact development. Buy one and get one free.

We should be incessantly fuming over air pollution concerns and foaming at the mouth over water quality impairments. And as rabid environmentalists, our efforts should be more than pint-sized. We can change all that. We <u>must</u> make the change.

The 'yuck' factor—

I have a personal repugnance for perfection. I really don't care if someone straightens the bookshelf or tucks in the bedsheets. Not that I'm messy, but I just have other priorities and see that time is a-waistin'. These tedious or menial acts don't drive me crazy, until the perfectionist becomes my direct supervisor. The sandpaper effect that I previously mentioned returns for an encore performance, and the prolonged agony of rough draft after rough draft remains abrasive, even if to a finer degree. At times I've even resorted to making things intentionally 'unperfect', striving for a crude idea or a new concept, and completely ignoring the orderly window dressing.

If the perfectionist is you, and you're committed to becoming a better environmental leader, then here's a recommendation—prior to making any correction, no matter how small, make a positive statement or pay a true compliment. Try keeping score (it shouldn't be too hard for your type). If you make two improvements or edits without giving equal consideration to the person expending the effort, you are still an agent of the BGB. Your actions and inactions have resulted in discouragement, disdain and disingenuous behavior. Is that what you were seeking when you reconfigured the alignment of the photo in the electronic document? Was your executive decision to change the background color worth the price? Does anybody (besides you) care if you spit out three, five or seven revised reports?

But here's the other thing—your soft, slight, yet repetitive 'corrections' are interpreted at first as criticism, next as disparaging remarks and ultimately as inhumane. Reverse the process, Scotty! Before the organizational aversion turns into vehemence and hatred, try the 'ole switcheroo approach—turn your growing incompatibility into, well, compatible ideas and actions. Show that not only can you coexist, but that you can indeed become harmonious. Don't chuck away the fundamental bread and jam, but pull out the supplemental Nutella and spread it with others. It might not stop some from loathing you, but it will make you feel better about yourself—not a bad thing!

Impunity (That's not what I ment)—

Though there are a vast number of interpretations, Aesop's Fable usually shares the parable where a cow, a goat and a sheep go hunting together with a lion. When it comes to dividing the spoil, the lion proclaims,

"I take the first portion because of my title as king; the second portion you will assign to me, since you are my subjects; then because I am the stronger, the third section will be served to me; and an accident will happen to anyone who touches the fourth."

Personally, I don't burn out—ever. But just as bad, I burn in. I get heated, irritated and restless. Then I slowly start to seethe, with my blood and bile starting to boil. I'm jealous with envy over that lion's share.

One thing we Environmental Leaders can easily do is request a seat at the discussion table. The requisition itself is a statement of will and desire. While we are waiting, we might browse around and examine the occupants. You will surely find some permanent fixtures that refuse to budge and who scoff at eviction notices. With more chairs, you might expect some elbow room. Perhaps we need to get rid of all the chairs and create a 'standing room only' situation. At least we won't be standing alone.

We work for a department—we take it for granted, but is that a good thing? Being a division of a complex organism or system may make some of us distinct, a few of us distinguished, and the rest of us extinguished. Your unit or branch cannot feasibly (nor sustainably) function as a segmented studio apartment for very long. Whether we recognize it or not, there's a point when privacy results in deprivation. Alas, we should always strive for unity and 'togetherment'. We shouldn't feel compartmentalized or detained, yet push for the removal of barriers and continue to seek mutuality and collective leadership attainment.

If someone starts a conversation with *'Let me be brutally honest with you...'*, you can bet that the next few lines will not be very reassuring. We need to acknowledge that the pieces don't fit, and as E-leaders, we need to reshape, reconfigure, recreate. We shouldn't conform, but instead carve out unique opportunities. As E-leaders, are we taking some heed or making headway? Are we following orders or making progressions? Can we concurrently do a- told while making significant forward strides?

Sure, we can, if we share EL responsibilities, along with EL fascination! Once we are enamored, there will be moments, special moments, when we are swept off our feet. We can mutually become attracted, attached and committed to a generous conservation cause, rooted in common ground. Environmental Leadership can be excruciating, mesmerizing and overwhelming— but EL cannot be under-whelming, pain-free, compulsory or obtuse. Take your life, before others take it from you.

> *You can fool some people sometimes*
> *But you can't fool all the people all the time So now we see*
> *the light...*
> *We gonna stand up for our rights!—*
> *Bob Marley / Peter Tosh*

Taking the Plunge--

There's a difficult (class IV) section of the Upper Arkansas River in Central Colorado known as 'The Numbers'. I've kayaked and unintentionally swam sections of this frigid, rocky whitewater, and it scares me to this day. Putting things into perspective, above The Numbers is an even more extreme river rapids section (class V) known as 'The Fractions'. I gawk at the skills of these kayakers, knowing that they're way out of my league.

We are often compelled to feel subservient to The Fractions at the top of our organizational food chain. Yet as Environmental Leaders, we need to conjure up or finagle a way to scale Mr. Everest and summit the sleeping mountain. One way is to integrate community fractions into a united, substantial and potent element—turning fractions into factions, so to speak. Perhaps there's a way to get those proverbial lions to actually share?

How we go about creating contentious debate and galvanizing support (that might defy conventional logic) is going to be a common denominator for many of our environmental strategies. Merely creating greener objectives will surely face uproars and objections. Proposing potential solutions do not always equate with our social and economic determinants. Commitment and reassurances won't hurt.

It reminds me of a famous quote by J. Wellington Wimpy:

*"I'll **gladly** pay you Tuesday for a hamburger today."*

Popeye's colleague Wimpy never comes to the restaurant on Tuesdays, of course. None of us can keep all of our promises, but what mighty Environmental Leaders do keep is the integrity of their intent. There will be hurdles and mishaps along with unconscionable efforts (by others) to stave off our environmental prowess and progress. But there are some advocacy actions that we can't afford not to do. In the interim, encourage courage!

Yeast and desist--

When mislead, we can feel like that one green-tainted potato chip in the entire bag—distinct in the eyes of some, damaged in the minds of others. We are part of the same packaged contents, but unmistakably different. Price reduced for quick sale, undervalued and worth less by the day.

Toxic leadership is akin to experimenting with unknown varieties of mushrooms. And if you have any problem relating to this mycological analogy, then try a comparison with flammable situations (inflammatory remarks), ignitable arguments (fueled by contention), or reactive situations (triggered by unwarranted actions). Sometimes you never know what's going to happen next. But more often than not, there are supervisory episodes that you can count on like clockwork. The human pressure cookers start to boil, then hiss, then scream at ear-piercing levels. Something's gotta give…

Fresh clove garlic is a gourmet treat—but place a tainted bulb in an airtight bottle of extra virgin olive oil, and you're inviting Clostridium Botulinum to the party. Environmental detonations can be vociferous (James Watt, Scott Pruitt) or solitudinous (carbon monoxide, radon gas), but both cause us to fend for ourselves and run for the hills.

Our external fuzziness is largely misunderstood. Aged steak, vintage wine, cured ham, bleu cheese, fermented kombucha, … the list goes on. Most molds are harmless, and others are very beneficial—but only to those with open minds and receptive taste buds.

Personally, the term 'permutation' sounds much prettier than a 'mutation'. One is a possible variation or change in arrangement, the other is the actual transformation. We are mincing words at best. Both involve disorder, alteration, altercation and a version of metamorphosis. The conversion can be from an immature form to a more-developed adult stage, or, from a distinct ability into something drastically different. Think of environmental leadership as a goulash of butterflies and Frankenstein, or as vinegar and chickenpox.

Tanks a lot!—

I headed up to Vallecito Lake in La Plata County, Colorado to inspect a mom & pop grocery store before the tourist season got going full swing. Still traces of snow on the ground (I've seen it snow in Colorado every month of the year), I trudged over to an above-ground 200-gallon gasoline tank. The containment tank below it (in case of a leak or spill) was a mere 50-gallon horse trough and was full of snowmelt at that. Shaking my head, I walked into the grocery store to talk with Elmer. He recognizes me, gives me a nod, and finishes his conversation with a friend at the diner counter. I say howdy, yes, it's that time again for another inspection (minimum of twice per year, maybe once if you're squeaky clean).

C'mon back into the kitchen and do your thing. Find a food violation or two, write it up, provide some potential solutions, and get the hell out of my store. That's the usual vibe. I told Elmer that I was more concerned about the fuel storage tank than the burger grill, and that the containment needed to be at least as large as the 200- gallon gas tank (actually bigger, but I'd cut him some slack).

"Why didn't you find this on your last inspection?"

"Because I didn't observe it—maybe it wasn't there." My humor was getting me nowhere.

"Those dang tanks cost a lot of money, and they don't ever leak".

This is where the 'dealing with difficult people' part comes into play on the job description. The tension in the air grows thicker and the citation book in my arms feels like an encyclopedia. I don't want to quote the regulations to Elmer, I just want him to get a larger freakin' containment tank in the next couple of months, before the snow flies again. I notice a huge lake trout mounted on the wall, and I start to feel small, almost guilty, for no reason of my own.

"Can I get a cup of coffee?", I ask.

Elmer pours two cups of okay java, and we sit down. I mention the fish, and he goes on a diatribe about one of the best days of his life. We drink more coffee, and I redirect the conversation back to the fuel tank situation.

"Well, I never fill the dang thing with more than 50 gallons."

I can't ensure that's the case, plus the regulations call for maximum containment. Time for a third cup of coffee, but better get some pie. Elmer doesn't want my money, but I pay for the pie, take him up on the free java.

"What if I just buy a new 50-gallon fuel tank to replace this bugger? It's 400 bucks cheaper than the big boy… I can sell the current beast, maybe make some money on the deal."

Hmmm… why didn't I think of that.

"Elmer, that's a great idea. Now can I use the restroom?"

"Sure, but we're fresh out of soap at the hand-sink…"

We shake hands, smile and say adios.

I get a kick out of the salty beliefs and convictions of the real characters in our world, as well as their peppered approach. You've heard me refer to our daily leadership toils as the functioning of our personal 'skeptic tanks', deciphering between nutrient loading and waste disposal. We have the capacity, yet not always the tenacity to take on environmental challenges. Digesting bile necessitates being able to process information and to identify potential beneficial uses. We expect our environmental leaders to have such abilities and to exercise them routinely. Surfacing from the depths of sludge-mindedness, we seek clarity above the daily muck and just below the pompous scum layer. Environmental leaders must be able to duck-dive, but then gravitate towards brighter horizons.

The X-Factor-

If a baseball slugger gets three swings, and a quarterback gets four throws, which athlete has a greater chance of success? I'm not going to do the math, as I've forgotten how those permutations work. But obviously, the more opportunities you have to succeed, the greater your chance for success. However, the feat of hitting the ball on your own differs greatly from throwing to a receiver and having him haul it in. The quarterback has more opportunities than the batter, but he is more dependent on others to complete the task--collaboratively, methodically and progressively moving the ball down the field.

If success is not important to you, then maybe you shouldn't be on the team. And if you are not given an opportunity to succeed, maybe you shouldn't be on the team either! Having skills, desire and ambition, but serving as a benchwarmer, will be an exercise in patience, humbleness and humility. Waiting for a break (like the shortstop fracturing his arm and you coming into the game) can happen at any time. For most of us, we can't expect to get traded to a team that can make better use of our skills. We need to become valuable, and then convince others of our value. Sometimes you can roll the dice, other times you get rolled over (hopefully not steamrolled!).

Larger organizations may need three or four quarterbacks and may offer financial incentives to jump ship and join their crew. Smaller, leaner groups are nimbler and more streamlined, potentially giving you greater attention and responsibility. You need to decide how successful you want to be. As they say, the proof is in the pudding. Are your expectations being met? You have to try something to see if you will like it, and this pertains as much about environmental work as to other adventures. Taste the pudding!

Induce Labor--

Ironically, pudding traditionally referred to stuffed sausage. So, when you're 'grinding it out' in the environmental workplace, think about the raw ingredients that it takes to make success, and how long it might take to become seasoned and reach perfection (if such a thing exists)!

By now you're past the stage of engagement with your environmental love affair and have conceived at least one if not eight environmental concepts that will, in your mind and spirit, lead towards environmental progressions. These ideas are your brainchild—you grasped an abstract thought or feeling, so yes, you do have a clue. Such engrained notions and personal concepts are impregnated in your daily thought patterns, sometimes kicking and screaming as if ready to be delivered to the real world. You can give birth to your beautiful belief, or you can abort at any time.

Environmental leaders strive towards hatching newborn ideas with an uncanny ability to comprehend that gestation and birth are followed by nurturing, caring and growth.

Ideas are not in their infancy if they are never introduced to the natural environment—they remain as infertile thoughts and dreams. Your task is to determine when ideas and strategies are in their final trimester and are ready to be born. If others adopt your ideas and they are willing to put the time and energy into its development, then why the hell not let them? In fact, they have probably been partially responsible for parts of the idea in the first place. Creation and ownership are less important than healthy growth and development. You can order a pizza, you can assemble the toppings and you can get a sense for the finished product—but at some stage in life, you must deliver.

Oye, oye, don't try to be so coy, eh? —
Your Magistrate

And the Dish ran away with the Spoon..—

There is little evidence that people slip on banana peels. In fact, the interior skin resembles an octopus that clings rather than slips. But as a peel starts to rot and slime starts to grow, the potential for a slide dramatically increases. Environmental and conservation organizations face a rather simple balancing act—remain rigid, firm and solidified, or risk facing that slippery slope of unexplored territory. Yet a slip is rarely a dramatic departure from the truth. We've discussed errors and failures, as well as the positive actions of escape. So, unleash or unpeel your potential!

Some of our environmental leadership desires and actions will be nothing short of blasphemy to the righteous desk jockey and the short-order Executive Chef. If we remain obedient and comply with their barking orders, they will probably throw us a bone from time- to-time. If your green leadership tendencies are anything like mine, you'll be trying to figure out how to be a proactive go-getter, not a retriever. There's nothing scandalous about adding a groundwater monitoring aspect to your on-site wastewater permitting program. While you're at it, consider an educational component that includes water conservation. Are you still thirsty? Think about convening monthly meetings over coffee with your local soil conservation district (plan on buying the doughnuts).

Yes, you just upset the apple cart. The team leader is now starting to wriggle around in her armchair. You kept her informed, of course—but she had no idea that you would make good on your intentions and ambitions. Now others are looking over your shoulder, waiting for your fledgling efforts to stub their toes, go head-over-heels and grind to a screeching halt—and one or more of those efforts usually does, so it's a good thing that you are committed to a collaborative approach that involves and invites others to share both wealth and royal screw-ups.

Does it get tiresome after a while, all this prolonged effort and not much to show for it? Not really—just for a day or two maybe. Then it's back to making puppy eyes to that green flash. Your adoration with our natural and human environment is omnipotent, so don't try to hide or disguise it.

It's very rare that medium efforts are well done—
Woojuu

Environmental Expectorants--

During the period of the Black Death of the 14th century, Venice established the system of 'quarantine'—requiring ships and manpower to be anchored for forty days before landing. If the crew were able to survive the confinement, they probably were not infected or infectious. What must it have been like, unable to escape from your ratty shipmates, taking it one sunrise and one sunset at a time? I would guess that many of us enviro leaders can relate to such lock-down conditions, not knowing what to expect next, except the inevitable.

How clever are we? Are we routinely honing our environmental skills? Are we shedding wasteful tendencies and attempting to be keen? Or are we straining to convert that onion into an apple? Was your latest incredible performance unbelievably super, or downright amazing, or barely justifiable? In order to avoid confusion, we E- leaders need to know wherein lays the befuddlement--astonishingly simple, yet true.

I'm all too-familiar with our laundry list of environmental impediments—resource shortages, fear of the unknown, backstabbing, complacency, lack of ambition and leadership shortcomings to name a few. It's a convoluted wrecking ball that swings wildly and with great force. Are we thriving as fluid, interconnected organisms, or barely surviving as trapped, vacuous globules? Sacre bleu! Our green tour of duty builds upon our yesterday, confronts today and stealthily peers at tomorrow. The onus to lead the charge for change is on us, and in our lifetime—so let's have the time of our lives!

Our makeshift revisions can be both entrepreneurial as well as practical—streamlining processes, creating enhanced products, manufacturing ideas, addressing risks, creating challenges and generating profitable ventures (depending on your definition of profit). Yet whether we opt for beer puns or watershed metaphors, remember that we have that one, dare I say "Huge" commodity— thirst.

Despite the chronic presence of political phlegm and managerial mucous, we environmental leaders should expect our concentrated efforts to become substantive and effective. It may take many doses of Tonic Water prior to observing any positive response, and yes, there will certainly be those unappreciated side effects. Yet we still need to instill hope and great expectations.

Start a franchise—

Subway is one of our most successful and affordable U.S. fast-food franchises, and often a healthier option than the Colonel. Subway nails their success down to a science, because it is a science. Food science, economics and market share are based on affordability, accessibility and acceptability. Environmental leadership can learn a thing or two by observing what people want—I call it 'Counter Intelligence'. Our communities are often disenfranchised from our local and regional decision-makers, segmented into piecemeal programs and projects that resemble an auto salvage yard. Nope, there won't be much one-stop shopping here.

Hold on for a second—at first, I'm challenging you to be unique and original, and the next moment I'm urging you to get in-line and order your stupid sandwich? You might be missing the point—we need to have a true understanding of our desires, while simultaneously exploring the pros and cons of environmental opportunities. It is okay to construct a model, and it is just as okay to destruct that model—the harmonic process will require assembly or disassembly and will provide you with hands-on environmental leadership experience. For example, if I was in charge...

> * A baseball game would have 3 balls, 2 strikes and 8 innings, as I believe there is more than adequate opportunity to perform, entertain, win or lose.

*   Barstools would have handrails—if you don't need them, then don't use them.

*   Spaghetti would be served with fishballs—the taste and texture are memorable.

*   Bagels would include a margarita variety—no stagnation here.

*   Candy bars would serve chocolate beer.

*   Bowling a gutter ball is worth 1 point (hey, you tried!).

*   Cinco de Mayo would be replicated to include an Ocho de Octobre green chili harvest fest.

*   Toothpaste would double as shaving cream—I just saved six bucks per month.

I've got news for you—I'm not in charge of most things. But I continue to dream, hope, aspire and share. If environmental leaders can dream, hope, aspire and share, they are more than halfway there. Where you leaders go from here, well that's up to you!

I'd like to make a toast—

Since 1924, Toastmasters International has been assisting individuals to become better public speakers. With more than 340,000 memberships in 135 countries, Toastmasters is undeniably a leader in effective communication. The organization aptly claims to 'give voice to your potential', and that 'leaders are good communicators'. Where I disagree is with their subsequent sentence:

"Leadership is the art of persuading others to do what you wish to be done …".

Nope, that's not leadership. That is persuasion or coaxing or convincing, creating action or reaction without proof of true sincerity or deep belief. Leadership is not about winning a debate— it's about creating a debate, by unveiling potential, examining alternatives and pondering possibilities.

I challenged Toastmasters to come up with a new age definition of leadership—one that bolsters thought and intent by verbal sharing with inclusive audiences, and with invitations for diverse responses. Ironically, the response I received from this linguistics forerunner was via email—the message simply said: *'thank you for communicating with us.'* That's burnt toast, to say the least.

Persuading and / or convincing others of your opinion and beliefs are often a daily occurrence in our green world. We make the case (with wads of scientific evidence) that global warming is really taking place—in our lifetime, and until we discover otherwise. But what about the other 90% of environmental leadership—what embodies the daily specials on our green menu?

> *   EL encourages others to 'form' personal opinions and then make 'informed' decisions.

> *   EL is just that—mental examination of enviro concepts, gravitating towards taking personal actions in support of your conservation convictions.

> *   EL is un-wasted, protected, promoted and valued beliefs in sustainable practices, including cooperative efforts and extended education.

Green leadership seizes leadership traits and concepts, then tweaks them to be environmentally relate-able, usable, affordable, functional, agreeable and at the same time, unpredictable. We lead not solely for others to join the Conga line, but for fellows and followers to live and experience their unique dreams with fewer inhibitions or repercussions. It's a sort of environmentally conscious, three-ring circus for the greatest earth on show.

Did you get the invoice??--

There is a mental reminder that we're either doing too much of something or not enough of another, and it usually comes in the middle of the night. It's that inner voice again, crying out for change. I refer to it as my 'taunted house'. You awaken, and can vaguely remember that you are supposed to do something—maybe take out the trash, or clean the litter box? We get easily confused, as there are so many prompted, cajoled and baffling situations in our daily lives. We become mesmerized and desensitized, unconsciously ignoring critical deadlines and essential communications. Yet times have drastically changed.

Over forty years ago, the famous self-help author Zig Ziglar wrote out a warning in his motivational book 'See You at the Top':

'…Charles Manson's motivation for the sadistic murders of Sharon Tate and other innocent people was planted in his mind by the message in a Beatle recording. This is one of the major reasons no one should go to sleep with the radio playing…'

Ziglar's concern was that a mind entirely open to any and all possibilities could be prone to hypnosis and warped interpretations. I would argue that while individuals are susceptible to outside influence, most of us make conscious decisions and conscious indecisions based on our level of desire.

The inner voice—that's what comes and goes, morphing from front page news to classified ads. Who was attacked today, and who is soliciting for help wanted? Guilt can motivate, but so can hope. Our emotions play around with sympathy, empathy, aspirations, despair and desires, eventually realizing that we are the owners of way-too- many excuses. We all have cracks in our leadership, yet we are able to aim for environmental progressions in areas where others have declined to participate. The in-voice is what you owe to yourself, so take careful notice.

Sitting and wishing makes no man great,
God sends the fishes,
But you must dig the bait--

1969 World's Fair

Being Hamstrung—

Sure-as-shootin', we need to have some meat on our enviro bones. Just as important, we need to have flexible tendons that attach muscle to that bone! Enviro leadership is that brawny, thick bungee cable of connective tissue—a band that can withstand tension, weather storms, right ships, and lead teams.

Flabby, flaccid leadership is prone to experiencing sprains, creating chain-reaction instability, slip-sliding and bruised egos. Underuse and lack of leadership messaging, delayed massaging and ignored honing are surefire ways to cripple any possible leadership lunges.

While ligaments attach bone-to-bone-to-bone, and provide a fine degree of stability, it is the tendons that attach the muscle to each bone. Managers are ligaments that ensure the necessary support, but tendons go one step further, by pulling bones into motion!

Furthermore, tendons absorb some of the shock that muscles incur, allowing and encouraging us boneheads to spring into action! Lack of environmental leadership, like a weak or torn tendon, can be our Achilles heel. Environmental tenacity might very well be that new leadership kindred and saving grace that we've been searching for. Green leadership staunchness, green guts and a leader's determination all have a strong 'tendoncy' of avoiding managerial lameness and ossification. Any strained relationships are quickly repaired through willpower, resoluteness and intestinal fortitude.

Arthritic leadership limps and lumbers along, often with less than a full environmental deck to shuffle. Make no bones about it—if you play your cards right and muscle-up on your E-leadership endeavors, we will become enmeshed within the very tissue and fabric of our communities. I guess I'll be sinew later…

> *Charity is the bone shared with the dog,*
> *when you are just as hungry as the dog—*
>
> Jack London

Belize it or not—

When the Queen of England came over to visit her former colony, her Belizean hosts thought it quite fitting to serve her a meaty meal of gibnut. The fatty muskrat (Agouti paca) can be very tasty— especially when you don't know that it is a whiskered rodent on your plate. From that day on, the roasted critter was referred to as 'the Royal Rat'.

Environmental leadership has no finishing stroke, and unquestionably no death knell. Despite the despicable annoyance of our psycho-leaders, they can't make mincemeat of us--there are too many of us gibnuts out there. We just need to figure out who our friends are, and how to deal with voracious appetites for money and monuments (the bad kind). What is near and dear to many leaders may be banana cream pie, along with making excuses for second helpings. More essential and vital resources may be out of reach, but as enviro leaders, we now know how to extend our efforts and enthusiasm—by becoming undertakers.

From polluted creeks to deforested hillsides and depleted aquifers, our conservation leadership challenges are gargantuan. When our ecological proposals appear dead-on-arrival (due to budget constraints and competing priorities), should we contact that expert rehabilitator? Surprise, surprise—that would be you!

Don't try to burrow your way out of this one. We've already dwelled on 'excavating and energizing leadership capacity' (within our conservation communities). This can be looked at as a huge undertaking, or, perhaps by others as an overburden. Are we environmental leaders primed and prepared to unearth suppressed opportunities? Can we untangle those pretzeled attitudes and embark on a joint mission? Can we ferret out waste and nonsense from the conservation tasks at-hand? Should we exhume King Tut, and perhaps perturb our heavily embalmed leaders? Much will depend on your leadership, your life.

Paradoxically, our unearthing of environmental snares and inhumane entrapments can produce earthly leadership footholds— opportunities to snag greener sentiments, and to release bluer freedoms of thought and conservation decision-making. Rooting up the ominous brilliant green bile is a major undertaking. There will be days of upheaval, tumultuous moments and thunderous occasions. Forward paddle, brace, back paddle, then recover. I'm not going to tell you what to say, nor how to think— that's the job of your gang-green leadership.

To reiterate for the umpteenth time, this EL guidebook is committed to excavating and energizing leadership capacity within our conservation communities. We offer an organic formula that conservation custodians can utilize to aggressively combat the moldy, lingering and stagnating environmental deficiencies that we invariably slog through. As the previous generation used to say, '*Can you dig it, man!*'

Road Tripping--

Someone once told me that the term 'hobo' was derived from transients riding the rails and catching trains to faraway places, yet eventually, after a full plate of experience and a can of cocktail franks, turning 'homeward bound'. He's a travelling wayfarer, a drifter dishwasher, a migratory human being, a curious pedestrian with a pack. The very image pastes a stark picture in my mind—a form of temporary satiation, with the awareness that a certain wandering hunger will return in due time.

You can embrace change or you can strangle it. Many of us are able to place a choke hold on change, due to our authority, connections and precious powers. Others seek the holy grail of change and are helped or hindered during this search for glory. Your environmental odyssey might truly be an oddity. I would bet that your fearless adventures will strike that excitable chord, transforming your inhibitions into environmental ambitions, and ultimately recognizing the clouds of bile for what they truly are.

To admit is to enter-- to gain entrance into a potentially positive mechanism for environmental enhancement. Not every-thing is probable, but most everything is possible. Take charge. Test the waters and take calculated risks. Go wading, despite the dangerous currents. Prepare yourself for the evitable. Exploit your inner sanctity, or deal with the eventuality of your efforts (some worthwhile, most a waste of time) becoming quicksand itself, where you latch and hold on to others. You will sometimes suck! Relinquish a slice of your personal pizza-like authority. You can always make more, but I believe that you'll find that less is more.

From riptides to whirlpools to sinkholes, environmental perils abound. Be perceptive in identifying suppressed flows of ideas and oppressed channels of communication. How many times do we need to bathe in the same tub of stagnant thoughts?

6 Simple Ways to Lower Morale:

1. Don't address priority problems.

2. Ignore underlying causes.

3. Make light of serious stuff.

4. Take all the credit, none of the fault.

5. Recognize the pieces but ignore the puzzle.

6. Postpone the inevitable.

Weapons of Mass Construction—why Matter Matters!—

We're always seeking the keys to successful environmental interventions—we examine grassroots initiatives, consider youth involvement, peruse opportunity costs, and seek devices to open new green doors. That's all fine and dandy. But let us not overlook the very locking mechanisms and alligator moats that offer continued resistance, presenting tough fortresses to penetrate.

What do many environmental leaders suffer from? Insecurity. What do locking devices provide? Security.

Why do skunks eat the heads off chickens, leaving the body to rot? Damned if I know!

Weak enviro leaders are afraid of being robbed—robbed of their prized possession: authority. They are afraid of being robbed not at gunpoint, but at vantage-point. So, they subsequently arm themselves and disarm others. I only wish there was a Robin Hood- esque methodology that could 'borrow' small-yet-considerable amounts of power from the upper echelon, and provide it to the impoverished, starving environmental workforce. Maybe there is. By repudiating organizational oppression and touting inverted pyramid approaches, we can embrace ecological endeavors, spice up bland programming, re-align conservation alliances, fortify grassroots support and engage in healthy environmental dialogue. Yeah, we can! Environmental Leadership can provoke thoughts, evoke responses and invoke solutions. Perhaps we are the boyz in the hood.

And perhaps Einstein was wrong. Perhaps matter can be created and destroyed. Perhaps matters can also be grown, harvested, ingested, defecated and composted again. Matter occupies space, and while matter can be defined as a physical body (distinct from mind & spirit), matters always occupy space in our minds. Bob Marley chanted about a natural mystic blowin' in the air, and I think it involved more than smoke and mirrors. Perhaps it's the shared amalgamation of nature and culture—an eco-infusion that unlocks our environmental leadership potential and releases green aura. It's also in our land and water, alluring our environmental leadership capacity or appetite, and daring us to address the tainted politics and administrative quagmires that entrap us.

With greater environmental leadership from top to bottom, we can make something momentous, something epochal. Sure, we shouldn't expect a Churchill-like performance from the get-go, but let's commit to sincere, unparalleled environmental efforts that hoist green flags—let's take the lead!

What's the matter? Don't you have a semi-fertile conservation project plan in mind? No worries—all you need is some personal spatial analysis, and you'll come up with something meaningful (at least to you)! They say that possession is nine-tenths of the law, so I assume that the leadership cap you are sporting is your-own. Adding personal energy to matter causes a physical alteration, along with a mental challenge. Go beyond sustenance, and commit to enhancing the integrity of your environment, our environment.

Going to Mass—

Not only does matter occupy space (and time, and brain cells), but it has mass. Some matters have little interest or concern while others have 'mass appeal' and 'mass support'. Enviro leaders often work on mass balance equations without even realizing it. What's happening to us and around us? How about key environmental entry points, inclusive stewardship circumstances, critical habitat concussions, organizational internal incidences, and a zillion other palpable conservation issues—green stuff happens!

On the other hand, poor leadership can be considered a weapon of mass destruction, or at least obstruction. Consider that the Greek mathematician Archimedes discovered the principle of buoyancy-- objects will float when the upward force is equal to the weight of the fluid displaced by the object. Therefore, when downward force exceeds upward mobility, we sink!

This is just me expounding, and if you don't follow my rationale, that's okay, because you're not reading this tonic book to follow the leader. But just to beat a dead horse, in order to occupy space, matter incorporates not only mass, but volume as well. So go on— occupy space, discuss what really matters, and speak volumes!

> *Without matter, there is no earth,*
> *And without the earth, nothing matters—*
> W. Urbonas

There oughtta be a law—

That you are awarded some mere pittance for the timely and professional completion of every arduous, unsuccessful grant application—

'We are sorry that you were not selected for our Pollution Prevention community-based grant, but here's a hundred bucks for trying, and keep up the good work!'

Wouldn't that be awesome! I'd probably be six thousand dollars richer by now! It wouldn't be a retirement fund, but a replenishment award that pays for your dinner and just dessert. If you can deal with adversity and promote diversity in the face of uncertainty and environmental disarray, then there's always a possibility of becoming a living, breathing Environmental Troubadour!

Chant a green psalm today! Rid us of that professional management ennui that has lulled our conservation communities into comas. Take out that anti-bile defibrillator and defame those leadership stunt doubles. Don't squander, sidestep or blow environmental opportunities! Help us detect true blue-green environmental chiefs from amongst the slew of invasive managerial mongooses. Welcome defectors from the dark world. Raise consciousness within our disparate, multi-cultural lives and times. Try to walk on water—at least try!

> *"It is not your responsibility to finish the work of perfecting the world, but you are not free to desist from it either."*
> *Rabbi Tarfon, Pirke Avot 2:21*

Dupe of Earl—

Is it just me, or do these melodies sound somewhat similar:

Ooooooh I heard it through the grapevine….

Oooooh I'm a rebel just for kicks now….

Subconscious thoughts attempt to build upon the positive and flee from the negative. We enviro leaders beg, borrow and steal in order to create the leadership gumbo that resembles our organization (or our organizational endeavors).

The nodding of the heads—does it signal acknowledgement, or perhaps even some semblance of agreement? One would hope so, but it would be a mistake to conclude that concurrence will 'lead' towards contributions, commitment, involvement or actions. Your project concept was conceived and is starting to grow legs, but who will be the cornerstone? Was he / she designated? How strong and intense is the desire? Are we being misled into believing that we have full-fledged support, while what really exist are informational ideals without any appreciation for its value? Will our community roots come to our rescue and prevent others from lopping off our leadership limbs? Is our support to-date genuine or disingenuous?

Working as a conservation director for an enviro partner organization, Earl had it pretty good—an above-average salary, flexible work hours, great benefits and the ability to make significant program decisions (so he thought).

The easy part of Earl's leadership role involved promoting and supporting those generally endorsed, non-controversial environmental grab-bags such as volunteer projects, outings and film festivals (man, enough with the film festivals already!). Getting people to attend events took a creative and amiable marketing flair and a gift for gab. Earl had it in spades.

The problem that Earl discovered, was how to keep the attention of these same people, hopefully converting them from 'attendee' to 'constituent'.

"*I felt like I was given the key to a combination lock…*", Earl confided.

"*We're on the same tug-of-war team, but I can't tell how hard each of us is individually tugging…; we don't seem to be making any progress*".

Earl's confidence was slowly slipping away, and he was extremely worried about his inability to ratchet things up to the next level. I don't know if he thought that I could help or if he was just heavily venting.

I liked his combo lock comparison, so we sat and talked about how many combinations it might take to open up new opportunities. We settled on four:

1. Physical presence—a giant leap past emails and text messages.

2. Desire—opening the Welcome door for others to come on-board.

3. Direction—not necessarily a destination, but a proposed route to take.

4. Ignition—planning for a takeoff, worrying about the landing later.

We then quickly discovered that our brains had already taken the liberty to create the above sequence, so we now knew how many combo turns might be needed, and in what specified order. Then we got lost in the details and decided to call it a day—but we left with a better understanding of the possibilities out on the horizon.

Earl called me up two days later and exclaimed that he had miraculously come up with the combination, and that he couldn't have done it without me. I thanked him for the compliment but didn't know what had gotten into him in the past 48 hours to produce this euphoric solution.

"Don't you see... it's not our lock. It's obviously a combination, but the key is in coming up with the combination in agreeable terms, and then ensuring that everyone has access to this community of sequences... anyone can then open the door, anytime they'd like! I can provide instructions, but following them is completely optional."

Earl no longer felt hoodwinked or deceived, and confided in me that he felt like a human can of Red Bull, ready to take on new challenges. I observed Earl's tactics from near and far, coming to the early conclusion that his leadership possibilities were endless— in fact, they always were, but it was a matter of not feeling like a victim or a chump. If we didn't dupe ourselves, there would be no brick walls, only doors that we could handle.

A fearless leader is also referred to as a psychopath--
Truth or Dare

Floors, walls & ceilings—

1. Life is short.

2. There are appetizers, entrees, desserts and death (not by chocolate).

3. You pay to park your butt nearby your chosen destination.

4. You take strides, while veering closer, then further, then closer...

5. You open the door and peer inside—scoping, sensing & cautiously entering.

6. The door closes behind you—not locked, just shut & contained.

7. You impatiently wait to get a seat at the table.

8. You wonder if you've come to the right place.

9. You examine your menu options and make a choice.

10. You indulge, piece-by-piece, morsel-by-morsel.

11. You pay a mighty price, leaving a tip or two.

12. You are ushered out the door, filled but not fulfilled.

Superior Leadership:	Inferior Leadership:
*Unbound & unconfined	*Insecure & hobbled
*Alive & tangy	*Stale & rancid
*Free & creative	*Greedy & reluctant
*Open & inviting	*Fearful & decayed
*Jubilant & visionary	*Loathsome & comatose
*Involved & thriving	*Reticent & complacent

Is there a mid-range between the two extremes? Sure, but why go there? That would be like swallowing a less-lethal pill, handcuffing one hand, or jumping halfway into the air. Environmental leaders need to practice what they preach. Go hide and seek in nature's lost and found—lose your worries, find your passion. Environmental leaders shouldn't stash their lives away, and then over time, forget where they put them. We need to find ways to shed our deadweight and demand a refund on piss-poor environmental protection efforts.

But life does not normally work that way. Our old nemesis bile can configure its own design and dimensions, ranging from environmental incompetence to conservation incontinence. Leading the environmental charge requires more than goodwill, more than money and more than words-on-paper. Wise decisions and sustained actions rely on continuous efforts and ambidextrous approaches. Cheap is expensive, and expensive is cheap.

You have 2 ceilings:
The one that you will never reach,
and the one that you set for yourself—
Kiswahili proverb

Spiteful or Insightful?

Maureen was preparing to have an intense, internal procedure performed. She was advised to get plenty of rest, eat healthfully, stay hydrated and minimize alcohol consumption for at least two weeks leading up to the event.

When the big day arrived, Maureen decided it was best to say 'thank you' to her peers and 'I love you' to her close friends. Yet only four days later, Maureen looked like a new person, expressing a small-yet-sincere grin from side-to-side. The procedure was successful. Maureen had performed self-reflection and open-mind surgery.

I may have not specifically referred to self-reflection, but we have examined personal fortitude, environmental desire and community chemistry at the watershed level. We discussed working towards 'breakpoint levels' that can appear to make things worse in the short-term. Team chemistry and environmental equations can be complex and in need of simplification.

We deliberated over the structure and selection process of environmental agencies and organizations, asking what concentrations of technical capacity, educational ability and social skills can produce the 'preferred results', and whether such preferences are echoed throughout the organization. We discussed EL transparency and veiled attempts to paint green images over internal combustion engines (hearts and desires).

We delved into rivers of thought and finding common ground with edu-technical watershed approaches. We sought, and continue to seek sustainable passageways while swimming upstream, with the ultimate goal of spawning EL potential. Tonic Water provides the EL challenge and the conservation encouragement, yet puts the onus on you the reader, you the omnipotent.

More Ruth, please! —

'Every strike brings me closer to the next home run.'—
George Herman 'Babe' Ruth

Despite his legendary 714 home runs, Babe Ruth struck out 1,330 times. In 1923, the Babe broke records for the most home runs, the highest batting average and also the most strikeouts. His persistence earned him induction into the Baseball Hall of Fame, and his genuine love for children has enshrined him in the hearts of all Americans.

Our world is chock full of cruel, merciless and ruthless people. Don't be afraid to step up to the plate and swing away. Please continue (or start) to show compassion towards the misery of other humans or living creatures. 'Da more Ruth, 'da betta!

Another American hero of mine is Woody Guthrie. Woody's original lyrics for 'This Land was Made for You and Me' included the following compassionate phrases:

Was a high wall there, that tried to stop me,
A sign was painted, said: Private Property,
But on the back side, it didn't say nothing —
~~God blessed America for me. (original lyric)~~
[This land was made for you and me.]
One bright sunny morning, in the shadow of the steeple,
By the Relief Office, I saw my people —
As they stood hungry, I stood there wondering, if
~~God blessed America for me.~~
[This land was made for you and me.]

It's normally a good idea to put things into context, but obviously include your own personal perspective. The next time you get depressed, you might try reeking some havoc within your environmental belief system—swing away at the bile piles, toy with contradictory approaches, spoon out a tad of mayhem and hum a few bars of greener waves of grain, from sea to shining sea.

Jousting, Jesting & Jowling—

We all have certain linguistic tendencies—Hillary regularly says 'ya know', Californians repeat 'like' all the time, adding interrogatives to basic phrases. My tongue releases copious amounts of 'okay'. I didn't realize it until I observed Zairois children mimicking me in my Peace Corps village, 'Okay, OK!'—I sort of liked it! No harm, no foul.

When Hawaiians converse informally, they refer to the process (that I previously mentioned) as 'talk-story'. It's an extremely accurate description, as the conversation centers around the lives and tribulations of people—what they did, what they're up to, and their account of the situation. Granted, like most storytelling, things can get a bit contorted or exaggerated along the way—but that's okay, because the narrative is simply a lead-in to connect with another person. It's an offering, so to speak. The best stories include lots of pidgin English, as it's the preferable way to speak local lingo and down-to-earth. And even if the anecdote is not the greatest, it must be acknowledged and accepted with an eyeful of attention and a smile of appreciation. Then it's your turn.

Environmentalism is supposed to be enthralling. We should be confabulating stories that would make Aesop grin, and then add to. We're always looking for the pieces to our environmental puzzle, and when something is missing, we tend to freak out, as if we are incomplete and desperate for solutions. No time for lollygagging, we'd better find a fix or blame someone else.

Environmental leadership recognizes that some pieces of our worldly puzzle are missing, while others are warped or tattered. After all, we are promoting ecological sanity in a disturbed habitat. We need to be creative and able to craft, figure and then reconfigure, wash, lather, rinse, repeat. If you do it as part of your creative thinking routine, you'll be less apt to have a conniption. Emerge from your cocoon, and don't dither! Environmental Leadership can be talented or toxic, daring or dysfunctional, never mediocre. Environmental Leadership should be scrumptious and contagious--if the performance is lackluster, then let's add luster to what's lacking!

Some folks have no clue when we talk about 'the greater good', or 'environmental costs' or 'intrinsic value'. We need to take a very deep breath, and then try to break it down into fundamentals. Conservative viewpoints can be convinced of conservation values, but as they get closer to agreeing with you, they often take credit for your ideas. That's okay, or at least, that's the least thing to be concerned about. When you hear other people speaking and sounding like you, perhaps you've transferred a dose of environmental affection. Proliferation takes zany routes.

Sometimes, it just rains----
Ambient

Non-nuclear Reactors--

I was thinking about how interesting-yet-simplistic a yo-yo is. Let 'er drop from a string and not much happens. But wind it up and add just a little snap and you are pleasantly rewarded with a polite and crisp response. It makes you want to do it again and again! You start to experiment with your style and technique—around the world, rock the baby, walk the dog … you name it. You quickly discover the energy, coordination and direction needed to produce intended results. But throw it at your brother, and you'd better run for cover!

Actions and reactions—physical see-saw battles, chemical combustion, biological reproduction, mental fortification-it all takes energy, the proper stuff (pounds, sperm, eggs, oxygen, heat, light, love, pain), and normally quite a bit of effort. Do you recall discussing PEE? How about that home-brewed IPA? It's about time to conjure up your own mantra and put it to daily enviro-benefit. Unleash the green-powered beast inside of you and take on the nuclear tiger. Shower fireworks of leadership over watershed health. Radiate a communal glow of green hope and positivism. Dance the tango with conservative county commissioners. But don't take it all on! You decide how to lead yourself into environmental temptation and deliver us from the bile of evil leadership. For you are the power and the glory! Happy trails and prevails!

Last but not Least:

One of these days when I'm out on one of my trail-run vision quests, I'll keel over, collapse and croak. Just before I go, an owl (pueo) will hover closer, out of curiosity. One of us will wink, one of us will shriek, and the world will continue to change. In the meantime, I wish you full stream ahead!

Aloha and Mahalo Nui. A hui ho….
Wano u.

'How long shall they kill our prophets, while we stand aside and look?
Some say it's just a part of it, we've got to fulfill the book.
Won't you help to sing, These songs of freedom?
'Cause all I ever had, Redemption songs— '
Bob Marley